THE PINES OF MEXICO
AND
CENTRAL AMERICA

THE PINES OF MEXICO AND CENTRAL AMERICA

Jesse P. Perry, Jr.

Associate Director
Agricultural Sciences Program
The Rockefeller Foundation
Retired

TIMBER PRESS
Portland, Oregon

ISBN 0-88192-174-2
Printed in Hong Kong

TIMBER PRESS, INC.
9999 S.W. Wilshire
Portland, Oregon 97225

Library of Congress Cataloging-in-Publication Data

Perry, Jesse P.
    The pines of Mexico and Central America / Jesse P. Perry Jr.
        p.   cm.
    Includes bibliographical references.
    ISBN 0-88192-174-2
    1. Pine--Mexico. 2. Pine--Central America.   I. Title.
QK494.5.P66P45 1990
    585'.2--dc20   90-10774
                                                               CIP

CONTENTS

FOREWORD

For close to a half-millenium, the region we now refer to as Mexico and Central America has lured European treasure hunters. Precious metals and souls were the first prizes. Next were maize, cacao, and other food plants unknown to the Old World. Around the middle of the last century, a new breed of treasure hunter ventured into the forests where a bewildering profusion of pines awaited them. The seed collectors, botanists, and foresters collected, studied, and wrote. As a result, certain of the pine species were grown as exotics in various of the temperate, sub-tropical and tropical areas of the world. Successful pine emigrants from the region have motivated increasing and continuing exploration and study.

Few, if any of the students of pines in this region have had both the long-time and geographically comprehensive *field* acquaintance which Jesse Perry draws on as a guide through these pine forests and woodlands. His book, to an extent unusual in botanical manuals, recognizes the dynamic nature of the pine populations in an area of great physiographic, climatic, and cultural complexity, where new species of pines are still being found and extinction of species is a constant threat. It is hoped that this book will assist in the efforts under way to conserve the rich but precarious diversity of the pines of Mexico and Central America.

J. W. Duffield

PREFACE

Since 1949 when I started to work in Mexico, the Mexican pines have fascinated me. My first pine collections were made in the mountains near Mexico City where I could not identify a single specimen. Fortunately, the second edition of Professor Maximino Martínez's book *Los Pinos Mexicanos* was published about that time and with this comprehensive work as a guide, I embarked on a study of the Mexican and Central American pines that was to last for 40 years.

This book presents a great deal of what I learned about the pines during that period, from numerous collecting trips in the field, laboratory research, studies of herbarium specimens, and information published by botanists and foresters.

Descriptions of the trees, leaves, cones, and seeds are based on personal collections and observations made in the field and laboratory combined with published information by other authors. Distribution and habitat of the different species is based upon my collections and field observations combined with published maps and collections by other authors. In many instances new information is presented about a particular species; for example, a significant extension of the range or a change in altitudinal distribution or species interrelationships.

Information in this book on "Where to Find" a species is taken almost entirely from my own experiences; of course it does not imply that there are not other, perhaps better, collection localities. In fact, in some of the localities listed, the trees may have since disappeared due to cutting, fire, and insect attacks.

In the "Notes and Comments," information is often included on important nomenclatural and taxonomical problems. Also special attention is called to those species that clearly should be placed in an "endangered category."

Much of the data on turpentine analyses present information previously unpublished. While turpentine analyses will not assist field identification of the various species and varieties, it is helpful in confirming identification when differences in morphological characters may not be clear. In addition to chemo-taxonomic value, these chemical compounds are becoming increasingly valuable in countries wherever pines are harvested commercially.

With the exception of Baja California Sur, I collected and photographed the pines where they occur in every Mexican State. In Guatemala my collections cover the distribution of pines very well and in El Salvador I collected and photographed the pines in their most important areas of distribution. In Honduras and Belize my collections have not been as intensive as in Mexico and Guatemala; however, the number of different species occurring there are far fewer than in Mexico and Guatemala. I have not had an opportunity to collect or photograph the pines in Nicaragua. Fortunately, however, the taxonomy and distribution of the few pine species found in that country is well documented. A few photographs were borrowed and the source is gratefully indicated in each case.

Rather than a highly technical work, I have prepared a book that will serve as a reliable and up-to-date source of information on the Mexican and Central American pines. It is hoped that botanists, taxonomists, foresters and individuals "just interested in pine trees" will find this a useful, informative, and interesting book.

For those readers interested in more detailed studies of a particular species, I have included a Selected Bibliography.

ACKNOWLEDGMENTS

I do not know of a book of this kind that was written without the help of friends, associates, institutions and organizations. This book is no exception.

The memory of my conversations with Professor Maximino Martínez, his advice and counsel on the pines of Mexico, I will always recall with deep appreciation. My conversations in 1950 with John Miller as we surveyed bark-beetle kills on the slopes of Popocatepetl helped me more than I knew at that time.

For Nick Mirov's interest, advice and encouragement on starting this book, I am deeply grateful. To Dana Bailey for his help with field collections and information on the piñon pines. I express my sincere gratitude.

To W. M. Mittak I acknowledge a debt of gratitude for his help with collection of pine specimens and oleoresin in Guatemala.

I find it difficult to express the debt of gratitude I owe to Bruce Zobel and Jack Duffield. Without their advice, encouragement and reviews of drafts of the manuscript, this book might not have been completed. I am indebted to Jim Hardin for making available herbarium specimens at North Carolina State University.

To Paul Mangelsdorf I express my deep appreciation for his suggestions, advice, and encouragement.

For Tony Squillace's assistance and suggestions regarding turpentine analyses, I am deeply grateful. I am thankful too, for John Drew's notes and comments on turpentine analyses.

For Peter Stevens' generous assistance at the Harvard University Herbaria, I am most appreciative. I thank too Betsy Schmidt for her editing of my papers published by the Arnold Arboretum and used in this book.

To Bill Critchfield I express my appreciation for information on many of the pines of Mexico and the western United States. I am grateful too, to Tom Ledig for permission to study a number of the hybrids at Placerville and particularly for his collections of oleoresin from a number of hybrid pines.

To Bill Dvorak, Director of Central America and Mexico Coniferous Resources Cooperative (CAMCORE), I express my deep appreciation for assistance with field collections of specimens and oleoresin in Mexico, Guatemala and Honduras. My appreciation is also extended to Jeff Donahue and Ernesto Ponce, CAMCORE field staff for their generous help with field collections particularly in Oaxaca, Chiapas, and Honduras.

To Xavier Madrigal Sánchez for his help with numerous collections of specimens and oleoresin in Michoacán, I express my deep appreciation. Jorge Alberto de la Rosa was generous with his help in collecting pine specimens and oleoresin in Jalisco.

I extend my thanks to Teobaldo Equiluz Piedra for information he provided on many of the Mexican pines.

I am most appreciative of Jerzy Rzedowski's courtesy and kindness in making available for study pine specimens at the herbarium of the Instituto Politécnico Nacional.

I am grateful for Javier Jil Flores' assistance with pine collections in a number of particularly isolated and inaccessible areas of the Sierra Madre Oriental of Mexico.

To officials of the Instituto Nacional de Investigaciones Forestales (INIF), I express my gratitude for their interest and help with pine collections in Mexico.

To the Forestry Department, Banco de Semillas Forestales (BANSEFOR), Guatemala, I am grateful for access to their herbarium and for assistance with field collections.

I am particularly grateful to Dr. Reuben Guevara, Director, Escuela Nacional De Ciencias Forestales at Siguatepeque, Honduras for his interest and encouragement with pine collections in Honduras. My deep appreciation is expressed here for the many kindnesses shown by Ing. Oscar Ochoa Mendoza, Director of the Banco de Semillas at the Escuela Nacional De Ciencias Forestales. His help was indispensable in making some of my pine and resin collections in Honduras.

I am grateful for Connie Millar's generosity with photographs and information on *Pinus muricata* in Baja California Norte.

To Mr. Oscar Rosado, Principle Forestry Officer for Belize, I express my appreciation for his interest and assistance with my pine and resin collections at Mountain Pine Ridge, Belize.

To Willy and Magdi Mittak, I wish to express my deep appreciation for their hospitality and many acts of kindness during my collecting trips in Guatemala.

For Norm and Margaret Borlaug's unstinting hospitality during my collecting trips in Mexico, I offer my sincere thanks. To Ruth Brunstetter I express my appreciation for her fine drawings.

I acknowledge with gratitude two grants from The Rockefeller Foundation that provided financial support for a number of collecting trips in Mexico and Guatemala.

I am most grateful for a grant from The American Philosophical Society that provided partial support for the costs of turpentine analyses.

Special thanks are expressed here to the Harvard University Herbaria for permission to use illustrations from Shaw's works on *Pinus*.

J. P. Perry, Jr.

CHAPTER 1

INTRODUCTION

The first Europeans to see the pine forests of Mexico were Hernan Cortes and his followers, when, in 1519, they began their historic march from the Gulf of Mexico to Tenochitlán, ancient capital of the Aztecs. Bernal Díaz, a member of that group, recorded their progress as they slowly ascended the pine-forested slopes of the mountains surrounding the great valley of Mexico.

Since that time, information about the pine forests of Mexico and Central America has accumulated, at first slowly and haltingly, then more rapidly up to the past 100 years when our knowledge about the origin and nature of these pines expanded enormously. Now from research and studies of geographers, geologists, paleobotanists, geneticists, taxonomists, and botanists, a fairly clear picture of the origin and development of pines in the North American continent has emerged. Time and space does not permit a review of that information—a number of volumes would be required for that—here it will only be possible to touch on some of the landmarks of this history.

ORIGIN OF PINES IN NORTH AMERICA

Geographers and paleobotanists agree that during the Mesozoic and Cenozoic eras and up to the Middle Pleistocene era, North America was intermittently connected with northeastern Asia in the area of the present Bering Sea. During this period, North America was also joined to Northern Europe by land connections with Greenland and Iceland. These connections provided migration routes for pines from northeastern Asia to North America and from northeastern North America to northern Europe as well.

During the Cretaceous period, pines were widely distributed in what is now Canada and the United States and were already differentiated into the species which constitute the two principal sub-genera, Haploxylon and Diploxylon.

In the Early Tertiary period, the Cretaceous seas that covered the west-central part of the United States and Canada and most of Mexico and Guatemala subsided. Plants then migrated southward from the eastern United States, around the Gulf of Mexico to Mexico and parts of Central America. During this same period pines were also migrating to Mexico from the western United States along the West Coast mountain ranges.

By the end of the Tertiary period, great uplifts had occurred in western North America radically altering the topography of the region. These monumental changes had equally important effects on the pine populations of that vast area. Many species disappeared entirely while others were reduced to relict populations.

The Quaternary period saw the advent of the great glaciers. In North America the ice sheet covered Canada and extended into the United States to the state of Washington on the Pacific Coast, to Long Island, New York on the Atlantic. In the east-central area it pushed as far south as southern Illinois and the present Ohio River (Fig. 1.1). During this period, the pine forests of Canada were wiped out, although a few species survived in small refugia in Alaska. Many eastern and western species in the United States, unable to adapt to the changing climate and different soil conditions, slowly disappeared. Many others adapted to the cooler climate and migrated southward.

MIGRATION OF PINES TO MEXICO AND CENTRAL AMERICA

As pointed out earlier, pines were already migrating southward into Mexico during the early Tertiary period. The advance and retreat of the great glaciers, only 2,400–3,200 kilometers (km) north of the present Mexico–United States border, added impetus to the southward migration. However, it should be pointed out that the southward migration was occasionally reversed as the glaciers advanced and retreated over a period of thousands of years. Many pine species took advantage of those intervals of warmer, drier climate and migrated northward, occupying open lands left by the retreating glaciers. There was, however, a general southward migration of pines into Mexico and Central America during this period (Fig. 1.2).

THE MOUNTAINS OF MEXICO AND CENTRAL AMERICA

There seems to be no doubt that pines migrated southward along the mountain ranges of Mexico and Central America.

In Mexico there are two important north–south mountain ranges: the Sierra Madre Occidental in the west (Fig. 1.3) and the Sierra Madre Oriental in the east. The Sierra Madre Occidental is a continuation of the western mountain ranges that extend southward from Alaska, Canada, and the United States. Most botanists and taxonomists believe that this broad, western mountain range was the principal migration route for western pines into Mexico and Central America.

In eastern Mexico, the Sierra Madre Oriental joins the easternmost ranges of the Rocky Mountains at the Big Bend area of Texas. For the first 400 km it is divided into a number of relatively low (1,000 m), arid, roughly parallel ranges. However, near the cities of Saltillo and Monterrey the mountains rise abruptly to altitudes of 2,000 m and more. Here a number of short, broken ranges extend in a westerly direction for about 250 km. In the Monterrey area the Sierra Madre Oriental is about 250 km from the Gulf of Mexico; however, as it continues southward, the distance to the coast narrows rapidly until at Veracruz, the mountains almost reach the Gulf. While this range is much narrower than the Sierra Madre Occidental, it is very rugged with a number of snow-capped peaks towering above 4,000 m and a narrow escarpment that drops abruptly to the coastal plain.

In northern central Mexico the western and eastern mountain ranges are separated by a broad, arid central plateau that extends from the Texas, Arizona–Mexico border south to about 19° N latitude. At that point the Great Cross Range or Volcanic Axis extends across Mexico, joining the western and eastern ranges with a chain of volcanic mountains reaching heights of 3,000 and 4,000 m. In the states of Michoacán, Mexico, Morelos, and Puebla, the southern slopes of this Great Cross Range drop rapidly into the dry, tropical Rio Balsas Basin.

On the west the Sierra Madre del Sur continues along the Pacific Coast as a narrow range of mountains that rise almost from the sea.

In the east the Sierra Madre Oriental, after joining with the Great Cross Range in Puebla, continues southeastward and merges with the Sierra Madre del Sur around the Valley of Oaxaca. At this point the mountain ranges extend eastward to the Isthmus of Tehuantepec.

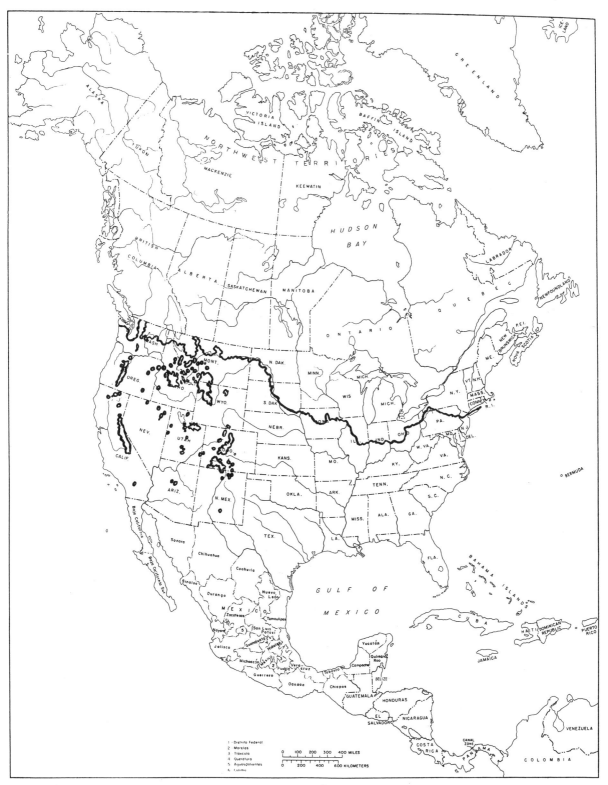

Fig. 1.1. Maximum extent of glaciation in North America during the Wisconsin glacial stage, Pleistocene epoch. From: USDA Forest Service Miscellaneous Publication No. 1146, slightly modified.

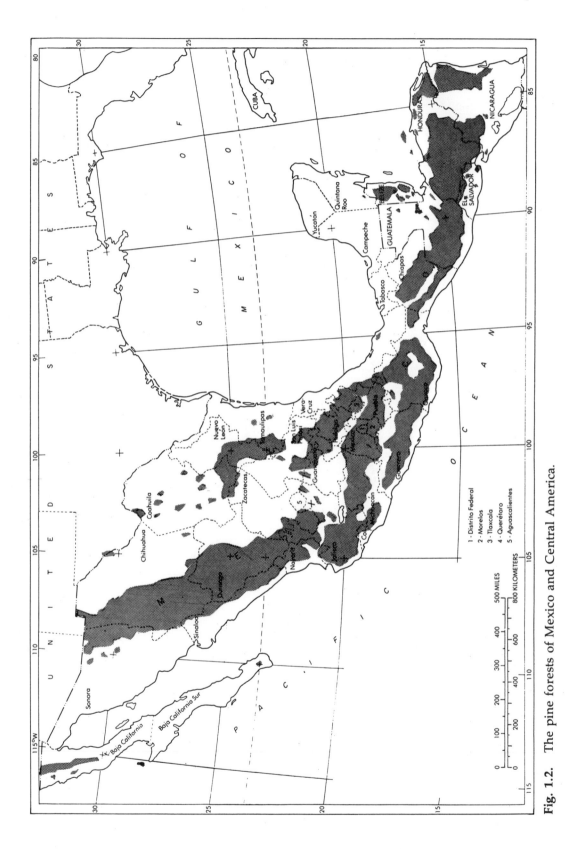

Fig. 1.2. The pine forests of Mexico and Central America.

Fig. 1.3. Looking west by north across the Sierra Madre Occidental near El Salto, Durango, Mexico.

The low-lying Isthmus has, during various periods of geologic history, been covered by the sea. During the Pliocene period the Isthmus re-emerged as a relatively low, hot, dry area. At present it appears to form a partial barrier between pines growing in the mountains of Oaxaca and pines of the Chiapas Highlands.

East of the Isthmus the mountains rise again to more than 2,000 m and again divide into two principal ranges, the Sierra Madre de Chiapas and the Mesa de Chiapas. The Sierra Madre de Chiapas continues southeastward along the Pacific coast until, at the Mexico–Guatemala border, it merges into the very high chain of volcanic mountains that extend along the Pacific coast of Guatemala. The Sierra Madre de Chiapas is separated from the mountain ranges of the Mesa de Chiapas by the hot, dry Rio Grijalva Basin. Those high ranges extend in a southeasterly direction to the Guatemalan border where they merge into the Sierra de Los Cuchumatanes. In northwestern Guatemala the Sierra de Los Cuchumatanes gradually turns eastward and divides into two smaller parallel ranges, the Sierra de Santa Cruz and the Sierra de Las Minas. Both are rather isolated ranges that extend eastward from central Guatemala to the Gulf of Honduras. Los Cuchumatanes and the two eastern ranges are closely joined to the chain of volcanic mountains along the Pacific coast by many short interconnecting mountains and small mesas. In Northern Guatemala the Sierra de Los Cuchumatanes and the Sierra de Santa Cruz slope gradually downward to the hot, tropical lowlands of the Peten.

In the southeastern area of the Peten, near Poptun, a small range of hills rises to about 800 m and extend eastward across the Peten–Belize boundary. This range, known as the Maya Mountains, gradually rises to 1,000 m and extends northward in Belize parallel to the Gulf of Honduras for about 100 km. These are the only mountains in Belize.

In southeastern Guatemala the range of high volcanic mountains continues eastward along the Pacific and merge into a similar volcanic chain extending along the Pacific coast of El Salvador. Although the volcanoes in El Salvador are not as high as those of Guatemala, they form an impressive range along the edge of the Pacific ocean.

From central Guatemala in the Jalapa area, a series of short, broken ranges extend southeastward to the Guatemala–El Salvador–Honduras border. Here they merge into a broad, irregular mountain range that forms the border between El Salvador and Honduras. This range, with peaks reaching 2,000–3,000 m, follows a southeasterly direction and is joined by El Salvador's volcanic coastal range at the Gulf of Fonseca where the borders of El Salvador, Honduras, and Nicaragua meet on the Pacific coast. This same broad range of mountains extends along the short (about 100 km) Honduran Pacific coast (the Gulf of Fonseca) and, following a southeasterly course, continues into Nicaragua.

In western Honduras, beginning near the Guatemala border, a series of roughly parallel broken ranges extend north and eastward from the high, broad western rampart to the Caribbean coast. The Sierra de Celaque is perhaps the least known and most isolated of these short broken ranges. The Cordillera de Montecilla is another short, more accessible range, with the well-known Cerro Santa Bárbara rising over 2,800 m above Lago de Yohoa. Along the north coast, the Sierra Nombre de Díos extends eastward for about 200 km. Similar west–northeast ranges are Sierra La Esperanza and Sierra de Agalta. The Cordillera de Jalapa, Cordillera Entre Rios, and Montañas de Colon extend along the Honduras–Nicaraguan border with their northeastern terminus at the coastal plain known as the Mosquitia.

The Mosquitia of Honduras is a broad, generally level area, slightly above sea level, about 100 × 150 km, bordering the Caribbean Sea on the northeast and Nicaragua on the south.

The western mountain range of Honduras continues southeastward along the Pacific coast of Nicaragua. A line of relatively small, volcanic cones follows the Pacific coast; however, they do not form a part of the principal mountain range that lies east of Lago de Managua and Lago de Nicaragua. As in Honduras, a number of smaller parallel mountain ranges extend northeastward and eastward from the broader western range. In the north, the Cordillera Isabella parallels the Nicaragua–Honduras border for about 150 km. The next range south, the Cordillera Dariense extends eastward for about 150 km. The Montañas de Huapi also extends eastward for about 100 km. The most southerly range, the Cordillera de Yolaina extends eastward from Lago de Nicaragua to the Caribbean Sea. South of this range, the mountains drop slowly to the lowland area of the Nicaragua–Coasta Rica border.

In northeastern Nicaragua, the Mosquitia lowlands of Honduras continue southward along the Caribbean coast for about 300 km to the port of Bluefields. This is a tremendous area averaging about 100–150 km in width. Only one pine, *Pinus caribaea* var. *hondurensis* (Senecl.) Barr. et Golf, grows in the entire Mosquitia from Punta Patuca on the Honduras coast to Bluefields on the Nicaragua–Caribbean coast, a straight north–south distance of about 400 km. The southern limit of North American pines occurs here at 12° N. latitude.

CLIMATE

The pines of Mexico and Central America occur between latitudes 12 and 32° N. The Tropic of Cancer crosses Mexico at about the center of the country, so most of the pine areas with which we are concerned could be considered tropical. However, that is true only in a geographic, but not a climatic sense. Mexico and Central America are predominantly mountainous countries and so present a multitude of climates that range from humid tropical on the narrow coastal plains of the south, to cold temperate on the high mountains of the northern ranges and even boreal conditions on the high, snow-capped peaks. The bold topography of the mountain ranges, often dropping rapidly from 3,000 to 1,000 m and less, results in dramatic changes in the climate over very short distances. In this respect, altitude rather than latitude is the more important factor controlling climate, which in turn, affects species and genetic diversity in the pines.

It is not possible to present here the multitude of climates of these tremendous mountain ranges and valleys. It is possible, however, to give a general picture of rainfall and temperature conditions for some broad, geographic areas. Throughout most of Mexico and Central America there is a rainy season between June and October. In some areas the rains may begin in May and last until November, in others rain falls only during July, August, and September. However, in general, the summer months are the months when most (70–90%) of the rain occurs. The remaining seven or eight months are generally quite dry (Fig. 1.4).

Baja California Norte, Baja California Sur, and northwest Sonora are desert areas that receive about 200 mm of rain annually. However, in Baja California Norte, the Sierra de Juárez and Sierra San Pedro Mártir are exceptions. These two small mountain ranges reach altitudes of 1,000–3,000 m and annual rainfall increases to 600 mm. Here are found the southernmost limits of a number of California pines.

In the northern ranges of the Sierra Madre Occidental, in eastern Sonora, and western Chihuahua, snow, sleet and rain commonly occur during the winter months and annual rainfall may reach 500–1,000 mm. Further south along these same ranges snow may occur during winter storms as far south as the high mountains of the Great Cross Range in the states of Colima, Jalisco, Michoacán, Mexico, and Puebla. In these areas annual rainfall increases to 1,000–1,400 mm.

In the low ranges of the northernmost Sierra Madre Oriental, near the Big Bend area of Texas, snow, frosts, and some rain occur during December and January. This is desert area with annual rainfall of 250–300 mm. Further south where the mountains rise abruptly near Saltillo and Monterrey, rainfall increases and snow and sleet occur on the high peaks during the winter months as far south as the 4,000 m mountain, Peña de Nevada at the

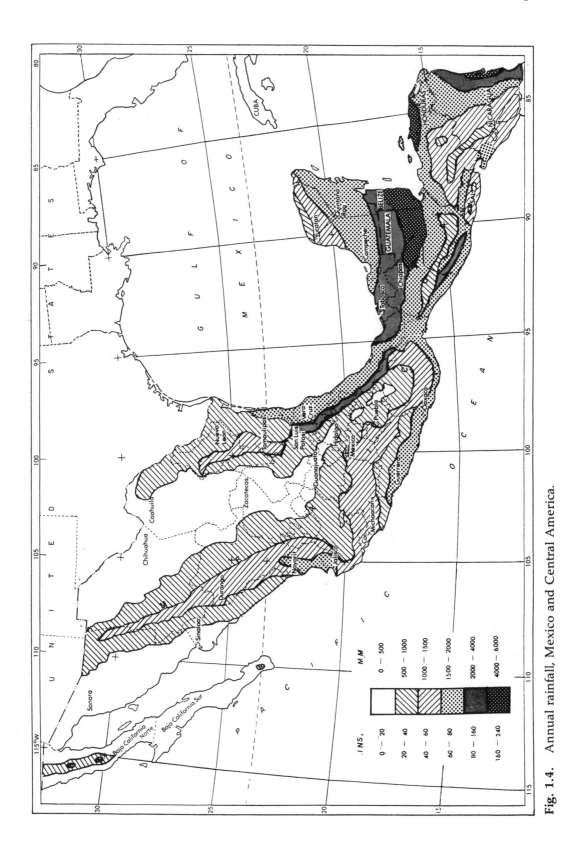

Fig. 1.4. Annual rainfall, Mexico and Central America.

border of southern Nuevo León and San Luis Potosí. Rainfall along this range is 900–1,500 mm annually.

On the lower (1,000 m) western slopes of these mountains, annual rainfall is 300–500 mm. However, the eastern slopes that face the moisture-laden winds from the Gulf of Mexico and the Caribbean have much higher rainfall—1,500–3,000 mm. This high rainfall occurs mostly in the long, narrow escarpment area that extends along the mountains from west-central Tamaulipas southward into Veracruz, Hidalgo, Oaxaca, Chiapas, Guatemala, and Honduras.

The broad central mesa separating the eastern and western ranges is quite dry. The northern part of the mesa near the Texas border is desert country with annual rainfall of 200–250 mm. Further south near Durango and Zacatecas, annual rainfall increases to 500–600 mm. In the high mountains of the Great Cross Range, rainfall increases to 1,000–1,500 mm. Annual rainfall in the hot, Rio Balsas Basin is 700–900 mm. Southeastward in the low, hot Oaxaca Valley, rainfall is 500–800 mm and further south in the Grijalva Basin of Chiapas, annual rainfall is 700–900 mm.

The Sierra Madre del Sur and the Sierra Madre de Chiapas follow the Pacific Coast of Southern Mexico and have annual rainfall of 1,500–2,500 mm with most of the moisture falling on the high, southwestern slopes facing the Pacific winds. The Mesa de Chiapas also receives 1,500–3,000 mm of rain and this pattern extends south and eastward along the Cuchumatanes Mountains in Guatemala.

In the more southerly latitudes (Guatemala, Belize, Honduras, and Nicaragua) annual rainfall is generally somewhat higher than in most of Mexico. However, a similar pattern appears, i.e. the eastern and northeastern mountain slopes facing the Gulf of Mexico and the Caribbean Sea have the highest annual rainfall 2,000–4,000 mm. The low-lying Peten area of Guatemala has about 1,500–2,500 mm annually. This pattern extends into Belize where the Maya Mountains receive 2,500–1,000 mm annually. In dry central-southeastern Guatemala (the departments of Sacatepequez, Guatemala, Japala, and Chiquimula), rainfall ranges from 500–1,000 mm. The high mountain range that extends along the Pacific coast receives 3,000–4,000 mm, mostly on the high southwestern slopes facing winds from the Pacific. The coastal and central mountain ranges continue southeastward into El Salvador and Honduras. Here, too, the high mountain slopes receive the most rain—1,500–2,000 mm annually. In Honduras the northeastern mountain slopes facing the Caribbean Sea have the highest rainfall. The mountains forming the border between Honduras and El Salvador cast a rain shadow into northern El Salvador. Thus El Salvador is dependent for most of its rainfall on winds from the Pacific. A few of the highest mountain peaks may receive moisture from both the Caribbean and the Pacific. At El Salvador's Federal Park, Monte Cristo, located at the boundary junctions of El Salvador, Honduras, and Guatemala. I was told that winds from the northeast and from the southwest brought clouds, mist, and rains. Annual rainfall was estimated at 3,000–4,000 mm. I found the peak covered with typical broadleaf cloud forest and the lower slopes (2,500 m) pine forested.

At Cerro El Pital, on the western Honduras–El Salvador border, I was told that the peak was covered with cloud forest. In June, 1972, while collecting on the lower southwestern slopes at an altitude of 2,200 m, I found the slopes pine-forested and the peak shrouded in clouds.

The mountains of northern Nicaragua are a continuation of the Honduras–El Salvador range and have a similar effect on the rainfall in that area. In general though, the mountain ranges become lower as they extend southeastward along Lago de Nicaragua and rainfall decreases as well.

In all of these Central American countries Guatemala, Belize, Honduras, El Salvador, and Nicaragua, the rainy season generally begins in May and continues into October. The hottest months are March, April, and May. As the rainy season gathers force, temperature decreases slightly in June, July, and August. The coldest months are usually November,

December, January, and February with temperatures reaching the lowest levels at the highest altitudes.

SUMMARY

From Canada and the United States pines migrated southward into Mexico and Central America along two mountain ranges, the Sierra Madre Occidental in the west and the Sierra Madre Oriental in the east. Between these ranges lies the high, arid Mesa Central that extends from the Mexico, Arizona–New Mexico–Texas border south to about 19° N. latitude. Here the great Volcanic Axis extends across Mexico from the Pacific to the Gulf of Mexico. This rugged, broken range was formed, as its name implies, by volcanic activity. Here are found the spectacular volcanic peaks of Nevado de Colima (4,300 m), Tancítaro (4,200 m), Nevado de Toluca (4,600 m), Malinche (4,500 m), Tláloc (4,200 m), Popocatepetl (5,500 m), Ixtaccihuatl (5,300 m), and Orizaba (5,700 m). The eastern and western ranges continue south and eastward and merge in Oaxaca where they slope eastward to the Isthmus of Tehuantepec. They rise again in Chiapas as two roughly parallel ranges, one extending along the Pacific coast of Chiapas, Guatemala, and El Salvador; another broader, inland range extending from Chiapas to Guatemala and Honduras. In southwestern Honduras the two ranges merge and continue southeastward through Nicaragua to the border of Coasta Rica.

In Guatemala, Honduras, and Nicaragua a number of roughly parallel broken ranges extend eastward from the broad central range of mountains. In eastern Honduras and Nicaragua a broad, lowland area known as the Mosquitia, extends southward along the Caribbean coast to Bluefields, Nicaragua. Here at 12° N. latitude, is the southernmost point reached by the genus *Pinus* in North America.

Rainfall and temperature often change abruptly over these mountain ranges with rapid changes in altitude. Despite these myriad microclimates of low valleys and high mountains, the climate of Mexico and Central America is best described as biseasonal, i.e. a rainy season and a dry season. In general, most rainfall occurs between May and October. The driest months are usually November to April. There are, of course, many exceptions; in northern Mexico (Baja California Norte, Chihuahua, and parts of Sonora) winter rains, sleet, and snow contribute about one-third of the annual rainfall. Another exception to the rainy season–dry season is the climate of the high mountain slopes. Here at 3,000–4,000 m, frost, sleet, and rain often occur during any month of the year. The narrow escarpment area of Veracruz, Oaxaca, and Chiapas is yet another exception since mists, clouds, and rain shroud those slopes most of the year.

Throughout the entire area, the hottest months are usually March, April, and May, i.e. just prior to the onset of the rainy season. The coldest months are generally November, December, January, and February. Here again altitude has a profound influence on climate and vegetation; at altitudes of 2,000–3,000 m frosts are common during the nights of the coldest months; at lower elevations, 500–1,000 m nights are frost-free and the climate is subtropical to tropical.

CHAPTER 2

CLASSIFICATION

HISTORICAL

Classification of the pines can be traced back to Ancient Greece when Theophrastus, about 300 B.C. described a number of different pines as evergreen plants with a woody cone and linear leaves, best propagated by seeds. The classical Latin name *Pinus* has been credited to the Roman, Pliny the Elder, a native of northern Italy, who lived during the first century A.D. During the period 1500–1600, Andrea Cesalpino gave a general description of the "genus *Pinus*" and recognized two groups of pines—wild and cultivated.

It seems clear that during these early years, despite many descriptions of different pines, there was no clear concept of a genus *Pinus*. However, in 1719, Tournefort defined and then described the genus. In his *Species Plantarum,* Linnaeus (1753), listed the genus *Pinus* in which he included only five species. Perhaps his greatest contributions were the consistent use of a nomenclatural system that could be applied to all plants, and that flower structure provided a common base for the classification of seed-bearing plants, since plants with similar flower parts possessed other similarities indicating a common lineage. This type of classification, i.e. based on presumed relationships, is called a "natural" system. Botanists and taxonomists endeavoring to unravel the intricate and ancient relationships of plants, developed many "natural" classification systems. As new information about older, recognized species became available and as new species were discovered, old systems were discarded and replaced by newer systems.

As more detailed studies are made of individual plants and populations of plants, a better and more complete understanding of their relationships emerge. This may require changes in the system of plant classification. It is clear then that a system of plant classification is not static, nor can it be, as long as reliable studies continue in the fields of plant ecology, genetics, plant chemistry, paleobotany, geographical distribution, botany and taxonomy.

From the diverse efforts to construct plant classification systems, general, though not complete, agreement on a system for grouping related plants has developed. Classification of a variety of *ayacahuite* pine illustrates the positions or "rank" of the different categories.

Kingdom—Plant
  Division—Spermatophyta
    Subdivision—Gymnospermae
      Order—Coniferales
        Family—Pinaceae
          Genus—Pinus
            Species—*Pinus ayacahuite* Ehrenberg
              Variety—*Pinus ayacahuite* var. *veitchii* Shaw

NOMENCLATURE

Since we will be concerned with the "genus" *Pinus* and with descriptions of "species" and "varieties" of pines, it is important that these words be clearly understood. Here we define "species" as groups of similar, interbreeding populations that are generally, but by no means always, reproductively isolated from other such groups.

Varieties of species are generally distinguished as the result of minor variations in length of leaves, number of leaves, cone size and so forth, however, the varieties often interbreed with the species. *Variety* as used here is thought of as a stage in the development of a *species.*

Genus is a group of related species and *family* is a group of related genera and on upward through the higher categories. Thus the terms "species", "genus", "family" and "order" etc. are categories that designate a rank or level in the classification system used here.

Individuals placed within a "species" category must be formally recognized by being described under a designated name. Without a clear description and identification (name), it would be impossible to pass on information about living organisms. Taxonomists have, among other things, developed a scientific method for naming all living organisms. Linnaeus, in 1753, published his *Species Planatarum* in which he listed nearly 6,000 species in 1,000 genera. While he did not invent binominal nomenclature, his consistent use of binary names employing precise Latin terminology provided the starting point for modern botanical nomenclature.

Under the Linnean binomial system, the scientific name, always in Latin, for all plants and animals consists of two words. The first word names the genus which is a group of closely related species. The second word is the species. Scientific names are always italicized, the generic name always begins with a capital and the species name with a small letter. Each scientific name is followed by the full or abbreviated name of the person or persons who first correctly described and published the name and description of the plant. The author's name is never underscored or italicized. An example of a scientific name is *Pinus teocote.* Martínez. The only way to unambiguously refer to a plant (taxon) is to give the genus name (in this example *Pinus*), species epithet (*teocote*) and author of the name (Martínez).

In this book the species is considered the basic unit of classification, though varieties and forms are also described when they differ significantly from the typical species. The varietal name always follows the specific name, and is followed by the name of the person who first described the variety; for example, *Pinus ayacahuite* var. *brachyptera* Shaw.

Local or common names are also given for a number of the pines; however, these can seldom be used to identify with certainty a particular species. For example, throughout Mexico, Guatemala and Central America, when inquiring about the location of groups of pine trees, two "standard" words were found to apply to all pine trees: "ocote" which is a corruption of the Nahuatl "ocotl", and "pino", Spanish for pine. Although there are local names for many species of pines, these are often confusing, since in a different locality the same name may be applied to a different pine species.

Rules governing the use of scientific names and development of new ones are now set forth in the *International Code of Botanical Nomenclature* (1978). This code was developed at a series of International Botanical Congresses. The first meeting was held in Paris in 1867 and provided, among other things, that a plant could have only one valid scientific name, that two different species or two different genera could not have the same name and that generic and specific combinations should be followed by the name or names of their authors. At one of the congresses it was pointed out that "the essential points in nomenclature are (1) to aim at fixity of names; (2) to avoid or to reject the use of forms and names which may cause error or ambiguity or throw science into confusion." With this advice in mind, the scientific names used throughout this book are those generally accepted by botanists and taxonomists.

IDENTIFICATION

When attempting to identify the pines of Mexico and Central America it is very important to remember that no two pine trees are ever exactly alike, there is always some variation. Among the pines of a particular species, leaves of individual trees may be shorter than those of other trees, the bark slightly different, the cones slightly different in size or shape and so on. One needs then, to obtain some "feel" for the range of variation to be expected within a species. This can be accomplished in a number of ways. Probably it is best to first read the descriptions and study photographs and drawings of the different species. Then visit herbaria to examine specimens of cones and leaves, and visit arboreta where some of the pines are growing. Finally and most importantly, go into the field with a good key to identification and if possible, a guide already familiar with the species, and study the trees in their natural habitat. It is also important to study the pines over their entire range. Granted, this may not be possible during a single field trip, still every trip leads to a better understanding and greater knowledge of the different species particularly when they are seen under differing ecological conditions such as altitude, site, temperature and moisture.

In the descriptions of the pines of Mexico and Central America, botanical terms such as leaves, bracts, resin canals, cone scales, apophyses, umbo, peduncle, seed wing, etc. are used to describe each species. The following definitions of these words may be helpful when reading the descriptions.

THE TREE—Pines range in size from occasionally low and bushy to usually tall, straight, evergreen trees with a single bole. In mature trees the crown is usually pyramidal though often rounded to flat-topped. In young trees the branches are generally regularly spaced in whorls and the form is distinctly pyramidal.

BARK—While bark of most pine species varies greatly, it remains a very important identification character. Although the outer bark is dead, it still performs the vital function of protecting the living inner bark and cambium. Bark is often distinguished as "early formation" or "late formation" and this distinction serves as a general but by no means precise rule for distinguishing between the Hard Pines and the Soft Pines. In the Hard Pines bark formation begins very early and the trunks of young trees are soon covered with gray, scaly, rough bark. In the Soft Pines bark formation is delayed for many years, thus the trunks of young trees remain very smooth. Rough, scaly bark formation usually first appears at the base of pines and with age gradually extends upward on the trunk. However, in Soft Pines the upper trunk or stem is invariably smooth and in Hard Pines the upper stem is almost always rough and scaly. There are other differences that readily separate the Hard Pines from the Soft Pines. These will be discussed later.

Bark thickness generally increases with age and may reach 5–10 cm in some species. Thickness together with texture, size and shape of the plates and color are important characteristics: In *Pinus arizonica* Engelm. the bark is thick, deeply fissured and formed into large, roughly rectangular, reddish brown plates. In *P. patula* Schl. et Cham., bark on the upper stem or trunk is always very thin and scaly and reddish-yellowish brown; on the lower trunk it is thick, deeply fissured, very rough and brown-grayish brown.

Color of the freshly cut inner bark is often useful in distinguishing some species. For example, *P. lawsoni* Roezl. has very distinctive reddish purple inner bark. Also the color of the inner surface of scales or platelets of mature bark can occasionally be helpful; in *P. douglasiana* Mart., they are sulfur-yellow, while in *Pinus teocote* Schl. et Cham., they are reddish brown.

BRANCHLET—As used here they are thought of as an entire season's growth from a single bud. This begins in the spring with the buds at the ends of the past season's branchlet.

Branchlet length varies a great deal ranging from a few centimeters to 50 cm or more. It is on the new branchlets that male (staminate catkins) and female (pistillate, conelets) flowers are borne together with the young leaves.

Smoothness or roughness of the branchlet is an important character in determining to which group of pines a species belongs (Fig. 2.1). Branchlets are smooth when bases of the leaf bracts are not decurrent; instead of becoming dry and scaly and eventually falling, the bases of the bracts gradually become submerged into and form a part of the smooth bark on the young branchlet. When the branchlets are rough, the opposite occurs; bases of the leaf bracts become dry and scaly and eventually fall from the branchlet, leaving the surface very rough. Smooth branchlets are characteristic of all the Soft Pines and, with a few exceptions, the Hard Pines have rough and scaly branchlets.

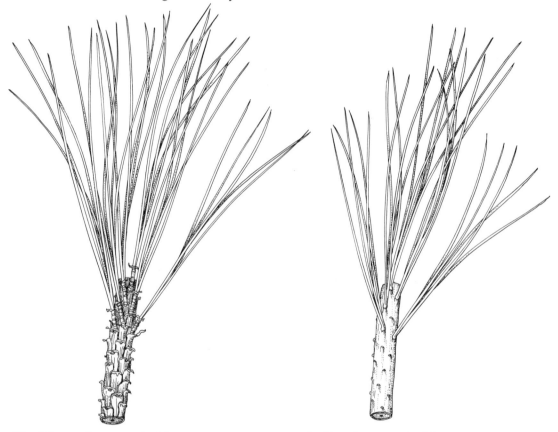

Fig. 2.1.   **a.** Decurrent leaf bracts.   **b.** Non-decurrent leaf bracts.

LEAVES—Botanists distinguish three kinds of leaves; the first to appear after the seed germinates are the cotyledons or "seed leaves" (Fig. 2.2). These may range in number from 3 to 24 and, though the number is variable for a particular species, it is still helpful in identifying some species. For example, *P. contorta* subsp. *murrayana* found in Baja California has 3–8 cotyledons while *P. maximartinezii* Rzedowski, in central Mexico, has from 18 to 24 cotyledons.

The second kind of leaves are called primary or "juvenile" leaves. These develop immediately after the cotyledons emerge and are small, solitary, spirally arranged and in most species, shed in a few weeks. However, before the juvenile leaves fall, the secondary or adult leaves, which form the evergreen foliage that is characteristic of the genus *Pinus*, begin to develop. These are borne in a basal sheath of scales termed the "needle sheath" or

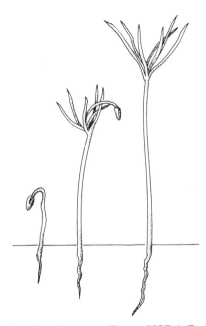

Fig. 2.2. Pine seedling, cotyledon development. From: USDA Forest Service Handbook No. 450, Fig. 4, p. 629, slightly modified.

"fascicle". In some species the sheath is deciduous (most of the Soft Pines) and in other species it is persistent (most of the Hard Pines). Some species have very long, sticky or gummy sheaths while others have short, scaly or papery sheaths. Thus the sheath or fascicle is very useful in identifying some species.

The number of leaves in a fascicle varies from 1 to 8; very rarely 1, mostly 2, 3, 5 and occasionally 4, 6, 7 and 8. The number in a fascicle is fairly constant in most species, and thus forms a helpful characteristic in species identifications. It is wise, however, in making needle counts to take a large number of samples from many different locations in the crown.

Length of pine leaves varies a great deal even within a given species. However, some species always produce short needles (the *Cembroides* group), others are characterized by medium length needles or leaves (the *Montezumae* group) and a few have very long needles (*P. michoacana* Mart. and *P. nubicola* Perry). As in the counting of numbers of needles, a reliable measurement of needle length requires a large number of samples from various locations in the crown rather than a few leaves from a single, low branch. Leaves taken from the ground directly beneath an isolated tree also provide a good foliage sample.

The flexibility of leaves is another helpful character in identification (Fig. 2.3). Some species always produce stiff, erect leaves (*P. hartwegii* Lindl.). Others always have flexible, slightly drooping leaves (*P. pseudostrobus* Lindl.) and still others have very flexible, pendent leaves (*P. patula, P. lumholtzii* Rob. et Fern.).

All pine leaves have minute openings through the outer layer of cells (Fig. 2.4). These openings, called stomata, permit the movement of carbon dioxide and oxygen from the atmosphere into the living cells within the leaf. In most of the Soft Pines, stomatal openings occur only on the ventral surfaces of the leaves and in some species the openings form minute, silver–white lines that give a characteristic silvery color to the ventral surfaces of the leaves. This is particularly evident in *P. ayacahuite* and its varieties *veitchii* and *brachyptera.* In the Hard Pines stomata are found on all surfaces of the leaves.

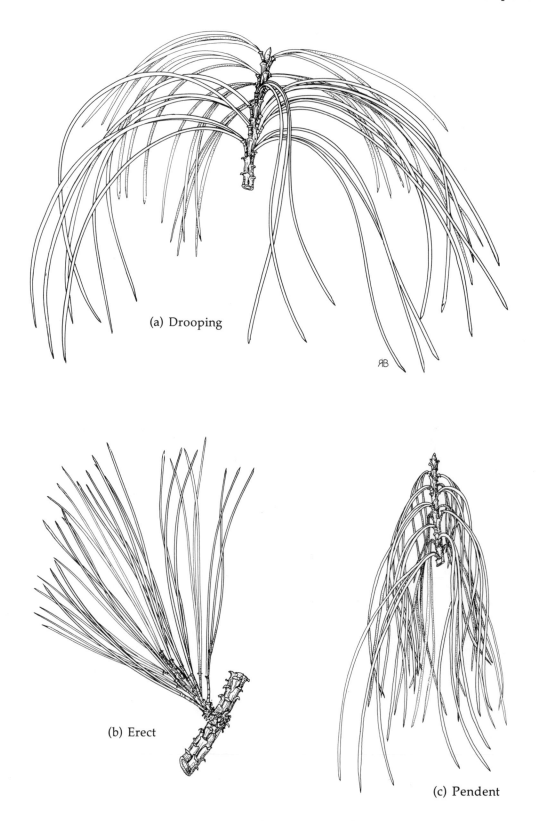

(a) Drooping

(b) Erect

(c) Pendent

Fig. 2.3. Leaf habit.

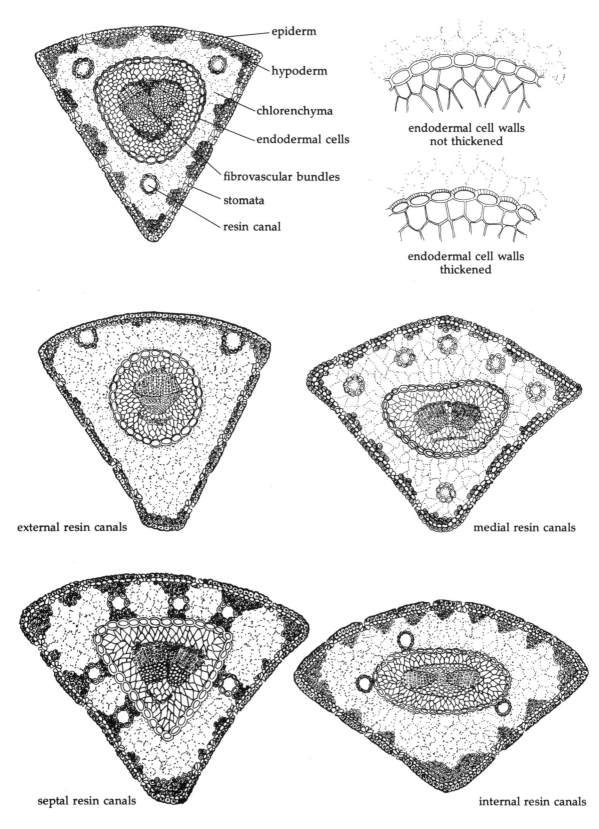

Fig. 2.4. Pine leaf anatomy.

In descriptions of the different species reference is often made to internal characters of the leaf such as the endodermal cells, the resin canals and their location and number, and the fibrovascular bundles. While it is usually not possible in the field to accurately determine the position and number of resin canals and fibrovascular bundles, sample leaves can be sectioned and examined under a low power microscope or a hand lens to accurately locate the endodermal cells, resin canals, and the fibrovascular bundles. For this reason information has been included here on those important diagnostic characters.

Resin canals are found in the green tissue of the leaves (Fig. 2.4). Their location within the tissue is described as:

(a) External—against the outer cells (the hypoderm),
(b) Internal—against the cells surrounding the fibrovascular bundle (the endoderm),
(c) Medial—not touching the hypoderm or the endoderm,
(d) Septal—touching both the hypoderm and the endoderm.

Occasionally leaves have resin canals, mostly external with one or two that are medial; other leaves may possess mostly medial canals with occasionally one or two internal. Similarly, leaves with septal canals may occasionally have an internal canal that is not septal. Rarely some leaves may be found that do not have resin canals, but this condition is not associated with any particular species. (*P. Donnell-Smithii* Mast. may be an exception, since many leaves were found without resin canals).

Location of the resin canals is an important diagnostic feature. Many of the Soft Pines always have external resin canals. Only two North American species of Hard Pines possess external resin canals, most of the others have internal or medial canals. On the other hand only a few species within the Hard Pine group have septal canals, while none of the Soft Pines possess them. The number of resin canals within a leaf is quite variable in some species and in others fairly constant. Among the different pine species, location of the canals appears to be a more reliable identification feature than number of canals; however, the two characters used together are very helpful in identifying many species.

The fibrovascular bundle is located in the center of the leaf and, as its name implies, consists of a number of cells arranged in a group or bundle. In the Soft Pines there is a single fibrovascular bundle in each leaf (Fig. 2.5). In the Hard Pines there are two fibrovascular bundles in each leaf. The two bundles in the Hard Pines are often contiguous and may appear to form a single bundle; however, closer study will usually reveal a dual bundle. This distinction between the Soft Pines and the Hard Pines is so constant it is used as the basis for a major division of the genus *Pinus* into two subgenera.

Haploxylon—the Soft Pines having a single fibrovascular bundle in each leaf,
Diploxylon—the Hard Pines, having two fibrovascular bundles in each leaf.

FLOWERS—in the pines, male and female flowers are borne on the same tree. Male flowers known as "staminate catkins," occur in crowded clusters on new shoots at the ends of the branches and are pollen-bearing. Female flowers known as "pistillate flowers," are generally borne laterally on new shoots and appear as minute cones. When ripe for fertilization by pollen shed from the staminate catkins, tiny scales of the pistillate flower open slightly so pollen grains may sift down between them. After pollination, the minute scales close and the conelet begins its development. The staminate flowers wither and fall after shedding their pollen.

CONELETS—Length of the conelet peduncle (stem) is often a help in identification; some species always have conelets with very long peduncles while other species have conelets with medium or short peduncles. In a few species, the conelet peduncle is reflexed rather than straight. Color is occasionally a distinctive character, some conelets being pale pink and rose, others reddish purple. Scales of the conelets vary too, in some species, the margins of the scales are rounded, in other species the scale margin may terminate in a

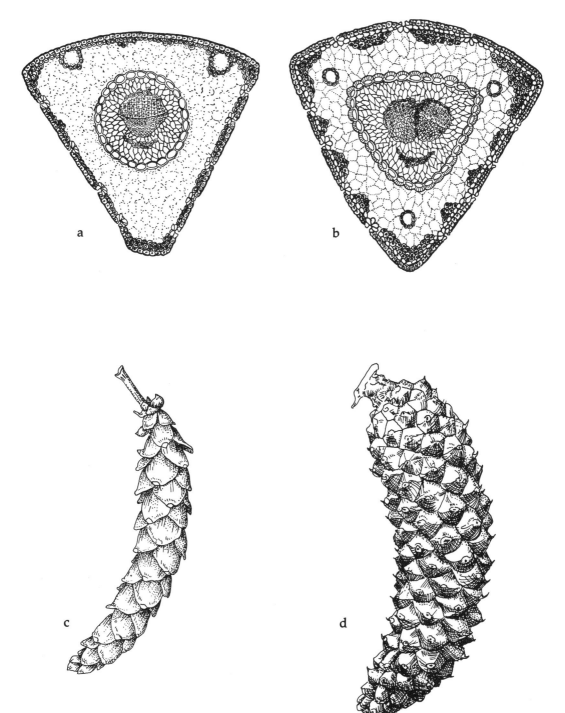

Fig. 2.5. **a.** Haploxylon, soft pine needle section with a single fibrovascular bundle. **b.** Diploxylon, hard pine needle section with two fibrovascular bundles. **c.** Haploxylon, soft pine cone. **d.** Diploxylon, hard pine cone.

spine or prickle.

CONES—The size, form and color of pine cones are important diagnostic characters. While they may vary a great deal within a given species, the fact remains that some species always have small cones (*P. teocote*), others have medium-sized cones (*P. pseudostrobus, P. rudis* Endl.), and others always have very large cones (*P. ayacahuite* var. *brachyptera, P. maximartinezii* (Fig. 2.5).

Cone color is also quite variable, but some species have cones that are always brownish gray to brown (*P. montezumae*), others have cones that are ochre-yellow to orange-red (*P. nelsoni* Shaw), and still others have cones that are yellowish to yellowish brown (*P. ayacahuite*).

Form of the cone is often distinctive too. Some species have ovate, symmetrical, erect cones (*P. pseudostrobus* var. *apulcensis* Mart.), others have long, rather slender, curved cones (*P. michoacana* var. *cornuta* Mart.), while still others have very hard, almost round, symmetrical cones (*P. oocarpa* Schiede).

PEDUNCLE—Character of the peduncle is also an important diagnostic character (Fig. 2.6). Some species have cones with long, slender, tough peduncles (*P. oocarpa*). Others have very short, tough peduncles that are barely visible (*Pinus greggii* Engelm); still others have cones with long, slender, delicate peduncles that remain attached to the cone when it falls (*P. chiapensis* (Mart.) Andresen)). Combinations of the characters mentioned here (and others) are all very helpful in identifying the various pine species. For example, *P. patula* has cones that are only medium in length (about 10 cm) conical, curved, asymmetrical; polished yellow-ochre color, with an extremely tenacious peduncle so short that it is hardly visible.

Pines also differ with regard to the time of maturity of their cones and subsequent seed dispersal. In most species cones mature during the fall of the second year. However, in a few species the cones require three years to maturity (*P. leiophylla* Schl. et Cham.).

In most species the cone scales open when cones mature, and the seeds are shed immediately, the cone soon falling to the ground. In a few species however, the mature cone may remain firmly attached to the branch (persistent) and unopened (serotinous) for years (*P. oocarpa, P. greggii*). In a few species the cones may mature and release the seed immediately, but the open cones are persistent for a number of years (*P. leiophylla*).

CONE SCALES—Since cone scales constitute the major part of the cone, their size and form are very important in identifying different pine species (Fig. 2.7). Three, occasionally more, features of the cone scales are used here; the apophysis, the umbo and the prickle or spine.

The apophysis is the visible exterior part of the scale when the cone is unopened. In effect, the sum of all the apophyses makes up the total visible surface of the unopened cone.

The umbo is the exposed part of the minute scale of the conelet; it represents the first or earlier growth of the mature cone scale. As the cone (and cone scale) grows during the second year, the cone scales enlarge to form the apophysis with the umbo retained as part of that surface. The position of the umbo as part of the apophysis is a very important diagnostic feature, since most of the Soft Pines have cone scales with terminal umbo. The exception is the Piñon or Nut Pine group which have cone scales with dorsal umbo. The Hard Pines all have cone scales with dorsal umbo.

The umbo is terminal when the margin of the apophysis is free. The margin may be rounded as in *P. chiapensis* or may taper to a blunt point as in *P. strobiformis* Engelm. Growth extension of the scale is always a terminal extension. The "tip" or extension of the cone scale bears the terminal umbo that characterizes the Soft Pines.

P. ayacahuite var. *brachyptera* is an example of a Soft Pine bearing cones with scales having an unusual extension of the apophysis free margin. In this case the margin has become prolonged and strongly reflexed; however, the umbo still forms the "tip" of the prolonged, reflexed scale.

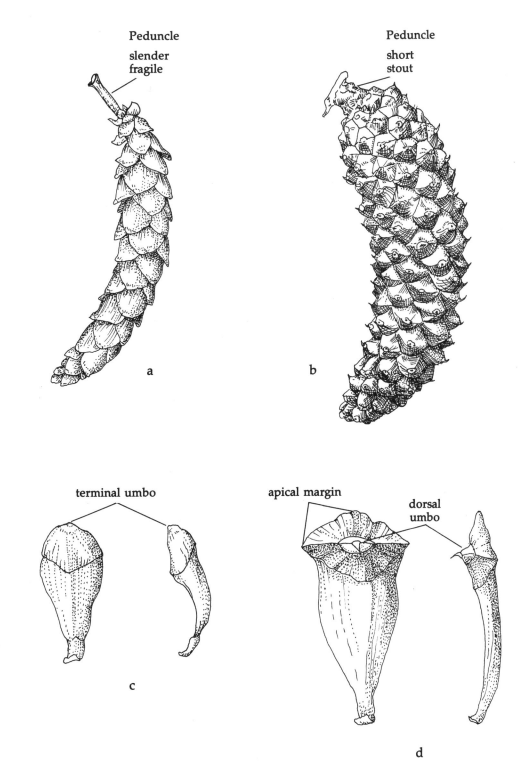

Fig. 2.6.   a. Soft Pine cone.   **b.** Hard Pine cone. From: Shaw (1914). *The genus pinus,* Plate V, p. 13, slightly modified.   **c.** Soft Pine cone scale.   **d.** Hard Pine cone scale.

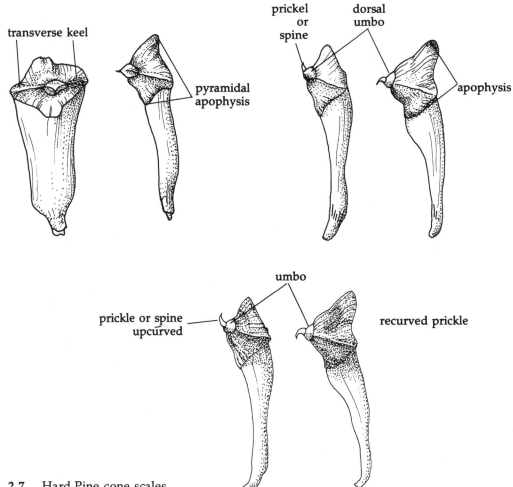

Fig. 2.7. Hard Pine cone scales.

The umbo is dorsal when all sides of the apophysis are tightly joined by the margins of other apophyses, thus no margin is free to grow or extend. Growth of the apophysis then is outward and results in a dorsal thickening or protuberance of the apophyses. The umbo forms the tip of this dorsal part of the apophyses and is characteristic of all the Hard Pines.

In some species the apophysis does not thicken with age but remains rather thin and flat with an umbo that is very small or even depressed in the center of the apophysis (*P. oocarpa*) (Fig. 2.8). In other species the apophysis may be thickened, unusually prolonged and reflexed (*P. oaxacana* Mirov). Other species may bear cones with apophyses that are thickened and pyramidal in form (*P. michoacana* Mart.).

In a number of species the shape and size of the apophysis differs on different parts of the cone. This occurs when the cone is oblique or curved in form, in which case scales on the upper side (adaxial) of the cone have larger, more thickened apophyses than scales on the lower side (abaxial). Also in some species, scales near the base of the cone have apophyses that are more prolonged or recurved than scales in the center area of the cone. Cones that are erect and symmetrical generally have scales with fairly uniform apophyses. In all of the Hard Pines the apophysis bears the umbo as a central and dorsal part of the prolonged or raised apophysis or, when the apophysis is thin and flattened, as a very small point in the center of the apophysis.

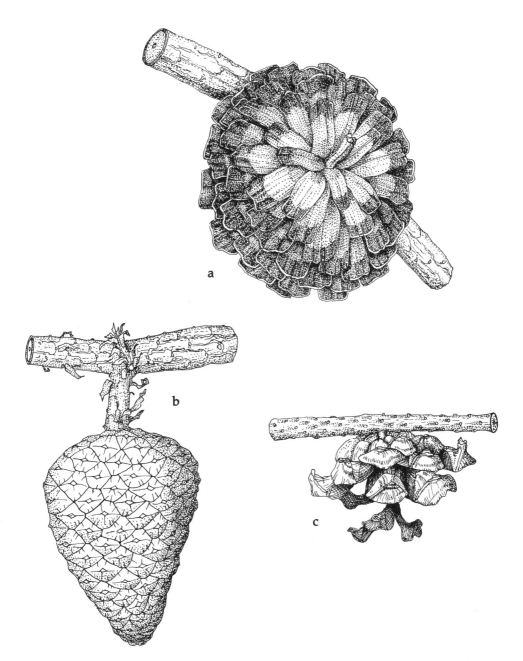

Fig. 2.8. **a.** Hard Pine cone, *P. oocarpa*, with scales widely opened in form of a "rosette". **b.** *P. oocarpa* cone; hard, smooth, the scales tightly closed, often for years; the peduncle stout, long, tough, and tenacious. **c.** Piñon pine cone, *P. cembroides*, early deciduous, sessile, the very small peduncle barely visible, the scales soon disintegrating after the cone falls.

In some species the umbo occurs as a sizeable (3–5 mm) projection of the apophysis (*P. oaxacana*) or erect as in *Pinus pseudostrobus* forma *protuberans* Mart.; or in some species, curved upward toward the apex of the cone or downward toward the base of the cone. In many species the umbo is barely discernible as in *P. maximinoi* and *P. hartwegii*; however, as a part of the apophysis, its size and form are important features in identification of the species.

In the Hard Pines, the umbo always bears a small prickle that is persistent or early deciduous. When persistent the prickle may be 1–2 mm long and very strong and recurved as in *P. arizonica* or erect as in *Pinus durangensis* Mart. When deciduous the prickle is usually very small and soon falls from the umbo (*P. lawsoni*, *Pinus herrerai* Mart.). In most of the Soft Pines the umbo is unarmed, i.e. without a prickle, the exception being the group of Piñon or Nut Pines.

SEEDS—Like many other characters of *Pinus*, the seeds also show a remarkable variability between the species (Fig. 2.9). Differences in size, shape, color, hardness, i.e. thickness of the seed coat or "testa"—all are important in species identification. Also some seeds are provided with a very effective wing as an aid to dissemination by the wind; other seeds are wingless and still others have only partial or vestigial wings. The method of attachment of the wing to the seed is also an important diagnostic character.

In most of the Hard Pines, the wing is attached to the seed by two hooks that contain hygroscopic tissue; when the air is dry and the cone scales open, the two hooks of the seed wing close tightly on the seed and it is dispersed by the wind when it falls from the cone scale. This type of seed wing attachment is termed "articulate".

Another method of seed wing attachment is found in many of the Soft Pines where the wing is firmly attached to the seed and cannot be separated from it except by actually breaking the membranous wing; this type of seed wing attachment is termed "adnate".

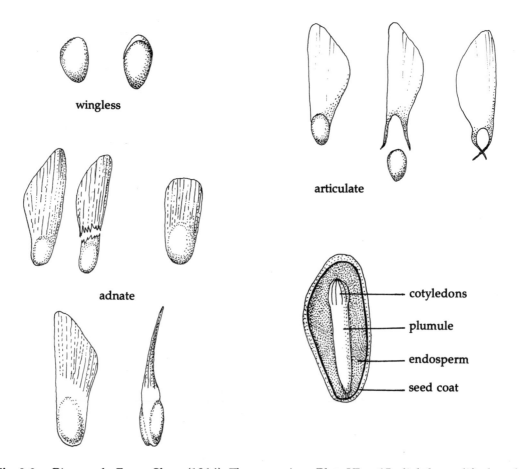

Fig. 2.9. Pine seeds. From: Shaw (1914). *The genus pinus*, Plate VI, p. 15, slightly modified; and USDA Forest Service Handbook No. 450, Fig. 3, p. 618, slightly modified.

WOOD—In the foregoing pages the terms "Hard Pines" and "Soft Pines" have been used a number of times to distinguish two major divisions or Subgenera of the genus *Pinus.* Originally the words "Hard" and "Soft" referred to the quality of the wood found in the main trunk or stem of the pine tree. Over the years the wood-using industry in the United States found the wood of the Eastern White Pine (*P. strobus* L.) and later, the wood of the Sugar Pine (*P. lambertiana* Dougl.), to be somewhat softer and more easily worked than wood from the Southern Yellow Pines (*P. palustris* Mill., *P. echinata* Mill., and *P. taeda* L.). While the terms "Hard" and "Soft" are far from precise and the wood from some of the Hard Pines is nearly as soft as that of the Soft Pines, anatomical studies of wood from each group revealed two important differences (Fig. 2.10).

<table>
<tr><td>Soft Pines</td><td>Hard Pines</td></tr>
<tr><td>Ray tracheids with smooth walls</td><td>Ray tracheids with dentate walls</td></tr>
<tr><td>Resin canals not numerous</td><td>Resin canals numerous</td></tr>
</table>

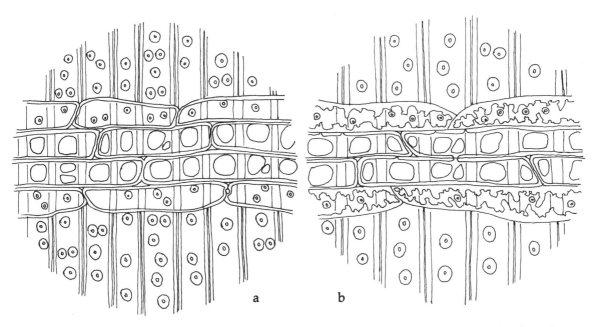

a   b

Fig. 2.10.   a. Soft Pine ray-tracheids with smooth walls.   **b.** Hard Pine ray-tracheids with dentate walls. From: Shaw (1914). *The genus pinus,* Plate VII, p. 19.

Although these characters are not identifiable in the field, still the terms Hard Pine and Soft Pine do have significance in the field since species in the Soft Pine group are much sought after in Mexico and Central America because the wood is considered to be "soft", not resinous and easily worked by hand.

On the other hand, the turpentine industry of Mexico and Central America, which is quite sizeable, is based on pine resin collected from species in the Hard Pine group simply because those trees have more resin canals and thus produce more resin than trees in the Soft Pine group.

In identification then, all characters and information about the species should be considered; some species are easily identified by a single character. Identification of other species may require detailed study of many characters from many specimens. It is helpful to remember that trees too are individuals and no two are exactly alike.

CLASSIFICATION OF THE MEXICAN AND CENTRAL AMERICAN PINES

Taxonomists, botanists and foresters are in general agreement on a major division of the genus *Pinus* into two subgenera: Haploxylon; also known as Soft or White Pines and; Diploxylon; also known as Hard or Yellow Pines. However, organization of the different species into groups and subgroups has shifted and changed a great deal over the years. Some authorities have used characters of the flowers, cones and leaves as the basis for a classification system. Others have used wood, pollen, chemistry, geography and crossability (some species readily intercross and produce fertile hybrids, others do not). Despite efforts to devise an all-inclusive, logical system of classification, there are still species that simply do not "fit" any of the groups or categories. Some species are extremely variable and appear to merge into another species, still others hybridize readily in the field and their fertile offspring may cross and recross with the parents, so the resultant trees do not "fit" any known species or variety. Finally new species are discovered, some of which do not fit any classification system. *Pinus rzedowskii* Madrigal et Caballero, described in 1969 from Mexico, is a classic example; this species possesses many Haploxylon and Diploxylon characters. *Pinus leiophylla* is a well-known Mexican pine that has many Soft Pine characters, yet even more Hard Pine qualities.

In Table 2.1, the Mexican and Central American pines are classed into subgenera, sections and subsections, based on studies of pine trees made during many field trips in Mexico, Guatemala, El Salvador, Honduras, and Belize, and from laboratory studies and studies of specimens in a number of herbaria. The taxonomic and botanical literature have also been reviewed and, although no single authority has been followed here, the arrangement follows in part that of Shaw, Martínez, Loock, Duffield, Little and Critchfield. With my own findings added to those of the authorities listed above, it is clear that the classification system used here is a combination of systems that seems to me to best "fit" the pines of Mexico and Central America at this time.

Table 2.1. Classification of the Mexican and Central American Pines

Subgenus Haploxylon or Soft Pines
  Section Cembra
      P. lambertiana Dougl.
      P. flexilis James
      P. strobiformis Sudw.
      P. ayacahuite var. *brachyptera* Shaw
      P. ayacahuite var. *veitchii* Shaw
      P. ayacahuite Ehrenb.
      P. chiapensis (Mart.) Andresen

  Section Paracembra
    Subsection Cembroides
      P. monophylla Torr. et Frem.
      P. edulis Engelm.
      P. remota (Little) Bailey et Hawksworth
      P. caterinae M-F. Robert-Passini
      P. cembroides Zucc.
      P. cembroides subsp. *orizabensis* Bailey
      P. discolor Bailey et Hawksworth
      P. johannis M-F. Robert
      P. lagunae M-F. Robert-Passini
      P. quadrifolia Parl.
      P. juarezensis Lanner
      P. culminicola Andresen et Beaman

    Subsection Pinceana
      P. pinceana Gord.
      P. maximartinezii Rzedowski
      P. nelsoni Shaw
      P. rzedowskii Madrigal et Caballero

Subgenus Diploxylon or Hard Pines
  Section Leiophyllae
      P. leiophylla Schl. et Cham.
      P. chihuahuana Engelm.
      P. lumholtzii Rob. et Fern.

  Section Ponderosae
      P. jeffreyi Murr.
      P. arizonica Engelm.
      P. arizonica var. *stormiae* Mart.
      P. engelmannii Carr.
      P. durangensis Mart.

  Section Montezumae
    Subsection Montezumae
      P. cooperi Blanco
      P. montezumae Lamb.
      P. montezumae var. *lindleyi* Loud.
      P. martinezii Larsen
      P. douglasiana Mart.

    Subsection Rudis
      P. rudis Endl.
      P. Donnell-Smithii Mast.
      P. hartwegii Lindl.

    Subsection Michoacana
      P. michoacana Mart.
      P. michoacana var. *cornuta* Mart.
      P. michoacana var. *quevedoi* Mart.
      P. michoacana forma *procera* Mart.
      P. michoacana forma *nayaritana* Mart.

  Section Pseudostrobus
    Subsection Pseudostrobus
      P. pseudostrobus Lindl.
      P. pseudostrobus forma *protuberans* Mart.
      P. pseudostrobus forma *megacarpa* Loock
      P. maximinoi H. E. Moore

    Subsection Oaxacana
      P. estevezi (Mart.) Perry
      P. pseudostrobus var. *apulcencis* Mart.
      P. oaxacana Mirov.
      P. pseudostrobus var. *coatepecensis* Mart.
      P. nubicola Perry

  Section Serotinae
    Subsection Contorta
      P. contorta subsp. *murrayana* (Balf.) Critchfield

    Subsection Patula
      P. radiata var. *binata* Lemm.
      P. muricata D. Don
      P. attenuata Lemm.
      P. greggii Engelm.
      P. patula Schl. et Cham.
      P. patula var. *longepedunculata* Loock

    Subsection Oocarpa
      P. oocarpa Schiede
      P. oocarpa var. *ochoterenai* Mart.
      P. oocarpa var. *trifoliata* Mart.
      P. oocarpa var. *microphylla* Shaw
      P. jaliscana Perez de La Rosa
      P. pringlei Shaw
      P. tecunumanii (Schwertfeger) Enguiluz et Perry

  Section Teocote
      P. teocote Schl. et Cham.
      P. lawsoni Roezl.
      P. herrerai Mart.

  Section Caribaea
      P. caribaea var. *hondurensis* (Sénécl.) Barr. et Golf.

  Section Macrocarpae
      P. coulteri D. Don

CHAPTER 3

DESCRIPTIONS

The genus *Pinus* embraces the most important species of trees that occur in Mexico and Central America. Pines are the primary source of wood for construction timbers of all kinds, the manufacture of pulp and paper, the production of turpentine, wood oils, tars and rosin; food for birds, animals and man; and perhaps most important of all, fuelwood for literally millions of people.

Mexico alone has the greatest number of pine species (including varieties and forms) of any country in the world. In the classification system used here I have listed 72 species, varieties and forms. These are divided into two major groups, namely, subgenus Haploxylon and subgenus Diploxylon (Table 3.1).

Key to the Subgenera, Sections, and Subsections
of the
Mexican and Central American Pines

A. Bases of leaf bracts not decurrent, leaves with one vascular bundle, sheaths of the leaves deciduous. Subgenus **Haploxylon.**
    B. Umbo of cone scale terminal, leaves borne 5 in a fascicle; Section **Cembra.**
    BB. Umbo of cone scale dorsal, leaves born 1–5 in a fascicle; Section **Paracembra.**
        C. Cones 2–5 (9)cm long, disintegrating soon after falling to the ground; Subsection **Cembroides.**
        CC. Cones 8–22cm long, remaining intact for some time after falling to the ground; Subsection **Pinceana.**
AA. Bases of leaf bracts mostly decurrent; leaves with two vascular bundles; sheaths of the leaves mostly persistent; Subgenus **Diploxylon.**
    D. Sheaths of the leaves deciduous; Section **Leiophyllae.**
    DD. Sheaths of the leaves persistent.
        E. Cones mostly opening at maturity and then deciduous.
            F. Cones very small to very large 2–35cm long, bases of leaf bracts decurrent, leaves in fascicles of 3–6, occasionally 7.
                G. Cones 6–17cm long, leaves mostly in fascicles of 3, occasionally 6–7, erect not drooping; Section **Ponderosae.**
                GG. Cones 6–30cm long. Leaves mostly in fascicles of 5, occasionally 3–4 and 6–7; Section **Montezumae.**
                    H. Cones 6–15cm long, leaves mostly in fascicles of 5, occasionally 6–7, fascicle sheath 1.0–2.5cm long, neither black nor sticky and gummy; Subsection **Montezumae.**

41

HH. Cones 15–30cm long, leaves mostly in fascicles of 5, occasionally 6, fascicle sheath 2.0–4.0cm long, often black, sticky and gummy; Subsection **Michoacana.**

   I. Cones 8–15cm long, dark brown to purplish-black, cone scales mostly thin and flexible, leaves mostly 3–5, occasionally 6–7; Subsection **Rudis.**

   II. Cones small, 2–8cm long, pale brown to brown, cone scales small, mostly stiff not thin and flexible, leaves mostly 3 per fascicle, occasionally 4–5; Section **Teocote.**

   J. Cones 5–12cm long, brown, cone scales small, thin, not hard and stiff. Leaves 3–4 per fascicle; Section **Caribaea.**

   JJ. Cones very large, 20–35cm long, cone scales large, thick, recurved. Leaves 3 per fascicle; Section **Macrocarpae.**

FF. Cones 6–18cm long, leaves mostly in fascicles of 5, occasionally 6–7; bases of leaf bracts not decurrent; Section **Pseudostrobus** (Fig. 3.1).

   K. Cones 5–18cm long; cone scales mostly thin and flexible; umbo mostly flat to depressed; Subsection **Pseudostrobus.**

   KK. Cones 6–15cm long; cone scales mostly thick, hard and stiff; umbo mostly raised to protuberant; Subsection **Oaxacana.**

EE. Cones mostly remaining closed, long persistent; Section **Serotinae.**

   L. Leaves 2 per fascicle, 4–6cm long; cones not serotinous; Subsection **Contorta.**

   LL. Leaves 2–5 per fascicle, 8–25cm long; cones mostly serotinous.

   M. Leaves 2–3, occasionally 4, per fascicle; cones mostly serotinous and sessile; Subsection **Patula.**

   MM. Leaves 3, 4, and 5 per fascicle; cones mostly serotinous and not sessile; Subsection **Oocarpa.**

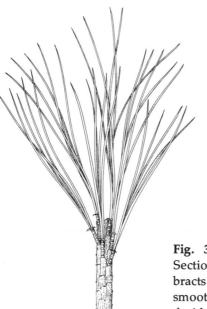

Fig. 3.1. Typical branchlet of pines in Section Pseudostrobus. Bases of the leaf bracts are not decurrent, and the branchlet is smooth. Fascicles of the leaves are not deciduous.

Table 3.1. Differences between the subgenera.

Botanical Feature	Haploxylon	Diploxylon
Fibrovascular bundle	Single	Double
Bark formation	Late	Early
Bark on upper trunk of mature trees	Smooth	Rough, scaly
Sheaths of the leaves (there are a few exceptions in both Subgenera)	Deciduous	Persistent
Position of the umbo	Terminal (except in Section Paracembra)	Dorsal
Bases of the leaf bracts	Not decurrent	Decurrent (except in Section Pseudostrobus)

HAPLOXYLON OR SOFT PINES

Subgenus Haploxylon is divided in this classification into Section Cembra and Section Paracembra. The cones of pines in Section Cembra all have scales with a terminal umbo. Cone scales of pines in Section Paracembra all bear a dorsal umbo.

Section Cembra

These are large trees 20–40 m tall with generally open, irregularly pyramidal crowns; bark on young trees is smooth for many years, branchlets are also smooth and bases of the leaf bracts are not decurrent. Leaves are borne in fascicles of 5 and are slender and flexible, the sheaths deciduous and resin canals are external. The trees are usually found at elevations of 2,000–3,5000 m growing on cool, moist slopes or in high valleys. One species, *P. chiapensis* is an exception since it grows under tropical to semi-tropical conditions at 500–2,250 m altitude.

Seven species are included in Section Cembra. These are listed in Table 3.2 with important distinguishing botanical features.

Table 3.2. Characteristics of Species in Section Cembra.

Species	Length of leaves, cm	Length of cones, cm	Cone scales	Seeds
P. lambertiana	5–10	25–50	Not recurved	Winged
P. flexillis	6–10	8–15	Not recurved	Wingless
P. strobiformis	6–10	10–20	Recurved	Wingless
P. ayacahuite var. *brachyptera*	10–18	15–45	Recurved	Wingless
P. ayacahuite var. *veitchii*	10–16	20–45	Recurved	Half-wing
P. ayacahuite	10–18	10–40	Recurved	Winged
P. chiapensis	6–12	10–15	Not recurved	Winged

Pinus lambertiana Douglas

Sugar Pine, Pino de Azucar, Ocote

THE TREE—Trees of this species are the tallest pines in North America reaching heights of 60 m or more and with diameters of up to 2 m. Crowns of mature trees are roughly pyramidal with the top rather flattened, branches large, irregularly spaced and mostly horizontal.

BARK—On young trees thin, smooth and grayish green; on old trees thick, up to 10 cm, reddish brown, rough and formed by deep, longitudinal and horizontal fissures into large, irregularly-shaped plates.

BRANCHLETS—Smooth, slender, rather flexible with the leaves borne mostly at the ends. Bases of the leaf bracts are not decurrent.

LEAVES—In fascicles of 5, thick, stiff, 7–10 cm long, bluish green, the margins serrate with very small teeth; stomata present on dorsal and ventral surfaces, resin canals 3, external with occasionally 1 or 2 medial; fibrovascular bundle single. Sheaths are deciduous.

CONELETS—Solitary and in groups of 2; borne on stout, erect peduncles; the small scales are wide without a prickle.

CONES—Borne at the ends of the branchlets, pendent, cylindrical, straight, 25–45 cm long, 8–10 cm wide when open, yellowish brown. When the cones mature, seeds are released but the cones remain on the trees for a number of months. When they fall the peduncle, about 8 cm long, remains attached to the cone.

CONE SCALES—Only medium-thick, stiff, wide ($\sim$ 30 mm), the apex rounded, often resinous, the apophysis straight, not reflexed; umbo terminal without a prickle.

SEEDS—Dark brown to almost black, 10–12 mm long, with a short wing 20–30 mm long and 12–15 mm wide, firmly attached to the seed (adnate); cotyledons are 11–18. Approximately 4,600 seeds/kg. They are sought for food by birds and rodents.

WOOD—Sapwood is soft, creamy-white, the heartwood pale brown and easily worked. Because of its large size, it has always been in great demand for general construction and interior woodwork. When freshly cut the wood has a pleasant, pungent odor.

DISTRIBUTION—In Mexico, *P. lambertiana* is found only in the San Pedro Mártir mountains of northern Baja California (Fig. 3.2). The major part of its range is in the United States within the states of Oregon, Nevada and California.

HABITAT—The trees occur at 2,000–3,000 m elevation on moist, well-drained, sandy to gravelly soils. Best growth is made in ravines and on cooler sites where adequate moisture is available.

WHERE TO FIND *P. lambertiana*—If driving to Baja California from San Diego,

P. lambertiana Tree   Bark   Cone

Thanks to the USDA Forest Service.

California, at Tijuana take Highway MEX 1 south along the Pacific coast to the city of Ensenada. There continue on Highway MEX 1 to the town of Colonet. A few kilometers south of the town, on the same Highway MEX 1, look for a dirt road on the left leading to the village of San Telmo.

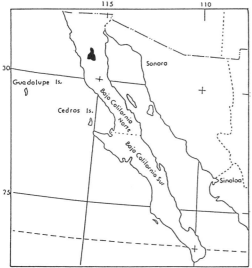

Fig. 3.2. Distribution of *P. lambertiana.*

From this village a narrow, rocky road follows the Rio San Telmo (mostly dry) due east. Look for signs indicating Parque Nacional Sierra San Pedro Mártir. However, before reaching the park, stop at the small village of San José (Meling Ranch) and inquire about accommodations at the ranch and a guide. At elevations of 2,000 m or more, look for *P. lambertiana* occurring as individual trees mingled with other conifers. Since the road is very rough and the area is very isolated, it is suggested that the trip be undertaken only during the dry season and in a vehicle with high clearance equipped with good tires, water and an adequate supply of gasoline.

NOTES AND COMMENTS—As mentioned earlier, this is a magnificent species. The tallest of the North American pines, and very old trees may attain diameters of 2 m. Though susceptible to blister rust, it is remarkably free from other diseases and insect attacks. It is easily separated from other white pines by its very long cones, the straight, wide cone scales and the seed with a very wide wing.

Pinus flexilis James

Limber Pine, Pino

THE TREE—A small to medium-size tree, 7–15 m in height and 20–40 cm in diameter, the trunk branching almost to the ground; in mature trees the crown is open and irregularly rounded, the branches long, tough, flexible. In young trees the crown is more dense and pyramidal.

BARK—On young trees smooth and grayish white; older mature trees have thin, rough bark divided by shallow furrows into small, scaly, polygonal plates, pale gray to brownish color.

BRANCHLETS—Grayish, smooth, becoming rougher with age; bases of the leaf bracts are not decurrent.

LEAVES—In fascicles of 5, stiff, erect, 6–10 cm long, the margins with very fine and widely spaced serrations—often entire. In its U.S. range, margins of the leaves are entire. Stomata are found only on the ventral surfaces (in the U.S., stomata are dorsal and ventral); resin canals 1–3, external; vascular bundle single. Fascicle sheaths are brown and deciduous.

CONELETS—Borne singly or in clusters of 2 or 3 on stout, scaly peduncles; the small scales wide and thin.

CONES—Long-ovoid, cylindrical, symmetrical, 8–10 cm long, yellowish to ochre color, resinous. They open when mature and are soon deciduous.

CONE SCALES—Thin, straight, not curved or reflexed as in *P. ayacahuite*, the apophysis only slightly raised, the apex rounded; umbo terminal and unarmed.

SEEDS—Oblong to ovate, 8–10 mm long,

P. flexilis Cone. *Collected by the author on Cerro Potosi, Nuevo Leon, Mexico.*

somewhat flattened, dark brown, generally wingless though occasionally bearing a vestigial wing. About 8,800 seeds/kg. Cotyledons number 8–11, mostly 8 and 9. They are sought for food by birds and rodents.

WOOD—Light, soft, pale yellowish sapwood, the heartwood a pale brown. Its habitat at very high elevations appears to rule out local use by humans.

DISTRIBUTION—*P. flexilis* has a very broad range in the U.S. extending from the Canadian border southward along the Rocky Mountains into New Mexico. Martínez reported it occurring in Nuevo León state (Fig. 3.3). I found a few cones near the summit of Cerro Potosí, Nuevo León and later searched for it unsuccessfully in the high mountains near San Antonio de las Alazanes, Coahuila. If the species occurred in Coahuila, the trees may have been destroyed by the disastrous forest fire of 1975 that swept through those mountains.

HABITAT—This species requires the cool climate of high mountain peaks where rain, sleet, snow and mists occur during most of the year. On Cerro Potosí cones were found at 3,400 m with *P. hartwegii, P. culminicola* and *P. ayacahuite* var. *brachyptera*. Here *P. flexilis* is a disjunct population about 1,600 km southeast from the southern terminus of its range in the United States.

WHERE TO FIND—*P. flexilis*—This taxon is so rare in Mexico, I would suggest that collections be made in the U.S. There are extensive forests in Colorado, Utah and Wyoming where roadside trees can be found.

NOTES AND COMMENTS—Not all botanists and taxonomists agree that *P. flexilis* occurs in Mexico. Many believe that *P. strobiformis,* not *P. flexilis,* extends southward into Mexico. However, Martínez cited specimens from Potosí peak Nuevo Léon, at 3800 m; 2.5 km northeast of Galeana, and the crest of Cerro Potosí near Galeana at 3420 m. The cones I collected near the summit of Cerro Potosí were clearly those of *P. flexilis.*

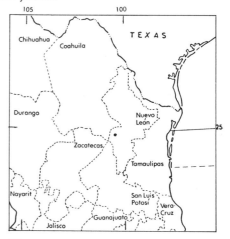

Fig. 3.3. Distribution of *P. flexilis*.

Pinus strobiformis Engelm.

Southwestern White Pine, Pino Blanco, Pinabete

THE TREE—Moderately tall, reaching a height of 20–25 m and diameter up to 1 m. The crowns of mature trees are generally rounded, rather open and irregularly branched. Branches are long, horizontal to pendent. In young trees the crown is dense and pyramidal.

BARK—On young trees thin, smooth, silvery-gray; on large mature trees, dark grayish brown, rough, divided into small irregular, rectangular plates.

BRANCHLETS—Long, slender, with smooth, greenish gray bark and leaves grouped mostly toward the ends. Bases of the leaf bracts are not decurrent.

LEAVES—In fascicles of 5, slender, flexible, 6–10 cm long; bright green in color; margins serrate with very small, widely spaced teeth; stomata present only on the ventral surfaces; resin canals 2–4, external; fibrovascular bundle single. Sheaths are deciduous.

CONELETS—Subterminal, borne singly and in groups of 2–4 on stout, erect peduncles about 2 cm long; scales wide with a small terminal prickle.

CONES—Variable in size ranging from 10–20 cm in length, rarely longer, mostly 10–15 cm; pendent, cylindrical to conical, straight to slightly curved, very resinous, yellowish to ochre color when mature; ripening in the fall and soon deciduous; the peduncle, about 2 cm long, falls with the cone.

CONE SCALES—Rather thick and stiff, apophyses elongated, the apex rounded or broadly triangular, usually curved but not strongly reflexed; umbo terminal without a prickle.

SEEDS—Dark brown, 10–12 mm long; wingless though occasionally with a very short, rudimentary wing 1–2 mm long; approximately 7,000 seeds/kg; cotyledons 12–13.

WOOD—Soft, not resinous, creamy-white with slightly darker heartwood; used locally for cabinetry, doors and window frames.

DISTRIBUTION—This species occurs in the U.S. in Arizona and New Mexico with a few small stands in the western corner of Texas. Its range extends southward into Mexico along the high mountains of the Sierra Madre Oriental in the states of Coahuila and Nuevo León and in the Sierra Madre Occidental in the states of Sonora, Chihuahua, Sinaloa and Durango (Fig. 3.4).

HABITAT—*P. strobiformis* grows at altitudes ranging from 2,000–3,500 m, occurring as small, pure stands or individual trees mingled with other pines and firs. It makes its best growth on moist, cool sites and in fact does not grow under hot, dry conditions. I found small groups of trees growing in Coahuila near San Antonio de las Alazanes at 3,000 m altitude. The trees were growing on north and northeast slopes with *P. hartwegii, P. rudis* and *P. ayacahuite* var. *brachyptera*. Small groups and individual trees were also observed on Cerro Potosí, Nuevo León, at 3,500 m; associated pines were the same species noted above with the addition of *P. culminicola*.

WHERE TO FIND *P. strobiformis*—If driving to Mexico from Laredo, Texas, go to the city of Saltillo and take Highway 57 south for a few kilometers. Look for narrow paved roads on the left leading to the

P. strobiformis Tree   Bark

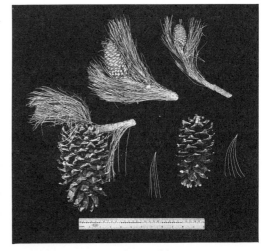

Branchlets, cones, conelets, and leaves

villages of Arteaga, Los Lirios and San
Antonio de Las Alazanes. Near these
villages the Sierra Madre Oriental rises
steeply to altitudes of 2,000, 3,000 and
3,5000 m. Narrow, winding, rocky roads
lead up into the mountains and to scattered
stands of pines and firs. *Pinus strobiformis*
will be found at about 3,000 m elevation,
mostly as single trees or very small groups
of trees mingled with *P. rudis, P. hartwegii*
and *P. ayacahuite* var. *brachyptera*.

Further south on Highway 57 at about
kilometer 130, look for a paved road on the
left that leads to the town of Galeana. A few
kilometers from Galeana there is a large isolated mountain, Cerro Potosí, its upper
slopes forested with pines and firs. A very
narrow, rocky, tortuous road leads to the
peak at about 3,500 m elevation. Much of
the forest has been cut; however, there are
still fine small stands of mixed pines and firs
at 2,000–3,500 m. *Pinus strobiformis* can be
found there in small groups and as single
trees mingled with the other conifers. In
western Mexico look for this species in the
high mountains of the Sierra Madre Occidental near the town of Madera, state of
Chihuahua. Near the town there are
narrow, rocky logging roads that extend
westward into the heart of the mountains. *P.
strobiformis* can generally be found on north
and northeast slopes at 2,000–2,500 m
mingled with other pines and firs. Further
south in the area near the mountain village
of El Vergel, scattered trees can still be
found growing with other conifers. At both
locations you will need a local guide and a
vehicle with high clearance. Allow at least a
full day for a trip into the mountains and
make it only during the dry season.

NOTES AND COMMENTS—The range of
P. strobiformis extends from Arizona and
New Mexico into northern Mexico and
overlaps the range of *P. ayacahuite* var.
brachyptera in Chihuahua, Durango,
Coahuila and Nuevo León. In all four states
I often found the two taxa growing together,
and with the wide range in cone size, scale
width and degree of curvature, it was difficult to make positive identifications. However, I did reach some rather general
conclusions: *P. strobiformis* cones were

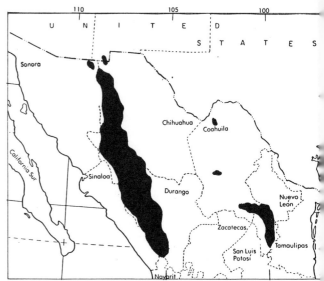

Fig. 3.4.   Distribution of *P. strobiformis*.

somewhat shorter than cones of *P.
ayacahuite* var. *brachyptera;* leaves of *P.
strobiformis* appeared to be rather shorter
and grouped more toward the ends of the
branchlets than leaves of var. *branchyptera;*
leaves of var. *brachyptera* seemed longer and
more flexible. In *P. strobiformis* cones, apex
of the scales was more rounded and not so
elongated or recurved as in var. *brachyptera*.

How to account, then, for this "merging
of characters"? I believe that in the Sierra
Madre Occidental of Chihuahua and
Durango, the two taxa have hybridized
producing fertile offspring that, in turn,
have backcrossed with the parents. In the
Sierra Madre Oriental of Coahuila and
Nuevo León, the situation is even more
complex. Here three related taxa, *P. flexilis,
P. strobiformis* and var. *brachyptera* occur
sympatrically. I believe these three taxa
have, over long periods of time, also
hybridized, producing fertile offspring that
have backcrossed with the parents.

Supporting these observations are the
successful crosses that have been made
between *P. flexilis* and *P. strobiformis*.
Crossing of *P. flexilis* with *P. ayacahuite* is
considered questionable since identification of the *P. ayacahuite* parent is uncertain. I
believe crosses between *P. strobiformis* and
P. ayacahuite var. *brachyptera* have not been
attempted.

Pinus ayacahuite var. brachyptera Shaw

Mexican White Pine, Pinabete, Pino Blanco, Ocote

THE TREE—This variety resembles typical *P. ayacahuite* in size, form, foliage, bark and branchlets.

CONES—Quite variable in size ranging from 15–45 cm in length, subcylindrical, and often curved. A few trees in the states of Michoacán and Jalisco were found with cones measuring 48 cm in length. As in the typical species, mature cones are very resinous, yellowish to ochre colored, ripening in the fall and soon deciduous, the long, stout peduncle falling with the cone.

CONE SCALES—Thick, stiff, wide; the apophyses are elongated and generally strongly recurved; the umbo terminal and very resinous.

SEEDS—Brown, 10–15 mm long, generally without a wing though occasionally bearing a vestigial wing 1–2 mm long.

WOOD—Similar to that of *P. ayacahuite* and the variety *veitchii*.

DISTRIBUTION—In the mountains of central Mexico and northward along the mountain ranges of the Sierra Madre Occidental and the Sierra Madre Oriental (Fig. 3.5). In western Mexico it has been collected in the states of Chihuahua, Sonora, Sinaloa and Durango. In northeastern Mexico it is found in the mountains of Nuevo León and Coahuila. In central Mexico it grows in the high mountains of Jalisco, Michoacán and Colima.

HABITAT—The variety *brachyptera* generally occurs as small groups of trees and as scattered individuals mingled with other pines and firs at elevations of 2,000–3,500 m. The trees grow best on moist, shady slopes of deep ravines and barrancas. Like other members of the *ayacahuite* group, this variety is not adapted to a hot, dry environment.

WHERE TO FIND—*P. ayachuite*—If driving from El Paso, go to the city of Chihuahua and take Highway 16 west to the town of Madera. Locate a guide and follow one of the dirt roads leading due west back into the high mountains of the Sierra Madre Occidental. This is a full day's trip and a vehicle with high clearance is required. Scattered trees can be found at altitudes above 2,000 m usually mixed with other pines and occasionally Douglas Fir varieties. Further south at the city of Durango, take Highway 40 west to El Salto; a few kilometers west of El Salto on the highway to Mazatlan, fine trees can be found growing as scattered individuals among other pines.

Driving to Mexico from Laredo, go to Monterrey and on to Saltillo. At Saltillo take Highway 57 south for a few kilometers, and look for narrow paved roads on the left leading to the villages of Arteaga, Los Lirios and San Antonio de Las Alazanes. These

P. ayacahuite var. *brachyptera*
Tree

Bark

Cone, conelets, leaves, and seed

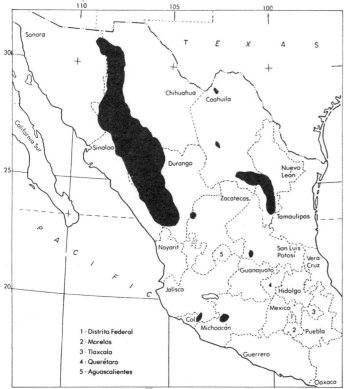

Fig. 3.5. Distribution of *P. ayacahuite* var. *brachyptera*.

1 - Distrito Federal
2 - Morelos
3 - Tlaxcala
4 - Querétaro
5 - Aguascalientes

onto a narrow paved road and go to the town of Galeana. Near the town there is a high mountain, Cerro Potosí, that dominates the landscape. There is a very narrow, tortuous, rocky road that leads to the summit at about 3,500 m altitude. Many of the slopes are forested with pines and firs. Large areas have been cut for lumber and then burned. However, at 3,000–3,400 m there are very fine, small groups of var. *brachyptera* mingled with *P. hartweggi, P. rudis, P. strobiformis* and *P. culminicola.*

NOTES AND COMMENTS—In central Mexico the range of this variety occasionally overlaps that of var. *veitchii.* However, the presence or absence of the seed wing distinguishes the two varieties. Some botanists believe that this variety should be identified as *Pinus strobiformis* Engelm, which occurs in the United States in Arizona and New Mexico and extends into northern Mexico. Certainly the ranges of the two taxa overlap in Sonora, Chihuahua, Coahuila and Nuevo León and specimens collected in those areas are often very difficult to identify.

I believe that in the overlapping zones, *P. strabiformis* and var. *brachyptera* hybridize producing fertile progeny which may also cross and backcross with the parents. In Chihuahua, Durango, Coahuila and Nuevo León, I found many trees with cones that were intermediate in their morphology between cones of typical *P. strobiformis* and typical *P. ayacahuite* var. *brachyptera.*

small villages are all in the foothills of the Sierra Madre Oriental and from them there are dirt roads leading up into the mountains. At 2,000–3,000 m, small groups and scattered trees will be found with other pines and firs. Also south from Saltillo on Highway 57 at about kilometer 130, turn left

---

Pinus ayacahuite var. *veitchii* Shaw

Acalote, Ocote, Pino

THE TREE—This variety, like the typical species, is one of Mexico's largest pines. The leaves, branchlets and fascicle sheaths are similar to *P. ayacahuite.*

CONES—Generally appear to be slightly longer and wider than those of *P. ayacahuite,* often reaching 45 cm in length. They are pendent, yellowish brown when mature, very resinous and ripen in the fall. When the seeds are shed, the cone soon falls with the peduncle still attached.

CONE SCALES—Generally thicker and stiffer than in the species and usually wider. The apophyses are prolonged and generally reflexed or curled; the umbo terminal and unarmed.

SEEDS—Dark brown, 10–13 mm long with a short seed wing 10–20 mm long; adnate.

WOOD—Very similar to that of *P. ayacahuite.*

DISTRIBUTION—Central Mexico in the

P. ayacahuite **var.** *veitchii* Tree   Bark   Cone, seed, and needles

states of Jalisco, Michoacán, Morelos, Mexico, Guerrero, Puebla. Tlaxcala, Hidalgo and Veracruz (Fig. 3.6).

HABITAT—This variety is found growing in small, scattered stands generally with other pines and firs at 2,000–3,000 m. At these altitudes, the trees are subject to occasional frosts and freezing rain. Best growth is made on moist, shady, cool sites. The variety does not grow well in hot, arid environments.

WHERE TO FIND *P. ayacahuite* var. *veitchii*—If in Mexico City, go to the Federal park, Desierto de Los Leones (Desert of the Lions) on the outskirts of the city. There are occasional large trees mingled with other pines and the fir, *Abies religiosa* Mart. Only a few kilometers from Mexico City on the highway to Puebla, there are scattered large trees at about 2,800 m altitude growing with pines and fir. Driving from Mexico City toward Cuernavaca in the state of Morelos, there are scattered trees mingled with other pines and firs growing on the high mountains before descending to Cuernavaca. East of Mexico City, in the state of Tlaxcala, go to the town of Apizaco and take Highway 119 north for about 15 kilometers. There is a small group of very large trees growing near the highway at 2,800 m altitude. Cones from these trees were very large, about 45 cm long. A one-day trip from Mexico City to the town of Amecameca leads to the road up to the two snow-capped peaks, Popocatepetl and Ixtaccihuatl. In the forest along the road up to the twin peaks, there

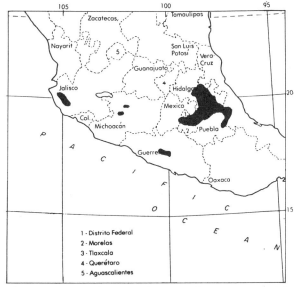

Fig. 3.6. Distribution of *P. ayacahuite* var. *veitchii*.

are very fine trees of var. *veitchii*.

NOTES AND COMMENTS—Central Mexico, where this variety occurs, is very densely populated, and this variety is rapidly disappearing since the wood is much sought after for construction of furniture, windows and doors.

The northern limit of the range of *P. ayacahuite* overlaps the range of var. *veitchii* and both taxa are occasionally found growing together. I found this particularly true in the states of Tlaxcala and Puebla. In those overlapping zones it is often difficult to distinguish var. *veitchii* from *P. ayacahuite*, and even length of the seed wing is not an invariable identifying character.

Pinus ayacahuite Ehren.

Mexican White Pine, Pinabete, Acalocote

THE TREE—This is a magnificent pine often reaching heights of 35–40 m with diameters of up to 2 m. Crowns of old, mature trees are open and irregular, the branches horizontal to pendent; the crowns of young trees are conical with the branches in regularly spaced whorls.

BARK—On young trees thin, ashy-gray and smooth. On large, old trees it becomes rough, grayish brown, scaly and divided into small, rectangular plates.

BRANCHLETS—Slender, smooth, light gray with the leaves generally grouped toward the ends; bases of the leaf bracts are not decurrent.

LEAVES—Slender, flexible, in groups of 5, 10–18 cm long; the dorsal surface bright green, the ventral surface glaucous; margins serrate with very small, widely spaced teeth; stomata present only on the ventral surfaces; resin canals vary from 2–4, occasionally 5–6, external; fibrovascular bundle single. Sheaths are pale brown and early deciduous.

CONELETS—Solitary or in groups of 2–4; erect on stout peduncles 10–15 mm long; scales thin, wide, without a prickle.

CONES—Almost cylindrical but tapering toward the apex; pendent, slightly curved, 10–40 cm long, yellowish brown color when mature and very resinous. They ripen in the fall and are soon deciduous, the peduncle, about 1–3 cm long, falls with the cone.

CONE SCALES—Thin, narrow, flexible, 5–7 cm long, the apophyses elongated with the apex rounded to obtuse, generally reflexed to curled; umbo terminal without a prickle and nearly always resinous; each scale bearing two winged seeds.

SEEDS—Light brown with darker spots; 5–8 mm long with a well-developed wing 30–40 mm long, strongly attached to the seed (adnate). Cotyledons (seed leaves) are 11–13; however, in seeds from Guatemala they were mostly 7 and 8.

WOOD—Soft, creamy-white, light and not very resinous. The timber is much sought after because it is easily shaped by hand; local carpenters prefer it for doors, windows, cabinets and furniture.

DISTRIBUTION—Mingled with other pines and firs in the mountains of southern Mexico to Guatemala, Honduras and El Salvador (Fig. 3.7). Sizable groups can still be found in Mexico in the mountains of Chiapas, Oaxaca and Guerrero. Small groups are also found in Puebla and Tlaxcala. In Guatemala scattered groups and individual trees occur at high elevations in the departments of Huehuetenango, Totonicapán, Quiché, San Marcos and Quezaltenango. In Honduras the species is found on high mountain peaks in the

P. ayacahuite Tree   Bark   Cone, conelet, leaves, and seed

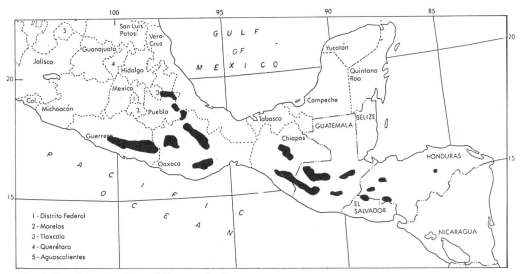

Fig. 3.7. Distribution of *P. ayacahuite.*

departments of Santa Bárbara, (Cerro Santa Bárbara, altitude 2,800 m), Lempira (Cerro Celaque, altitude 2,900 m), and near the village of Las Trancas in the department of La Paz. In El Salvador it occurs in the department of Chalatenango on the slopes of Cerro El Pital, (altitude 2,800 m). Since El Pital is on the El Salvador-Honduras border, the species probably occurs in Honduras at this location.

HABITAT—*P. ayacahuite* grows at altitudes of 2,000–3,200 m. It is found on all kinds of sites but reaches its greatest size on well-drained, moist, loamy soils. While it does grow in small pure stands, it is most often found mingled with other pines and firs. This species is not adapted to hot, arid environments but grows well under cool, moist conditions.

WHERE TO FIND *P. ayacahuite*—In Mexico, at the city of Oaxaca, take Highway MEX 175 north to Ixtlán. There are fine, mature trees in this area growing with *P. rudis, P. patula, P. patula* var. *longepedunculata, P. montezumae* and at 2,000 m *P. chiapensis.* Still further south in Mexico at the city of San Cristobal de las Casas in Chiapas, there are young trees growing near the highway leading to the town of Ococingo. Also south of San Cristobal de las Casas, scattered trees of this species grow along Highway 190 near the village of Teopisca.

In Guatemala, driving west from Guatemala City on Highway CA-1 at kilometer 168, there is a small group of *P. ayacahuite* trees growing on a steep, north-facing slope in an area appropriately called "Alaska"—altitude about 3,000 m. These are magnificent trees, many over 40 m tall and a few trees 1–2 m in diameter. Also on this same highway and north in the department of Totonicopán, in the Maria Tecum mountains, there are small stands of *P. ayacahuite.* Driving west from the city of Quezaltenango toward San Marcos, groups of these trees can be found along the highway.

In Honduras drive north on Highway CA-5 from Tegucigalpa to Lake Yohoa. There inquire about a narrow, winding road to the village of El Mochita, near the lake. Near the village, the volcanic mountain, Cerro Santa Bárbara (∿ 2,800 m, altitude) dominates the landscape. *P. ayacahuite* grows on the upper slopes of the mountain; however, ascent should be attempted only with reliable guides. The species is also found on Cerro Celaque (∿ 2,900 m, altitude) in the department of Lempira near the town of Gracias, on Highway CA-11A west from Tegucigalpa. This mountain, actually a small range, is virtually unexplored, and collections should only be attempted with reliable guides. Also west from Tegucigalpa near the villages of Santa Ana and Las Trancas (just east of Highway CA-7), *P. ayacahuite* can be found in small, isolated stands at elevations of about 2,100 m. Here too it is important to have a reliable local guide to assist with collections.

In El Salvador, drive north from the capital San Salvador, on Highway CA-4 to the town of La Palma. At La Palma a very narrow, winding, rocky trail leads eastward to the very small villages of Las Pilas, El Aguacatal and El Miramundo, all at an altitude of about 2,300 m. In the surrounding mountains *P. ayacahuite* is found in small isolated groups and as individual trees mingled with other pines and *Abies guatemalensis* var. *tacanensis* Mart.

When I last visited the area in 1977, the forests were being clear-cut for firewood to be sold in the capital, San Salvador. Many small stands of pines noted there in 1974 had disappeared completely in 1977, and the land was being heavily grazed by sheep, goats and cattle. It is quite possible that at this writing *Pinus ayacahuite* can no longer be found in El Salvador.

In both Honduras and El Salvador, collections should be attempted only in a vehicle (where trails are accessible) with high clearance and then only during the dry season, generally November through February.

NOTES AND COMMENTS—I have already described the two varieties of *P. ayacahuite*. However, they are mentioned here because their ranges overlap one another and var. *veitchii* overlaps the range of *P. ayacahuite*. They can generally be separated on the basis of development of the seed wing and seed size. As mentioned earlier, *P. ayacahuite* has small seeds with a long, firmly attached wing. *P. ayacahuite* var. *veitchii*, has larger seeds with a short, 5–15 mm seed wing and *P. ayacahuite* var. *brachyptera* has large, nut-like seeds without wings, or with vestigial wings 1–2 mm long. I should point out too that there is considerable variation in the size of *P. ayacahuite* cones. I have found cones from the same tree ranging from 15 to 30 cm in length with scales that are straight, slightly curved or strongly reflexed.

Pinus chiapensis (Mart.) Andresen

Pinabete, Ocote, Pino Blanco

THE TREE—A really magnificent white pine that often attains a height of 40 m and diameter of 1 m or more. Crowns of large mature trees are generally pyramidal with horizontal branches spaced in fairly regular whorls. In young trees the regular spacing of the branches is particularly apparent, so too is the pyramidal form of the crown.

BARK—On young trees the bark is smooth, greenish gray; on mature trees the upper stem is smooth and greenish gray, while bark on the lower stem is rough and divided into long rectangular plates, grayish brown in color.

BRANCHLETS—Smooth, slender with leaves grouped mostly toward the ends. Bases of the leaf bracts are not decurrent.

LEAVES—In groups of 5, slender, flexible, somewhat drooping, 6–12 cm long (averaging about 8 cm); bright green; margins serrate with very small teeth; stomata present only on the ventral surfaces; resin canals 2–3, external; fibrovascular bundle single. Sheaths are light brown and soon deciduous.

CONELETS—Almost cylindrical but tapering slightly toward each end, solitary and in groups of 2–4, erect on slender peduncles 20–30 mm long.

CONES—Brownish yellow, 10–15 cm long on slender peduncles 25–35 mm long; subcylindrical, tapering toward the apex, mostly straight and often resinous. They mature in early fall (August–October) and seeds are shed immediately. They are early deciduous, the peduncle remaining attached to the cone when it falls.

CONE SCALES—Thin, flexible, 10–15 mm wide; apophyses prolonged, with thin rounded apex often slightly curved inward; the umbo terminal without a prickle and usually resinous.

SEEDS—Dark brown, occasionally mottled, 6–7 mm long, 2–4 mm wide. Seed

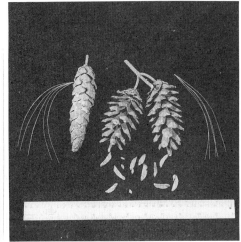
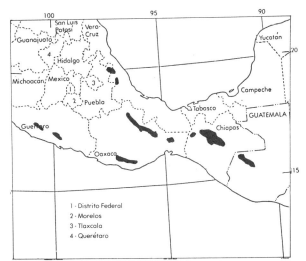

P. *chiapensis* Tree Bark Cones, seeds, and leaves

wing is 20–25 mm long and 4–8 mm wide, strongly attached to the seed (adnate). Cotyledons number 7–9, but are mostly 8. Seeds number 60,000–80,000/kg.

WOOD—Light, soft, creamy white with slightly darker heartwood. It is much sought after locally and, because it is easily shaped by hand, widely used for furniture, doors, window frames, and interior woodwork. Its specific gravity is .340–.360.

DISTRIBUTION—Eastern and southern Mexico into northern Guatemala (Fig. 3.8). In Mexico the species is found in the states of Veracruz, Puebla, Oaxaca, Guerrero and Chiapas; in Guatemala the departments of El Quiché and Huehuetenango. The northern limit of its range occurs a few miles from the Gulf of Mexico near the town of Tlapacoyan in the state of Veracruz. There I found it at elevations as low as 600 m growing with *Pinus maximinoi*, various species of oak, beech, sweet gum and other species including tree ferns, coffee and bananas.

In eastern Oaxaca it has been collected from as low as 500 m and up to 2,250 m altitude. Small groups have also been found in the Sierra Madre del Sur of Guerrero and Oaxaca. Its range is broken at the Isthmus of Tehuantepec but continues into the high central mountains of Chiapas and terminates in Guatemala along the border between the departments of Huehuetenango and El Quiché.

HABITAT—*P. chiapensis* grows at altitudes that range from 500 to 2,250 m. It

Fig. 3.8. Distribution of *P. chiapensis.*

makes its best growth on medium to steep mountain slopes of the Sierra Madre Oriental exposed to the moisture-laden northerly and northeasterly winds from the Gulf of Mexico. In the Sierra Madre del Sur, it is found on slopes of mountains exposed to the southwesterly winds from the Pacific. At most locations the species occurs as widely scattered individuals or small groups of trees often mingled with *P. maximinoi, P. pseudostrobus, P. patula* var. *longepedunculata, Pinus oaxacana, Liquidambar styraciflua, Quercus* spp., *Fagus mexicana,* and other broad-leaved species. Soils are mostly moist, well-drained sandy clays; climate is semi-tropical to tropical at lower elevations; however, at 2,000 m altitude it could be classified as warm-temperate; rainfall ranges from 1,500 to 3,000 mm annually with most occurring from June to September. However, during the drier months dense fogs and clouds blanket the entire eastern escarpment area of Mexico maintaining a very moist, humid atmosphere.

WHERE TO FIND *P. chiapensis*—In Mexico City take the toll road to the city of Puebla. Continue on this same highway for about 50 km beyond Puebla, then turn left onto Highway 140. This will take you to Perote. There go left on Highway 131 to the town of Altotonga. Here you are on the escarpment of the Sierra Madre Oriental and the city of Teziutlán is only a few kilometers to your left. Since the trip will require at least two days, plan to stay overnight in Teziutlán. From Teziutlán take the highway toward Tlapacoyan and look for *P. chiapensis* along the highway. It will probably be very cloudy and foggy, and since the road is steep and very winding, two persons will be needed, one to drive and another to look for the pines.

Also from Mexico City take Highway 95 south toward Acapulco. About 50–60 km south of the city of Iguala, at the town of Milpillas, turn right toward the village of Yextla. Approximately 50–60 km south of Yextla you will be in the heart of the Sierra Madre del Sur, and *P. chiapensis* can be found in the area. It would be advisable to have a reliable guide with you since this is a very isolated region.

Further south in Mexico at the city of Oaxaca, take Highway 175 north toward Tuxtepec. Near the town of Guelatao, the mountains begin to rise rapidly. You will need to cross the continental divide at over 3,000 m before descending to the fog and mist-shrouded escarpment area where these pines are found. Since the road is very steep, winding and narrow with visibility limited by fog and clouds, one person will be needed to drive and another to look for pines along the highway.

Still further south in Mexico one can drive on the Pan American Highway to Tuxtla Gutierrez, capital of Chiapas State. A few kilometers east of the capitol, turn left on Highway 195 to the town of Bochil and then to the village of Tapilula. Follow Highway 195 north for a few kilometers and look for *P. chiapensis* in small groups and as individual roadside trees. The altitude in this area is about 1,500–1,900 m. Obtain a reliable guide since this, too, is a rather isolated area.

In Guatemala drive northwestward from Guatemala City on Highway CA-1 to the city of Huehuetenango. Obtain a reliable guide to take you north of the city for about 30–40 km into the Sierra de Los Cuchumatanes. Here, too, the pines will be found on the north and northeast slopes where rainfall is highest and fog and clouds shroud the forests.

Since the area is very isolated and inaccessible, give considerable thought to a proposed trip before actually starting. Certainly the trip should not be attempted without one or two guides well known in the area.

NOTES AND COMMENTS—The species *P. strobus* L. is a well-known white pine that grows in the mountains of eastern Canada southward along the Appalachian Mountains to northern Georgia. *Pinus chiapensis* is closely related to *P. strobus* and, at the northern limit of its range, is separated from *P. strobus* by about 2,000 km. In Mexico and Guatemala *P. chiapensis* grows under tropical to subtropical conditions and, interestingly, a hardwood species, *Liquidambar styraciflua* L, which has a very wide range in the eastern United States, is associated with it over most of its range in Mexico and Guatemala. Botanists and taxonomists are not in agreement about the origin and relationships of these closely related though widely separated pine species. Did they originate in Central America and migrate northward, or did the periods of glaciation force many northern species southward into Mexico and Central America where they remained as isolated reservoirs of species that migrated northward again as the glaciers retreated? Although we do not have answers to these questions, we do know that *P. chiapensis* is rapidly disappearing over its entire range. Man is the principal offender since the wood is much sought after for use in construction of small homes. Even small groups of trees and individual trees are becoming rare and generally can be found only in very isolated and inaccessible areas. There is no question now that the species is rare and, during the past few years, may have become endangered. Fortunately, since 1984 CAMCORE (Central America and Mexico Coniferous Resources Cooperative) has made extensive and intensive seed collections from selected provenances over the entire range of the species, and these are now planted in carefully controlled areas in Brazil, Venezuela, Colombia and South Africa. Mexico and Guatemala are also planning to establish plantations under the supervision of their Forestry Services.

Jeffrey Donahue, field representative for CAMCORE, collected *P. chiapensis* in Oaxaca, growing with *P. ayacahuite* at 2,250 m altitude. I found *P. ayacahuite* trees near Totonicapán, Guatemala, with unusually small cones (approximately the size of *P. chiapensis* cones) and wondered about the possibility of hibridization between the two species.

No crosses have been attempted between *P. chiapensis* and *P. strobus*. The two taxa are very similar morphologically and might readily hybridize. In this connection, I have found that chemical analyses of turpentine from *P. chiapensis* reveal significant differences from that of *P. strobus*. Progeny from such crosses might possess resistance to some insect pests and diseases that now attack *P. strobus*.

Section Paracembra

In marked contrast to the tall trees of Section Cembra, the pines in this group are small and poorly formed, generally 5–15 m tall with broadly rounded crowns. Their branchlets are smooth and often slender to pendent; leaves are borne in fascicles of 1–5 and are mostly short, stiff and erect. Fascicle sheaths are generally (though not always) recurved into a "rosette" and then deciduous. Seeds are wingless (with one exception) with seed coats that range from thin to very thick. The "pine nuts" or piñones, are much sought after for food by birds, rodents and man. Trees in this group generally grow at elevations of 700–2,500 m on rocky, arid lower slopes of the mountains. *P. culmincola* is an exception, growing at 3,000–3,500 m altitude.

I have divided Section Paracembra into two clearly defined groups; Subsection Cembroides and Subsection Pinceana. The trees of Subsection Cembroides bear small cones (2–9 cm) that soon disintegrate after falling to the ground. Pines in Subsection Pinceana bear larger cones (8–22 cm) with larger scales that do not disintegrate quickly after falling to the ground.

Subsection Cembroides

In the classification used here, 11 species and one subspecies are included in Subsection Cembroides. During the past few years, intensive studies of the pines in this group by a number of botanists and taxonomists have resulted in descriptions of "new" species and subspecies. In Table 3.3, I have listed some of their distinguishing characters.

Table 3.3. Characteristics of Subsection Cembroides.

Species	Leaves per fascicle	Seed coat	Form of mature tree
P. monophylla	1	Very thin	Small tree
P. edulis	2	Moderately thin	Small tree
P. remota	2	Very thin	Small tree
P. catarinae	2	Thin	Shrubby
P. cembroides	2–3	Thick	Small tree
P. cembroides subsp. *orizabensis*	3	Thick	Small tree
P. discolor	3	Thick	Small tree
P. johannis	3	Thick	Shrubby
P. lagunae	3	Very thin	Small tree
P. quadrifolia	4	Very thin	Small tree
P. juarezensis	5	Thin	Small tree
P. culminicola	5	Thick	Low, prostrate

Pinus monophylla Torr. et Frem.

Singleleaf Piñon, Piñon, Nut Pine

THE TREE—A small pine up to 20 m tall but generally about 10–15 m; the trunk about 30 cm, occasionally 40 cm in diameter; generally short with stiff branches that occasionally extend almost to the ground; the crown is rounded and in young tress dense and pyramidal.

BARK—On young trees thin and smooth, on mature trees 1–2 cm thick with deep, irregular fissures and ridges, the surface broken into thin, reddish brown scales. The upper part of the trunk has relatively smooth, thin bark similar to the young trees.

BRANCHLETS—Orange to brown, smooth when young but becoming rough with age; bases of the leaf bracts are not decurrent.

LEAVES—Mostly solitary, occasionally 2 in a fascicle; 4–6 cm long, stiff, 1–2 mm thick; stomata present on the dorsal surface; resin canals 5–10, occasionally 12–13, all external; vascular bundle single. Fascicle sheaths 5–10 mm long, pale brownish yellow; recurved into a rosette and early deciduous.

CONELETS—Borne singly and in groups of 2–3 on slender peduncles; globose with thick scales.

CONES—Globose, symmetrical, 5–8 cm long, and 6–7 cm wide when open. Borne on a very short peduncle that falls with the cone. Mature cones are somewhat larger than cones of *P. cembroides* and *P. edulis*; yellowish orange, lustrous not dull colored; opening at maturity and soon deciduous.

CONE SCALES—Few but somewhat larger and stronger than those of *P. edulis* and *P. cembroides*. The scales are thick and strong, apophyses thick and pyramidal; umbo dorsal, rather depressed, with a small, deciduous prickle. Scales at the base and apex of the cone are often small and sterile in contrast to the larger, central, seed-bearing scales.

SEEDS—Sought after for food by birds and animals; dark brown, about 15 mm long, wingless, with a very thin seed coat, 0.1–0.3 mm thick; cotyledons 5–10, averaging 7. It is interesting to note that margins of the juvenile leaves are serrate. The endosperm is white.

WOOD—The wood is light, soft, not strong or resinous, pale yellowish brown color and used locally for firewood and fence posts. In years past, large numbers of the trees in their U.S. range were cut for mine props and charcoal for smelting silver ore.

P. monophylla Tree   Bark   Branchlet, cones, seeds, and leaves

DISTRIBUTION—*P. monophylla* occurs principally in the southwestern United States in California, Nevada, Utah and Arizona. In southern California its range extends southward into Baja California Norte along the Sierra Juárez and San Pedro Mártir Mountains where it occurs with *P. quadrifolia, P. juarezensis* and *P. jeffreyi* (Fig. 3.9).

HABITAT—This small nut pine grows at altitudes varying from 1,200–2,000 m on dry, rocky slopes. In the high mountains temperatures often drop to freezing during the winter months. At 1,600–2,000 m altitude, rainfall may range from 300–600 mm with about 30% occurring as snow and sleet.

WHERE TO FIND *P. monophylla*—Since this species has an extensive range in southern California and Nevada, there should be no problem finding specimens in those states. By contrast, the San Pedro Mártir Mountains of Baja California Norte are rather isolated and inaccessible. Collections there should be attempted only with a reliable guide, a high-clearance vehicle, spare tires, extra gasoline and water, and only during the dry season.

NOTES AND COMMENTS—This small piñon is widely used for posts and firewood. The seeds are very nutritious and sought after for food by man, birds and rodents. With its ability to survive under very harsh conditions of frost, drought and high summer temperatures, and still produce sizable crops of highly nutritious seeds, this species warrants special consideration for planting in arid areas that are presently unproductive. Its ability to cross with *P. juarezensis* and *P. quadrifolia* would appear to present very interesting genetic possibilities for the development of an improved hybrid piñon.

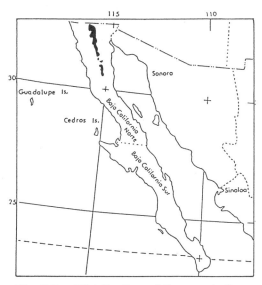

Fig. 3.9.   Distribution of *P. monophylla.*

Pinus edulis Engelm.

Piñon, Nut Pine, Colorado Piñon

THE TREE—A small pine 5–15 m tall and 30–60 cm in diameter; most often 10 m in height and 20–30 cm in diameter; the trunk usually short and soon branching, the branches thick and stiff, forming a rounded, rather compact crown.

BARK—On young trees thin and smooth, on older, mature trees about 1 cm thick, irregularly divided into shallow ridges covered with thin, reddish brown, scaly plates. The upper part of the trunk has thin, smooth bark similar to the bark on young trees.

BRANCHLETS—Light gray, rather stout and rough; however, bases of the leaf bracts are not decurrent.

LEAVES—Mostly in fascicles of 2, occasionally 1 and 3, often incurved, thick, stiff, 2–6 cm long, the margins smooth. Stomata on dorsal and ventral surfaces; resin canals mostly 2, occasionally 3 or 4, external; fibrovascular bundle single. Sheaths of the leaves thin, recurved into a rosette and early deciduous.

CONELETS—Borne singly and in groups of 2–4 on slender peduncles; globose with thick scales.

CONES—3–6 cm long and 4–7 cm wide when open, globose, symmetrical; borne on a very short peduncle 2–5 mm long that falls with the cone. Mature cones are ochre to reddish orange in color, opening at maturity and early deciduous.

CONE SCALES—Few, those at the base and apex of the cone generally sterile and smaller than the central, seed-bearing scales. Scales are thick, the apophyses pyramidal; umbo dorsal, depressed with a very small, deciduous prickle.

SEEDS—Brown, 10–13mm long, 6–8 mm wide; wingless with a moderately thin seed coat; about 3,000/kg. Cotyledons 8–9, mostly 8 and the endosperm is white. Seeds are widely sought for food by rodents, birds and man.

WOOD—Medium-hard, not strong, the heartwood pale yellowish brown, not resinous; used principally for posts and firewood.

DISTRIBUTION—This piñon pine is widely distributed in the southwestern United States, occurring principally in Arizona, Utah, Colorado and New Mexico. Smaller, outlying populations occur in southern Wyoming, western Texas and possibly in the northwestern corner of Chihuahua, Mexico (Fig. 3.10).

HABITAT—Generally found on foothills and mesas at altitudes ranging from 1,600 to 2,400 m. Like most of the nut pines, it occurs on dry, rocky slopes that form a transition zone between desert conditions and higher, more humid areas. Over its limited range in northwestern Chihuahua, temperatures fall

Branchlet, cone, seeds, and leaves

P. edulis Tree   Bark

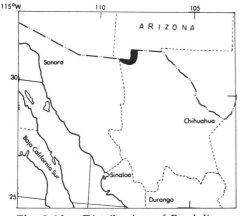

Fig. 3.10. Distribution of *P. edulis.*

well below freezing during the winter months. Annual rainfall varies from 300–600 mm with snow and sleet accounting for about 30%.

WHERE TO FIND *P. edulis*—Since the species is very common in the southwestern United States, there should be no problem in finding specimens in that broad area. Collections in northwestern Chihuahua might be made by crossing the border at El Paso and driving west on High-

way 2. Look for the piñon pines along the highway and in the hills near Laguna de Guzman.

NOTES AND COMMENTS—When the first silver mines were opened in the west, these trees supplied the mine timbers and charcoal needed for smelting the ore. Now the trees are widely used in the southwestern U.S. for fence posts and firewood.

Centuries before the arrival of Europeans, Indians of the southwest harvested the seeds for food, particularly for use during the long winter months. For millennia birds and rodents have stored the seeds for a food supply during the winter months.

With regard to the limited range of this species in Mexico, a number of taxonomists believe that *P. edulis* does not occur in Mexico. However, other authorities cite its range as extending across the border into northern Chihuahua and in the Big Bend area of Texas at the border of Coahuila. The distribution of *P. cembroides* and *P. edulis* apparently overlaps in northern Chihuahua, thus I have shown the range of *P. edulis* extending across the border into Chihuahua.

Pinus remota (Little) Bailey & Hawksworth

Paper-shell Pinyon, Texas Pinyon, Piñon, Nut Pine

THE TREE—A small, limby tree 3–8 m tall; mature trees have a rounded, irregular crown while in young trees the crown is much more dense and pyramidal in form.

BARK—On mature trees not thick but rough, longitudinally furrowed, forming dark gray, scaly plates; on young trees much thinner and smooth.

BRANCHLETS—Slender, light gray, bases of the leaf bracts not decurrent.

LEAVES—Mostly in fascicles of 2, occasionally 3, slender, flexible, 3–5 cm long, 1.3–1.8 mm wide, the margins entire; stomata present on dorsal and ventral surfaces; resin canals 2–5, mostly 2, external; fibrovascular bundle single. Sheaths are thin, pale brown and on young needles

reflexed or curled backward, early deciduous.

CONELETS—Borne singly and in pairs on peduncles about 4 mm long. The conelets are about 7 mm long, brown, transversely keeled; the umbo bears a minute prickle.

CONES—Small, globose, symmetrical, dehiscent and deciduous, 2.5–3.5 cm long and 3–5 cm wide when open; ochre to reddish orange color when mature. They are borne singly and in pairs on peduncles about 6 mm long that fall with the cone.

CONE SCALES—Few, rather thin and weak, the apical and basal scales small and generally sterile, the central seed-bearing scales larger, the apophysis thick, trans-

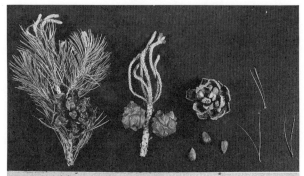

P. remota Tree in center   Bark   Branchlet, cones, seeds, and leaves

versely keeled but not protuberant; the umbo dorsal, very small, generally depressed and bearing a minute, early deciduous prickle.

SEEDS—Wingless, large, 12–15 mm long, 6–10 mm wide, the seed coat very thin, 0.1–0.4 mm thick, the endosperm white.

WOOD—Rather hard for piñon pines, the heartwood pale brown, slightly resinous, used mostly for posts and firewood.

DISTRIBUTION—This piñon is found in southwestern Texas and across the border in northeastern Mexico. In Texas it has been collected in Trans-Pecos (the Big Bend region) and the Edwards Plateau. In Mexico, northern and southeastern Chihuahua, northwestern Coahuila near the Big Bend area and southeastward into Nuevo León as small rather isolated populations (Fig. 3.11).

HABITAT—This species has the distinction of growing at the lowest altitude of any of the piñon pines. In the Edwards Plateau of Texas, the species has been found on rocky limestone soils at altitudes as low as 500 m; in Coahuila State, Mexico, it has been collected at 1,200–1,800 m altitude. Like most of the piñons, this species is adapted to semi-arid conditions. In the Big Bend area of Texas and northern Coahuila rainfall is generally quite low (300–500 mm), and temperatures often drop to freezing during the coldest months (December and January). Associated

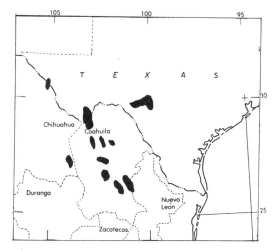

Fig. 3.11.   Distribution of P. remota.

species are P. cembroides, P. arizonica var. stormiae, Juniperus ashei Buchh. and Juniperus monosperma Sarg.

WHERE TO FIND P. remota—This small piñon can be easily collected in Texas. Trees can be found growing near Highway 277 about 30 miles north of the city Del Rio. In northwestern Coahuila, take Mexico Highway 53 to the town of La Cuesta. A few kilometers south of the town where the highway forks to the left, look for these small pines.

NOTES AND COMMENTS—The seeds are sought for food by birds, rodents and man; the very thin seed coat makes them especially attractive for human consumption. This piñon should be considered for intensive selection and breeding studies for production of fuelwood and posts and for production of very thin-shelled "pine nuts." Since it grows at fairly low elevations under very difficult environmental conditions, it could be used for planting in many areas that are now almost completely unproductive.

Little (1966) first described this taxon as a variety of *P. cembroides*. Bailey & Hawksworth (1979) raised it to specific status principally because of its low altitudinal requirements, leaves with occasionally 3 resin canals, a different type of curl-back of the fascicle sheath and of most importance, "its occurrence (near its upper elevational limit) sympatrically in west Texas with *P. cembroides* (near its lower elevational limit) without evidence of hybridization."

Pinus catarinae M.-F. Robert-Passini

Catarina Pine, Piñon, Nut Pine

THE TREE—A low shrubby tree, generally 2–4 m in height, seldom 6 m, with low, wide-spreading branches. The crown is rounded, low, wider than tall and more shrubby than tree-like.

BARK—Thin, smooth and gray in young trees, later becoming rough and scaly but not thick.

BRANCHLETS—Gray, rough when older, bases of the leaf bracts are not decurrent.

LEAVES—Thick, stiff, 2 and occasionally 3 in a fascicle, 2.5–5.0 cm long, the margins entire; stomata on dorsal and ventral surfaces; resin canals 2–4 mostly 3, external, dorsal; vascular bundle single. Fascicle sheaths pale brown and deciduous.

CONELETS—Borne on slender peduncles 5–10 mm long, generally curved inward; the conelets 4–8 mm long and 4–8 mm wide.

CONES—About 4 cm long when open; globose. Mature cones are pale lustrous brown, dehiscent but remaining on the branches for a number of months after opening; the small peduncle falls with the cone.

CONE SCALES—Few, hard, stiff; the apophyses pyramidal, transversely keeled; umbo dorsal, depressed; the prickle minute and soon deciduous. The central scales are seed-bearing, those at the apex and base of the cone are quite small and generally sterile.

SEEDS—Wingless, brownish color, about 12 mm long and 7 mm wide, the seed coat

P. catarinae Tree. *Thanks to M-F Passini.*

or shell 0.2–0.5 mm thick, the endosperm white.

WOOD—The sapwood is a creamy color and the heartwood pale brown. The shrubby trees are used for fuelwood.

DISTRIBUTION—*P. catarinae* has been found in a very limited area in the state of Nuevo León, Municipio de Santa Catarina, near the village of Santa Catarina, in the mountains between the cities of Saltillo and Monterrey (Fig. 3.12).

HABITAT—This small piñon, more shrub than tree, was found growing at an altitude of 1,140 m. The site is a rocky-gravelly limestone plateau and no other pines are asso-

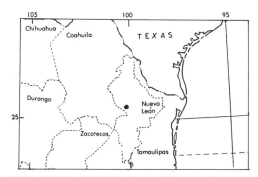

Fig. 3.12.   Distribution of *P. catarinae*.

ciated with the species. *Agave lecheguilla* was the only other "sizable" plant growing with *P. catarinae* at this site. Annual rainfall in the area is about 300 mm and average temperature is about 18° C. The coldest months are December and January and the hottest are May and June.

WHERE TO FIND *P. catarinae*—Like *P. johannis,* another dwarf piñon, this is not a common species. To find this taxon, take Highway 40 from Saltillo toward Monterrey for about 90 km (almost to Monterrey) and look carefully on the right for a turn off to the town of Santa Catarina.

In the town inquire about the location of an area known as Casa Blanca and hire a guide who is familiar with the area. Although the area is not distant from Monterrey, it is isolated and collection should be attempted only during the dry winter months.

NOTES AND COMMENTS—This small, shrubby piñon is used for firewood and, like all the nut pines, the seeds are collected for food. The species is found at a lower altitude than most of the Mexican piñon pines and manages to grow under very inhospitable conditions. It could be useful as a source of food and fuelwood in some areas that presently are unproductive.

Passini (1982) described this dwarf species from a single location in Nuevo León. However, Bailey & Hawksworth (1983) considered *P. catarinae* to be a synonym for *P. remota.* Apparently they found a number of good-sized, single-stem trees growing at the type locality and considered the dwarf, shrubby trees to be the result of a local soil problem. Pending further studies of this taxon, I have included *P. catarinae* as a part of subsection Cembroides.

Pinus cembroides Zucc.

Piñon, Piñonero, Nut Pine

THE TREE—Usually a small pine 5–10 m tall, though occasionally reaching 15 m, 30–60 cm in diameter; the crown irregularly branched, often rather open and rounded in mature trees. In young trees the branches are regularly spaced and the form is pyramidal.

BARK—On young trees thin and smooth, on older trees dark brown, with deep longitudinal and horizontal furrows dividing the bark into irregular, geometrically-shaped, scaly plates on the lower part of the trunk; on the upper part of the trunk the bark is thin and smooth.

BRANCHLETS—Slender, grayish, rather rough although bases of the leaf bracts are not decurrent.

LEAVES—In fascicles of 2–3, mostly 3,

stiff, often curved, 3–7 cm long and 1.2–1.6 mm wide; margins smooth; stomata on both surfaces, the ventral surfaces often glaucous, the dorsal surface generally dark green but occasionally pale to yellowish green. Resin canals 2, external; fibrovascular bundle single. Fascicle sheaths strongly reflexed forming a rosette, later deciduous.

CONELETS—Borne singly and in groups of 2–5, short slender peduncles; globose, the scales thick and bearing a small prickle.

CONES—Globose, symmetrical, when open 3–4 cm long and 3–6 cm wide; borne singly and in groups of 2–5; the peduncle, only 2–5 mm long, falls with the cone. Mature cones are lustrous reddish to yellowish brown, ripening in late fall to winter, opening when mature and soon

P. cembroides Tree   Bark   Cones, seeds, and leaves

deciduous.

CONE SCALES—Few; those in the center of the cone larger than the scales at the base and apex, the central scales seed-bearing, the others generally sterile. Scales are thick, the margins thinner; apophyses pyramidal, umbo dorsal, slightly raised, bearing a small prickle that is soon deciduous.

SEEDS—Sought for food by man, rodents and birds. They are dark brown, 13 mm long and 7–8 mm wide; wingless, with a thick hard seed coat 0.5–1.0 mm thick; number per kilogram varies from 2,500–3,000; cotyledons are 9–11, mostly 10. The endosperm is pink.

WOOD—Since most trees grow rather slowly on rocky, dry slopes, the wood is close-grained but rather soft, only slightly resinous, the heartwood pale yellow. Used locally in construction of mines, small homes, sheds, doors, posts and of course for firewood.

DISTRIBUTION—P. cembroides is very widely distributed in Mexico (Fig. 3.13). In the Sierra Madre Occidental, it ranges from the United States border (Arizona and New Mexico) southward in the states of Chihuahua, Durango, Zacatecas, Aguascalientes and Jalisco. There its range extends eastward into the states of Guanajuato, San Luis Potosí, Queretaro and Hidalgo. In the Sierra Madre Oriental, its distribution extends from the United States border (Texas) southward into the states of Coahuila, Nuevo León, and Tamaulipas.

HABITAT—Generally occurs on dry, rocky slopes of mountain foothills. Its range is so broad that no particular soil type appears to be associated with it; however, moisture and altitude are important ecological factors in its distribution. Its altitudinal range is 1,500–2,800 m; however, I found P. cembroides growing in association with P. nelsoni at elevations of about 3,000 m on the dry, south-facing slopes of Peña Nevada mountain on the Nuevo León-Tamaulipas border north of the town Miquihuana.

In the Sierra Madre Occidental, the species is found in a rather narrow band along the eastern foothills, generally in a transition zone between arid desert country and higher, more humid areas. Along the foothiils of these mountains, rainfall averages ᜠ 450 mm with a 7 month dry season. Temperature ranges from below 0° C to 22° C; the coldest months are December and January, the hottest May, June and July.

Along the Sierra Madre Oriental the species grows under similar ecological conditions, i.e., in a band along the western foothills of the mountains, between desert country and higher, more humid areas. In the foothills of these mountains, rainfall averages ᜠ 400 mm with an 8 month dry season. Temperature ranges from 0° C during the winter months to 21° C during the summer.

It should be pointed out that the very

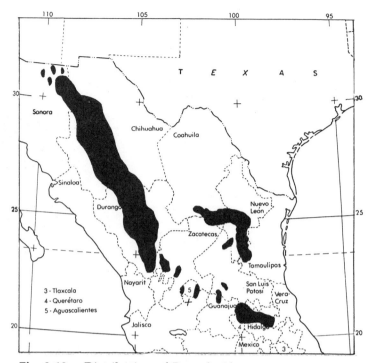

Fig. 3.13. Distribution of *P. cembroides.*

broad geographical range of this species encompasses an equally wide range of temperature and rainfall conditions; in some areas temperatures often fall well below freezing each winter and rainfall may reach 800 mm or more per year. The conditions shown here by the rainfall and temperature figures do represent "good average" conditions for the species.

Associated species in the Sierra Madre Occidental are *P. johannis, P. chihuahuana, P. engelemanii, Juniperus* spp. and *Quercus* spp. In the Sierra Madre Oriental associated species are *P. arizonica* var. *stormiae, P. nelsoni, P. teocote, P. pinceana, P. remota, Juniperus* spp. and *Quercus* spp.

WHERE TO FIND *P. cembroides*—Since this species occurs over a very broad area in Mexico, it is not at all difficult to find. In the Sierra Madre Oriental, the mountains near the city of Saltillo (west from Monterrey) have sizable stands of the species particularly 10–15 km south along Highway 57. Further south on this same highway, near kilometer 130, look for a paved road on the left leading to the town of Galeana; 10–12 km before reaching Galeana there are many trees on both sides of the highway. From the

town of Galeana there is a narrow dirt road northward that leads to the town of Dieziocho de Marzo. This road passes through a small forest of *P. cembroides;* the trees appeared to be rather taller than most stands of the species found in the area. This same area (near Galeana) is dominated by an isolated mountain, Cerro Potosí, that reaches an altitude of about 3,500 m; on the lower slopes and foothills of which are many scattered groups of *P. cembroides.*

Again driving south from Saltillo, but on Highway 54 to the city of Zacatecas (about 360 km), look for *P. cembroides* along the highway. They are scattered trees found only occasionally in a rather arid, desolate environment. At Zacatecas turn northward on Highway 45 to Durango. North of Durango near the village of Canatlan are open stands of the species in the foothills of the nearby mountains. From Durango continue northward on Highway 45 to the city of Hidalgo del Parral. There locate a guide to follow a narrow road west from the city into the foothills of the Sierra Madre Occidental. This is an all day trip and should be made only in a vehicle with high clearance. From Hidalgo del Parral continue north to the city of Chihuahua, then north on Highway 45 for about 150 km to the village of El Seco. There go left on Highway 10 to the town of Buenaventura. There are fine stands of *P. cembroides* in the foothills west of the town, particularly along the road toward the village of Ignacio Zaragosa. From Buenaventura back to Highway 45 and north to El Paso, Texas, is about 420 km.

NOTES AND COMMENTS—Although *P. cembroides'* small size and poor form make it unattractive to lumber producers, it fills a very important need in the lives of thousands of families, inhabitants of Mexico's high, semi-arid lands. Since it grows in areas of very low rainfall, it is often the only sizable tree to be found and thus serves almost daily for fuelwood, small hand-hewn timbers for local construction needs and, since the seeds are edible, as an important source of food. While *P.*

cembroides does not bear heavy seed crops each year, usually every second or third year will bring a very heavy yield of seed which forms an important part of the diet for humans, birds and rodents. In addition to their importance as a source of "local free food" the "piñones" or pine nuts, are harvested and sold in the markets, thus providing some ready cash.

The ability of this species to provide firewood, small, useful construction timbers and food, all under difficult environmental conditions, should place it high on a list of preferred species for reforestation in arid and semi-arid areas. Such is not the case; over most of its range stands are slowly but steadily diminishing. Man, through population pressure, land clearing and fire, is the most important factor tilting the scales against the species.

Pinus cembroides subsp. *orizabensis* D. K. Bailey

Orizaba Nut Pine, Piñon

THE TREE—A small piñon pine usually 8–10 m tall, the crown rather open and irregularly branched in mature trees.

BARK—On young trees thin and smooth; on large, mature trees rather thin with irregular, rather broad longitudinal furrows that reveal an orange colored inner bark.

BRANCHLETS—Slender, rough, rather dark; bases of the leaf bracts are not decurrent.

LEAVES—In fascicles of 3, occasionally 4, rarely 2; generally 4–6 cm long, rather thick but not stiff; stomata on both dorsal and ventral surfaces, the ventral surfaces quite glaucous, the dorsal surface dark green. Resin canals 2, external; fibrovascular bundle single. Sheaths of the leaves are curled backward into a rosette and later deciduous.

CONELETS—Borne singly and in groups of 2–4 on slender peduncles, the scales rather thick and bearing a minute prickle.

CONES—Globose, symmetrical; when

open 3–5 cm long and 4–6 cm wide; almost sessile, the very short peduncle falling with the cone. Mature cones are lustrous, light brown, opening when mature and soon deciduous.

CONE SCALES—Few; the central scales larger than those at the base and apex of the cone, the latter generally sterile. Scales are thick and hard, the apophyses raised, umbo dorsal, bearing a very small early deciduous prickle.

SEEDS—Brown, about 14 mm long and 7 mm wide, wingless with a thick, hard seed coat. The endosperm is pink in color.

When heavy crops are borne, the seeds are collected for food by humans, birds and rodents.

WOOD—Close grained, rather soft, only slightly resinous. It is used locally in construction of small homes, for posts, mine timbers and of course for fuelwood.

DISTRIBUTION—Subsp. *orizabensis* has the most southerly distribution of all the Mexican piñon pines (Fig. 3.14). It is found

P. cembroides subsp. *orizabensis* Tree

Fig. 3.14. Distribution of *P. cembroides* subsp. *orizabensis*.

in a rather limited zone west of Mt. Orizaba in the states of Tlaxcala, Puebla and Veracruz. An isolated population of this taxon is also reported from an area 15 km east of the city of Tehuacán, Puebla.

HABITAT—Like most of the nut pines, this taxon is found on the rocky, lower slopes of mountains. It grows at altitudes of 2,300–2,600 m, and the climate is rather cool and humid in contrast to the more arid environment associated with most populations of *P. cembroides* in northwestern and northeastern Mexico.

The hottest months are May and June

and the coldest months are December and January when temperatures may fall below freezing. Rainfall, mostly during the summer months, ranges from 800–900 mm. No other subspecies or varieties of Cembroides were found growing in association with subspecies *orizabensis*.

WHERE TO FIND subsp. *orizabensis*— Go to Mexico City and take Highway 150 (the autopista) to the city of Puebla (125 km) in the state of Puebla. From Puebla continue on the autopista eastward for about 40 km and look for a turn off on the left to Highway 140 near the town of Acatzingo. Follow Highway 140 northward for about 25 km to the village of El Seco. There ask for directions to the village of Soltepec, about 10 km southwest of El Seco. At Soltepec obtain a guide familiar with the area and search the surrounding hills for the piñons. Though not far from Puebla, collections should be attempted only during the dry winter months.

If the trees cannot be found at Soltepec, return to El Seco and continue northward on Highway 140 for about 15 km. Look for the junction with Highway 129 on the left and drive for about 15 km to the town of Oriental. A few kilometers north of the town on Highway 129, look for the small trees.

NOTES AND COMMENTS—The collection of *P. cembroides*, subsp. *orizabensis* near the city of Tehuacán, Puebla, at 18° 27″ N latitude is, at present, the southernmost occurrence of the piñon pines in North

America. The northern limit of the range of the nut pines is near the southern border of Idaho state ($\sim$ 42° N latitude), a north–south distance of about 3,000 km from southern Puebla, Mexico—a remarkable testament to the adaptability of these small pine trees bearing wingless seeds.

Pinus discolor Bailey & Hawksworth

Border Pinyon, Piñon

THE TREE—Like most of the nut pines, this is a small tree 5–10 m tall, the trunk 10–50 cm in diameter, the crown rather open and irregularly rounded.

BARK—On old mature trees the bark is dark gray, furrowed longitudinally and with smaller transverse fissures resulting in small, rough, scaly plates. At the base of the deeper furrows an orange colored underback can be seen. On young trees the bark is smooth and gray.

BRANCHLETS—Smooth, slender, light gray, bases of the leaf bracts are not decurrent.

LEAVES—Mostly in fascicles of 3, occasionally 4 and rarely 2; 2–6 cm long, 1.3–1.6 mm wide, straight, slender, flexible, the margins entire; stomata present on ventral surfaces only, the dorsal surface dark green, the ventral surfaces very glaucous; resin canals 2, external, dorsal; fibrovascular bundle single. Sheaths thin, pale brown, recurved into a rosette; deciduous.

CONELETS—Borne singly and in pairs on slender peduncles 4–8 mm long, light brown, the small scales lightly keeled and without a prickle.

CONES—Symmetrical, very small, 2–3 cm long and 3–4 cm wide when open; pale orange to reddish brown, opening when mature and soon deciduous, the short peduncle (3–6 mm) falling with the cone.

CONE SCALES—Like most of the nut pines, the apical and basal cone scales are small and generally sterile, the central seed-bearing scales are thick, the apophyses pyramidal, umbo small, dorsal, flat to depressed and without a prickle.

SEEDS—Small, wingless, 10–12 mm long, 7–10 mm wide; brown with a thick, 0.7–1.2 mm, hard seed coat and white endosperm. They are stored by rodents but not sought after by humans because seed crops are generally small and the seed coat is very hard.

WOOD—For years the trees have been

P. discolor Trees

Bark

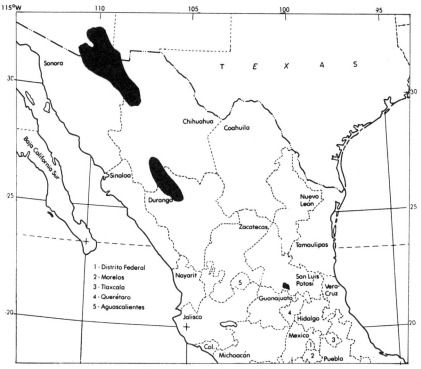

Fig. 3.15. Distribution of *P. discolor.*

cut for mine timbers and charcoal. They are now used for local construction of small homes, posts for doorways and window frames, fence posts and, of course, fuel. The wood is soft, not very resinous, and easily worked by hand.

DISTRIBUTION—The principal range of *P. discolor* is along the U.S.-Mexico border in southeast Arizona, southwest New Mexico, northeast Sonora and northwest Chihuahua (Fig. 3.15). A few populations have been found in southern Chihuahua, northwestern Durango and the San Miguelito mountains in southwestern San Luis Potosí.

HABITAT—The lower slopes and foothills of mountains, generally growing under arid conditions at 1,500–2,400 m altitude. This pine does not form extensive forests but grows in open woodlands as scattered individuals mingled with *P. arizonica, P. cembroides, Juniperus deppeana* Steud and *Quercus* spp.

Rainfall, including snow and sleet, may vary from 300–500 mm annually over most of its range. Along the U.S.-Mexico border, temperatures drop to freezing during November, December, January and February.

WHERE TO FIND *P. discolor*—This taxon can be rather easily collected in a number of the U.S. National Forests in southeastern Arizona and southwestern New Mexico. For example, in the Apache National Forest, along Highway 666 north of Clifton, *P. discolor* has been found growing with *P. edulis.* In Mexico, cross the border at El Paso and at Ciudad Juárez take Mexico Highway 2 west for about 200 km to the town of Janos. There take Highway 10 south to the city of Neuvo Casas Grandes. Hire a guide who knows the roads and trails west of the city toward the Sierra de Huachinera and look for small nut pines at altitudes of 1,500–2,000 m. This is isolated country so collections should be attempted only in a high-clearance vehicle with an adequate supply of gasoline and water, and only during the dry season.

NOTES AND COMMENTS—This small piñon was described by Little (1968) as *P. cembroides* var. *bicolor.* Bailey & Hawksworth (1979) gave it specific rank principally because of the very distinctive bark, quite different from that of *P. cembroides;* the pronounced silver-white color of the ventral leaf surfaces; leaves usually in fascicles of 3 (rarely 2); differences in flowering dates ("*P. cembroides* sheds its pollen almost 4–6 weeks earlier than *P. discolor*"); and important differences in chemical analyses of wood cores taken from *P. cembroides* and *P. discolor*. Bailey & Hawksworth state, "*P. cembroides* is high in α-pinene (89±5%) and low in both sabinene (2±2%) and p-cymene (1±1%), whereas *P. discolor* is low in α-pinene (35±10%) and high in both sabinene (22±14%) and p-cymene (12±7%). The percentages are means and standard deviations for 90 trees of *P. cembroides* and 120 trees of *P. discolor*."

Pinus johannis M.-F. Robert-Passini

Johannis Pine, Dwarf Piñon, Piñon

THE TREE—A small multi-stemmed shrubby tree, perhaps more shrub than tree since it is rare to find this taxon with a single, dominant trunk. The species seldom attains a height of 4 m, plants 2–3 m tall being more usual. It is quite spreading with branches extending outward from the ground line as much as 3–4 m. The crown is low, dense and rounded.

BARK—In young trees smooth and gray; in older, mature trees the multiple trunks-branches are rough and scaly, not deeply furrowed or ridged.

BRANCHLETS—Dark gray, rough; the bases of the leaf bracts are not decurrent.

LEAVES—Three in a fascicle, occasionally 2, rarely 4; 3–5 cm long, 0.9–1.2 mm thick; flexible, margins entire, stomata present only on the ventral surfaces, the dorsal surface dark green and the ventral surface glaucous. Resin canals 2, external, dorsal; vascular bundle single. Fascicle sheaths are gray, curled backward into a rosette and later deciduous.

CONELETS—Brown; 9–11 mm long and 5–7 mm wide; borne singly or in pairs on slender peduncles.

CONES—Oblong and quite resinous; 3–4 cm long and 2–3 cm wide when open. The peduncle is very short, 3–4 mm long and falls with the cone. Mature cones are a polished, chestnut brown, opening at maturity and soon deciduous.

CONE SCALES—Thick, hard, stiff; the apophyses thick, slightly raised; umbo dorsal, depressed, the prickle minute and soon deciduous. Only the central scales are seed-bearing. Those at the base and apex of the cone are generally very small and sterile.

SEEDS—Edible; brown; wingless; about 10 mm wide, the seed coat or shell thick,

P. johannis Trees

Bark

Leaves, branchlet, cones, and seeds

0.5–1.0 mm and hard; about 2,200 seeds/kg; cotyledons 6–11, averaging about 9. The endosperm is white.

WOOD—Pale yellowish brown, used only for fuelwood.

DISTRIBUTION—*P. johannis* was originally described as occurring only in a very limited area near the towns of Concepción del Oro and Mazapil, state of Zacatecas (Fig. 3.16). More recently a number of small populations have been reported in western Coahuila and in the area between the towns of Miquihuana and Aramberri, Nuevo León.

HABITAT—I examined this shrubby piñon at 2,700 m near the road between Concepción del Oro and Mazapil. The site

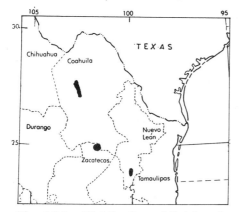

Fig. 3.16.   Distribution of *P. johannis*.

was a fairly steep slope of practically bare limestone. *P. cembroides* was the only other pine species noted in the area. Rainfall is approximately 300–400 mm annually and average annual temperature is about 16° C. In this area at 2,700 m, frosts are common during December and January.

WHERE TO FIND *P. johannis*—This is certainly not a common species in Mexico. However, it is not difficult to find by following Mexico Highway 54 south from Saltillo for about 112 km. Look for a turn off on the right to Concepción del Oro. The road is paved to Concepción del Oro (about 3 km), but from there to Mazapil it is narrow, steep and unpaved. Though the pines can be found only a few kilometers from Concepción del Oro, it would be best to plan collections during the dry winter months, November–February.

NOTES AND COMMENTS — The branches of this small piñon are occasionally used for firewood and the seeds are collected for food.

The trees I found north of the village Miquihuana in Nuevo León, though low and bushy, appeared to be rather larger than those found near Concepción del Oro. In Neuvo León they were growing with *P. nelsoni* at about 2,800 m. Bailey (1983) has also reported *P. johannis* as occurring in western Coahuila.

Pinus lagunae M.-F. Passini

Laguna Piñon, Nut Pine, Piñon

THE TREE—This is among the tallest of the nut pines; 12–20 m in height, the trunk slender and relatively free of branches up to the crown that, in mature trees, is open and irregular in form.

BARK—On young trees thin and smooth; on old, mature trees deep longitudinal and transverse fissures divide the bark into thick, geometrically-shaped plates that are a dark grayish brown color.

BRANCHLETS—On older trees rough and gray; bases of the leaf bracts are not decurrent.

LEAVES—In fascicles of 3, occasionally 2, averaging 7 cm in length, flexible; stomata present on the dorsal and ventral surfaces; resin canals 2, external. Sheaths are pale brown, recurved into a rosette and later deciduous.

CONELETS—Borne singly and in groups of 2–3 on slender peduncles; the scales armed with a very small prickle.

CONES—Globose to subglobose; about 4 cm long and 6 cm wide when open; symmetrical; borne on a short peduncle about 1 cm long. Mature cones open when ripe and

P. lagunae Trees   Bark   Branchlet, leaves, and cones.

Thanks to M-F Passini.

are soon deciduous, the small peduncle falling with the cone.

CONE SCALES—Small, thick, the apophysis rhomboidal; umbo dorsal, flat, bearing an early deciduous, minute prickle. Cone scales at the base of the cone are very small and sterile, the central and upper scales are larger and seed-bearing; roughly 60% bear 2 seeds/scale.

SEEDS—Sought for food by rodents and birds. Wingless; brown; about 13 mm long and 8 mm wide; approximately 3,800/kg. The seed coat is very thin, 0.2–0.9 mm; cotyledons average about 12 and the endosperm is pink.

WOOD—Rather soft, pale creamy-brown, used locally for firewood, posts and home construction.

DISTRIBUTION—*P. lagunae* is found only in a single, very restricted locality in Baja California Sur, about 90 km south of the city of La Paz, in the Sierra de la Laguna (Fig. 3.17). The Mexican Forest Service estimated the pine-oak forest at 20,000 ha.

HABITAT—This variety grows at altitudes of 1,200–2,000 m on semi-arid slopes. Annual rainfall in this area is about 500–600 mm. Frosts may occasionally occur during December and January, the coldest winter months. August is the hottest month with temperatures up to 29° C. Associated trees are *Quercus devia*.

WHERE TO FIND *P. lagunae*—This rare taxon is found south of La Paz, the capital of Baja California Sur. From La Paz drive

Fig. 3.17. Distribution of *P. lagunae*.

south on Mexico Highway No. 1 for about 40 km. When the road divides, take Highway 19 south for about 50 km to the town of Todos Santos. It would be wise to find a reliable guide there for a difficult trip into the Sierra de la Laguna. The trip should be undertaken only with a good supply of water, a high-clearance vehicle and good hiking boots.

NOTES AND COMMENTS—Passini (1982) has pointed out that seedlings from trial plantings of seed from *P. lagunae* have made double the height growth of seedlings from other provenances of the piñon pines. Apparently separate test plantings were made in Paris and at the school of agriculture at Saltillo, Mexico. It would be interesting to compare the growth of this taxon with *P. cembroides*, *P. edulis*, *P. monophylla*, and the subspecies of *P. cembroides* in more extensive test plantings.

P. lagunae was first described as *P. cembroides* var. *lagunae* by Passini (1981). More recently Bailey (1983) raised var. *lagunae* to the rank of subsp. *lagunae*. He justified this change in rank by noting slightly longer and thinner leaves with fewer lines of stomata, as well as longer and thicker cone peduncles and a minute prickle on the umbo. However, he considered the most important finding to be differences in the monoterpene chemistry (wood cores) of *P. lagunae*, *P. cembroides* and subsp. *orizabensis*. *P. lagunae* is high in sabinene and terpinolene as compared with *P. cembroides* and subsp. *orizabensis*. Both *P.*

lagunae and *P. discolor* are low in α-pinene as compared with *P. cembroides* and subsp. *orizabensis*. *P. lagunae* has very low amounts of p-cymene while *P. discolor* averages about 12%.

Following Bailey's (1983) paper elevating this taxon to the rank of subspecies, Passini (1987) raised it to specific status. In doing so she cited the longer needles, thin seed coats, rapid seedling growth, tall slender form of mature trees, thick, deeply fissured bark of old trees and significant differences in monoterpene chemistry.

Flowering and pollination occur from mid-May to mid June. Cones mature the following year and shed their seed toward the end of August or early September. It is interesting but not unusual, that this small, isolated piñon with very limited distribution has attracted such detailed scrutiny.

Pinus quadrifolia Parl.

Parry Piñon, Nut Pine

THE TREE—A small piñon 5–10 m tall, the trunk 20–40 cm in diameter. The branches are stiff, low and spreading, giving young trees a compact, pyramidal form. Older trees develop a more rounded, irregular crown.

BARK—Thin and smooth on young trees; on older trees dark, brownish red with deep furrows and scaly, small plates on the ridges.

BRANCHLETS—Gray and smooth when young, rougher when older; bases of the leaf bracts are not decurrent.

LEAVES—Borne 4 in a fascicle, occasionally 3 or 5; thick, 1.0–1.5 mm; stiff, sharp, generally curved inward, 3–5 cm long, the margins entire, stomata present on the ventral surfaces, occasionally on the dorsal surface; resin canals 2, external; fibrovascular bundle single. Sheaths are pale yellowish brown, curled backward and early deciduous.

CONELETS—Subterminal; globose on slender peduncles, borne singly or in clusters of 2–4, the small scales transversely keeled and bearing a minute dorsal prickle.

CONES—Globose, symmetrical; 3–5 cm long and 4–6 cm wide when open; the peduncle barely visible and falling with the cone. Mature cones are a lustrous pale ochre or yellowish orange color, opening at maturity and early deciduous.

CONE SCALES—Few, thick; the apophyses pyramidal but not protuberant; umbo dorsal, bearing a small, deciduous prickle. Scales at the base and apex of the cone are small and usually sterile while those in the central part of the cone are larger and bear 1–2 seeds.

SEEDS—Wingless, dark brown to pale spotted brown; 12–15 mm long and 8–10 mm wide; average number of seeds per kilogram about 2200; cotyledons number 6–8. The endosperm is white.

WOOD—Soft, close-grained, pale yellow, generally very knotty. Used mostly for firewood and fence posts.

P. quadrifolia Tree   Bark   Leaves, branchlets, and cones

DISTRIBUTION—This piñon occurs principally in Baja California Norte in the Sierra de Juárez and San Pedro Mártir Mountains (Fig. 3.18). Its range extends northward along the Sierra de Juárez, barely crossing the border into southern California.

HABITAT—*P. quadrifolia,* like many of the nut pines, grows in a transition zone between the hot, dry desert at lower altitudes and more humid areas found at higher altitudes. Throughout its range it is found at altitudes of 1,200–2,500 m (rarely at 2,700 m). During the winter months frosts occur at these altitudes and annual rainfall is about 300 mm at lower altitudes and 500–600 mm at 2,500 m.

WHERE TO FIND *P. quadrifolia*—Although this species occurs primarily in the Sierra de Juárez and the Sierra de San Pedro Mártir of Baja California Norte, there are a number of small populations in southern California where specimens can be collected more easily than in the rather isolated mountains of Baja California Norte. Both the San Bernadino National Forest and the Cleveland National Forest have small groups of these trees, often growing with *Pinus monophylla.* The dry season is the best time to search for the trees.

NOTES AND COMMENTS — Lanner (1974) reduced this species to hybrid status based upon studies of needle number, resin canal number, twig hairiness and stomata

Fig. 3.18.   Distribution of *P. quadrifolia.*

position. He concluded that *P. quadrifolia* is the result of hybridization between *P. monophylla* and a heretofore unrecognized five-needle piñon now named *Pinus juarezensis* Lanner. There are divergent opinions among botanists and taxonomists regarding these conclusions. Pending further studies of these taxa, I prefer to recognize *P. quadrifolia* as a separate species. It is interesting to note that this small nut pine is the most widespread conifer in Baja California Norte.

Pinus juarezensis Lanner

Sierra Juárez Pinyon, Nut Pine, Piñon

THE TREE—A small pine up to 15 m tall. In mature trees the crown is irregularly rounded; in young trees it is thicker and narrowly pyramidal.

BARK—In old trees, thick, scaly, divided by longitudinal and horizontal furrows; in young trees thin and smooth.

BRANCHLETS—Light gray, rough, pubescent; bases of the leaf bracts are not decurrent.

LEAVES—In fascicles of 5, rarely 4, slightly curved, 1.5–4.0 cm long, 0.5–1.5 mm thick; margins entire, stomata primarily on the ventral surfaces with an occasional row on the dorsal surface; resin canals 2, rarely 1 or 3, dorsal; fibrovascular bundle single; the leaves bright green on the dorsal surface and silver-colored (lines of stomata) on the ventral surfaces; connate (united) during the first year. Sheaths of the leaves 5–9 mm long, curled into persistent rosettes, later deciduous.

CONELETS—Borne singly and in pairs on slender, short peduncles; globose with thick, transversely keeled scales.

CONES—Subglobose; symmetrical; 3.5–5.0 cm long, 4.5–7.0 cm wide when open; yellow to ochre colored; dehiscent; deciduous when mature, the peduncle very small and falling with the cone.

CONE SCALES—Few; the apophysis rhomboidal, transversely keeled; the umbo dorsal, flat to depressed, bearing a minute early deciduous prickle. Only the central scales are seed-bearing.

SEEDS—Brown; wingless; 14–17 mm long, 6–8 mm wide; the seed coat very thin, 0.2–0.3 mm thick; the endosperm white. The rather large, thin-shelled seeds are gathered for food by birds and rodents. They are also sold on the market as pine nuts along with the seeds of *P. edulis* and *P. monophylla*.

WOOD—Like most of the nut pines, the trunk is short and small in diameter and thus hardly useful for sawn lumber. However, it is used locally for posts and firewood.

DISTRIBUTION—*P. juarezensis* has a rather limited distribution in southern California and northern Baja California. Its principal range lies in the Sierra de Juárez and Sierra de San Pedro Mártir in Baja California Norte (Fig. 3.19).

HABITAT—Found on semi-arid to arid foothills and mesas at altitudes ranging from 1,100 to 2,000 m. Rainfall at the lower elevations generally does not exceed 500 mm annually and temperatures may drop to freezing during the winter months. At the higher altitudes (1,600–2,000 m) frosts often occur during the winter and annual rainfall may reach 600 mm with about 30% occurring in the form of snow and sleet.

P. juarezensis Tree

Bark

Branchlet, cones, seeds, and leaves

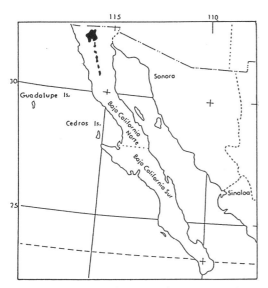

Fig. 3.19. Distribution of *P. juarezensis*.

Associated piñon pines are *P. monophylla* and *P. quadrifolia*.

WHERE TO FIND *P. juarezensis*—This species can be found in southern Cali-fornia, San Diego County, growing in the Laguna Mountains on Mt. Laguna, within the Cleveland National Forest at 1,800–2,000 m. South of the border in Baja California Norte, take MEX Highway 2 east from Tijuana to Tecate (also on the border). At Tecate take MEX Highway 3 south into the Sierra de Juárez and look for the trees along the highway at altitudes of 1,200–1,500 m. To collect at the type location, follow MEX Highway 2 east from Tecate toward the village of Rumorosa. About 2 km before reaching Rumorosa, look for this species near the road on the right.

NOTES AND COMMENTS—Lanner believes that *P. quadrifolia* is a natural hybrid resulting from crosses between *P. monophylla* and *P. juarezensis*. He reduced *P. quadrifolia* to hybrid status as *Pinus* × *quadrifolia* Parl. I found the two species growing together at the site described along MEX Highway 2, about 2 km west of village Rumorosa and prefer to treat these taxa (*P. monophylla*, *P. quadrifolia*, *P. juarezensis*) as separate species.

Pinus culminicola Andresen & Beaman

Potosi Piñon, Dwarf Piñon, Piñon

THE TREE—A low, shrubby, dwarf piñon 1–5 m high. In old trees the trunk may be 16–25 cm in diameter, low, twisted and often prostrate; the branches numerous, long, twisted, often extending along the ground; the crown low, very dense and rounded.

BARK—On mature trees the bark is thin, light brown, not fissured longitudinally or transversely but formed of small, thin, irregularly-shaped, scaly plates. On young trees the bark is thin and gray.

BRANCHLETS—Thick, stiff, rough, the leaves grouped in clusters at the ends.

LEAVES—In fascicles of 5, the dorsal surface bluish green and the ventral surface glaucous; the margins entire; thick, stiff, curved inward, 3–5 cm long, 1.0–1.3 mm wide; stomata only on ventral surfaces; resin canals 1, dorsal; fascicle sheaths 6–8 mm long, light brown and curled into rosettes but not completely deciduous.

CONELETS—Borne singly or in pairs on very short peduncles; ovate, 7–10 mm long; brown; the small scales bearing a minute prickle.

CONES—Small; globose; sessile; 3–4 cm long and about the same width when open; light reddish brown; opening when mature and soon deciduous.

CONE SCALES—Small; the apical and basal scales very small and sterile, only the central scales seed-bearing and those often with only a single seed; thick, the apophysis rhomboidal, transversely keeled, the apex obtusely angled, generally with small, unequal projections; umbo dorsal, flat to depressed, bearing a minute, deciduous prickle.

SEEDS—Wingless; 4–6 mm long; brown

Branchlet, leaves and cone

P. culminicola Tree

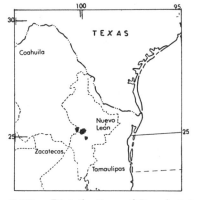

Pure stand of trees. Note the low
compact growth form. Most of
the trees are about 1.5 m high.

with a thick seed coat, the endosperm
white; cotyledons 8–11. Despite the thick
seed coat, the seeds are sought for food by
rodents and birds.

WOOD—The wood is hard and heartwood formation apparently begins quite
early. One of the very few pines that I have
not seen cut for firewood or local use, perhaps because it grows at such high altitudes and the trunk is so twisted and
contorted.

DISTRIBUTION—*P. culminicola* was first
collected and described from Cerro Potosí
at about 3,500 m, near Galeana, Nuevo
León, and for a number of years was
thought to occur only at that location. More
recently Riskind & Patterson (1975)
reported collections from Sierra Santa
Marta east of Saltillo, Coahuila, in the
department of Arteaga and from the mountains northeast of the village San Antonio
de Las Alazanes (Fig. 3.20). These areas are

Fig. 3.20.   Distribution of *P. culminicola.*

about 60 km (straight-line distance) northwest, north and northeast of Cerro Potosí.
The population at Cerro Potosí now
appears to be the southern limit of this
species.

HABITAT—This dwarf piñon grows at
the highest altitude of any of the

Cembroides group of nut pines. Its altitudinal range is 3,000–3,500 m i.e., on or near the summits of the mountains where it has been collected. The soils are shallow, rocky, gravelly limestone. Rainfall is quite high since rain, sleet and snow occur frequently throughout the year. Unfortunately at the very high, isolated locations where this taxon grows, temperature and rainfall measurements are not available. Near the summit of Cerro Potosí, the species does form an extensive scrub community and at the summit grows with *P. hartwegii*. This is not timberline area, though, since there are no higher grassland slopes above the *P. hartwegii—P. culminicola* association. Associated species are *P. hartwegii*, *P. rudis*, *P. ayacahuite* var. *brachyptera*, *Pseudotsuga flahaultii* Flous, and *Abies vejari* Mart.

WHERE TO FIND *P. culminicola*—Although a number of locations are nearer Monterrey and Saltillo, I suggest that collections be made on Cerro Potosí primarily because there are extensive populations of the species and because of the rare and interesting associations of conifers found on this isolated peak.

At Saltillo take Highway 57 south for about 120 km to a large gasoline station on the left. There, turn to the left onto Highway 60, drive about 18 km and turn left again onto a narrow paved road to the town of Galeana (about 3 km). Spend the night there (there is one small hotel) and arrange for a guide who knows the dirt road to Cerro Potosí and, best of all, to the summit. The road-trail up the mountain is very narrow, steep and rocky with hairpin turns and only occasional places where two vehicles may pass, so the ascent should be attempted only in a high-clearance vehicle equipped with very good, heavy-duty tires and in excellent mechanical condition. It is very important to remember that the very high altitude, 3,500 m, can be dangerous for some persons. The trip should be undertaken only during the dry winter months.

NOTES AND COMMENTS—This is a very interesting piñon, because it is so different from the other nut pines in the Cembroides group. The moist, cool, high-altitude environment is in marked contrast to the semi-arid conditions generally associated with the nut pines. *P. hartwegii*, *P. rudis* and *P. ayacahuite* var. *brachyptera*, all associated species on Cerro Potosí, are well adapted to the high altitude conditions; however, they do not have "close relatives" that are adapted to warmer semi-arid and arid conditions. *P. cembroides* grows in a wide area around the base of Cerro Potosí under hot, dry conditions. One wonders how *P. culminicola* adapted to such different conditions or perhaps it didn't change and we have here a relict of an ancient plant community. The unusual assortment of conifers on this lone peak also suggests this possibility.

P. culminicola has a very restricted range, and while not subject to intensive cutting for fuelwood, is, during long dry periods, very susceptible to fire. Several years ago I found a large community (more than 5 ha) on the northwestern slope of Cerro Potosí completely destroyed by fire. In 1978 I explored the mountain slopes east of San Antonio de las Alazanes and found that a disastrous forest fire had swept through the mountains as far as I could see (Fig. 3.21). Thousands of hectares of conifer forest had been destroyed, along with them (probably) some of the populations of *P. culminicola* reported by Riskind & Patterson (op. cit.). It is hoped that a few trees may have survived. On the slopes that I explored (∿ 3,300 m), a few "pockets" of *P. ayacahuite* var. *brachyptera*, *P. rudis* and *Abies vejari* had survived the flames and were bearing seed. There can be no doubt that *P. culminicola* is indeed a rare and endangered species.

Fig. 3.21.   Conifer forest killed by wildfire. In 1975 a terrible wildfire swept through these mountains near San Antonio de Las Alazanes in the Sierra Madre Oriental. Thousands of hectares of pines and other conifers were almost completely wiped out. Without doubt this was the finest conifer forest in northeastern Mexico. The loss in timber, wildlife, and watershed control is almost unimaginable.

Subsection Pinceana

Four species are included in this group and all are interesting and unusual pines. Both *P. maximartinezii* and *P. rzedowski* are rare and endangered species; *P. pinceana* and *P. nelsoni* are rare and may soon become endangered. With the exception of *P. rzedowski*, the trees are small with broad, rounded crowns. *P. rzedowski* is much taller than the other species in this group and its seeds are winged—more like the seeds of the pines in Section Cembra. However, its cone scales have a dorsal umbo rather than a terminal umbo; thus I have included it in Section Paracembra.

Each of the four species is so different from the smaller-coned cembroides group of piñon pines that there should be no difficulty in separating the two subsections. In Table 3.4 I have listed some of their distinguishing characteristics.

Table 3.4.   Characteristics of Species in Subsection Pinceana.

Species	Leaves per fascicle	Cone length, cm	Seed	Seed coat
P. pinceana	3	5–10	Wingless	Thick, hard
P. maximartinezii	5	18–22	Wingless	Very thick and hard
P. nelsoni	3 (connate)	8–14	Wingless	Thick, hard
P. rzedowskii	4	10–15	Winged	Soft, delicate

Pinus pinceana Gord.

Weeping Piñon, Ocote, Piñon

THE TREE—A small tree 4–10 m high, the crown thick, irregularly rounded; the branches are low, irregularly spaced on the trunk, long, flexible, pendent, often extending almost to the ground. Young trees have a dense, rounded crown that extends almost to the ground giving the tree a bushy appearance.

BARK—On mature trees, thin, divided by narrow, horizontal and longitudinal fissures into thin scaly plates. In young trees the bark is thin, smooth and grayish colored.

BRANCHLETS—Light gray, smooth, slender, long and pendent; bases of the leaf bracts are not decurrent. Leaves are borne in groups at the ends of the branchlets.

LEAVES—In fascicles of 3, occasionally 4, the margins entire, slender, 6–14 cm long, pendent, grayish green; stomata on dorsal and ventral surfaces; resin canals 2, dorsal, external; fibrovascular bundle single. Sheaths of the leaves are recurved into a rosette and later deciduous.

CONELETS—Borne singly or in pairs on long, slender peduncles; yellowish brown color; the small scales transversely keeled with a recurved minute prickle.

CONES—Oblong-ovate, 5–10 cm long, pendent, symmetrical; a polished orange color; dehiscent and early deciduous, the long, slender peduncle not falling with the cone.

CONE SCALES—Thick, hard, apophysis raised, transversely keeled; umbo dorsal bearing a small, thick, deciduous prickle.

SEEDS—Brown to yellowish brown; wingless; 10–12 mm long and 5–6 mm wide, the seed coat thick and hard. The seeds are collected for food along with those of *P. cembroides*.

WOOD—Because of the slow growth of this small piñon, the wood is close-grained but not very resinous. The wood is used locally for firewood.

DISTRIBUTION—Like *P. nelsoni*, this species has a limited range, being found only as scattered individuals on the very dry, rocky hills and mountains of the Sierra Madre Oriental (Fig. 3.22). It occurs principally in the state of Coahuila and as small, scattered populations in the states of Zacatecas, San Luis Potosí, possibly Queretaro and Hidalgo.

HABITAT—*P. pinceana* grows at altitudes ranging from 1,500–2,300 m on arid and semi-arid rocky hills and mountain slopes. Rainfall is 300–400 mm annually and occurs during the summer months. Average temperature for the year is about 18° C. The coldest months are December and January and the hottest months are May and June. The only pine associated with this taxon is *P. cembroides*.

WHERE TO FIND *P. pinceana*—This

P. pinceana Tree

Bark

Branchlets, cones, conelets, leaves, and seeds

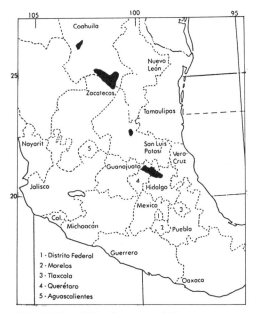

Fig. 3.22. Distribution of *P. pinceana*.

species is quite rare, occurring in very small groups or as widely scattered individuals. One small group of trees was located at a fairly accessible location in the state of Coahuila. From Saltillo take Highway 54 south for about 18 km and look for a sign on the left, "CUATEMOC"; turn left onto a gravel road and drive for 5–10 km into low, rolling hills. Look on the right for a few low, bushy trees on the slope and ridge of a low, arid, rocky hill; the trees are mostly *P. pinceana* mingled with *P. cembroides*. If not successful there, continue southward on Highway 54 toward the Zacatecas border; go through Carneras Pass and continue south for about 40 km. Look carefully on the left for a small ravine with small, bushy trees with pale green foliage. In 1976 there were 7–8 mature trees and a number of young trees in this group. The ravine is about 200 m from the highway. If not successful there,

continue southward on Highway 54 for about 70 km to the village of San Tiburcio. Turn left on a narrow paved road that goes eastward for about 100 km to Matehuala on Highway 57. There turn right and go southward on 57 for about 85 km to the village of Huizache; continue south on 57 for about 25 km and look carefully for a trail on the left that leads directly toward a high hill. Facing the highway up on the hillside is an old mine opening with a broad, whitish band extending down the hillside where white limestone had been dumped from the mine entrance. On top of this hill are a number of scattered *P. pinceana* trees. This is a very arid location and the hillside is covered with a spiny agave called "lecheguilla," so very heavy boots will be needed to make the ascent.

NOTES AND COMMENTS—This small piñon with its pendent branches, leaves and cones is very different from the Cembroides group of nut pines. Although it is sympatric with *P. cembroides* at some locations within its range, there is no evidence whatever of hybridization between the two species. All locations where this species was found were very arid and supported mostly a desert type of vegetation. On many trees the larger branches had been cut for firewood. Grazing by goats, burros and cattle was evident at all sites and reproduction was extremely limited. From the evidence at hand, it is clear that this species is now rare and endangered.

While certainly not a timber tree, the graceful, pendent branches, drooping foliage and interesting trunk form should make this taxon an outstanding candidate for many horticultural and ornamental sites particularly in those areas where lack of water is a recurring problem. The edible seeds also add to its desirable qualities.

Pinus maximartinezii Rzedowski

Large Martínez Pine, Pino, Ocote

THE TREE—Mostly small trees 5–10 m in height and 15–25 cm in diameter; the branches large, low and irregularly spaced, drooping; the crown rather open and irregularly rounded. One very large mature tree was found that measured 60 cm in diameter and 20 m in height.

BARK—On mature trees, thick, grayish brown, broken into geometrical plates by longitudinal and transverse fissures. On young trees the bark is thin and smooth.

BRANCHLETS—Long, pendent, slender, flexible; greenish gray color; bases of the leaf bracts not decurrent.

LEAVES—In fascicles of 5, slender, flexible, 8–10 cm long and 0.3–0.6 mm wide, borne in groups at the ends of the branchlets. Margins are entire, stomata present only on the ventral surfaces, the dorsal surface bright green, the ventral surfaces glaucous; resin canals 2, external, dorsal; fibrovascular bundle single. Sheaths are light brown, 6–8 mm long, curled back into a rosette and deciduous.

CONELETS—Borne singly on a long slender peduncle, the scales large and pointed, brownish green in color.

CONES—Symmetrical, very large and heavy, 18–22 cm long and 10–15 cm wide when open; long-ovoid, resinous, yellowish ochre to light brown color; dehiscent, deciduous when mature, borne singly and appearing pendulous on the long, slender, pendent branchlets.

CONE SCALES—The most unusual scales to be found among the nut pines; very large, thick, hard and strong, the apophysis unusually thick and protuberant (2 cm or more); flattened horizontally and appearing wedge shaped in the green cones; the umbo also unusually large and protuberant (10 mm) thick, strong, blunt to rounded, without a prickle.

SEEDS—Like the cone and cone scales, the seeds are unusually large; wingless; 20–25 mm long, 10–12 mm wide, oblong and very light brown in color. The seed coat is very hard and thick (1.5 mm), the endosperm white and cotyledons number 18–24. Despite the thick seed coat, they are sought for food by rodents and man.

WOOD—No samples were taken from this species and I saw no evidence of wood cutting on this high mesa.

DISTRIBUTION—*P. maximartinezii* is found at only one spot in Mexico, near the village of Pueblo Viejo in the southernmost area of Zacatecas state, on a small mesa in the Sierra de Morones (Fig. 3.23).

HABITAT—I observed this species growing on a small, very dry, rocky mesa at 1,900–2,200 m altitude. Rainfall is estimated to be about 500 mm annually occurring almost entirely during June, July

P. maximartinezii Tree

Bark

Branchlet, cones, seeds, and leaves

Fig. 3.23. Distribution of *P. maximartinezzii*.

and August. The coldest months are December and January. At 2,000 m frosts occur during the winter months. About 1 km from the group of *P. maximartinezii* trees, a small group of pines (*Pinus lumholtzii*) and oaks (*Quercus macrophylla*) were found. No other trees were found on the small mesa. The site was heavily grazed by goats, burros and cattle, and I found practically no reproduction of this strange pine.

WHERE TO FIND *P. maximartinezii*—This is a very rare species quite isolated in the mountains of southern Zacatecas and can be reached by driving north from Guadalajara on Highway 54 to the village of Juchipila. Near Juchipila a small dirt trail turns off to the left and winds westward through the dry hills to the Rio Juchipila. This must be crossed twice at rather deep, very rocky fords. After finally crossing the river, the trail winds upward toward a small village, Pueblo Viejo, situated at the base of a small mountain. Above the village, on top (a mesa) of the mountain, the only known population of this species is growing.

It is wise to hire a guide at Juchipila, and the trip should be attempted only in a high-clearance, 4-wheel-drive vehicle, with a good supply of gasoline and water and *only* during the end of the dry season when the river is at its lowest depth.

NOTES AND COMMENTS—This is one of the most unusual pines in Mexico. The very large wingless seeds borne in such massive cones (one green cone measured 26 cm long and weighed 2 kg), the short trunk and very wide-spreading "unconifer-like" crown, and its very limited range all indicate that this species represents a relic population that has survived in this small area for perhaps hundreds of thousands of years. There is no question that this is a very rare and endangered species. Every effort should be made to save these few remaining trees and to begin intensive seed collection and propagation efforts.

Pinus nelsoni Shaw

Nelson Pine, Ocote, Piñon

THE TREE—A small tree 5–10 m tall, the trunk 10–30 cm in diameter. On mature trees the crown is low, rounded and very bushy in appearance, the lower branches drooping almost to the ground, the central and upper branches horizontal and turning upwards. The branches are long, tough and remain attached to the trunk long after they are dead. In young, open-grown trees the branches grow sharply upward, giving the tree a narrow, pyramidal form.

BARK—On young trees, smooth, thin, grayish white; on old trees the bark is rather thin with shallow longitudinal and horizontal fissures forming small, scaly, rectangular plates, ashy gray and light brown in color.

BRANCHLETS—Long, slender, flexible, grayish white, rather smooth, long persistent even when dead; bases of the leaf bracts are not decurrent.

LEAVES—In fascicles of 3, growing at the end of the branchlets, rather sparse, and grayish green in color. The leaves are connate (united), giving the appearance of a single needle; however, they are easily

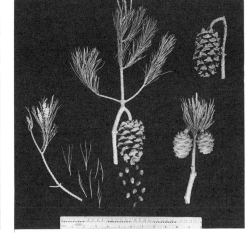

P. *nelsoni* Tree   Bark   Branchlet, cones, conelets, seeds, and leaves

separated by rolling them between the fingers; 5–10 cm long, the margins finely serrate, stomata on dorsal and ventral surfaces; resin canals 1 and 2, external, dorsal; fibrovascular bundle single. Sheaths of the leaves pale brown, 0.5–0.8 cm long, persistent and not recurved into a rosette.

CONELETS—Borne singly and in pairs on thick, curved peduncles 3–5 cm long. The conelets are quite large, 5–6 cm long with wide, thick, keeled scales and prominent apophyses. An unusual character of this species is the great increase in size of the conelet during its first season.

CONES—Symmetrical, cylindrical, 8–14 cm long and 5–7 cm wide when open; borne singly or in pairs on long (3–6 cm) sharply recurved, thick peduncles. They are yellowish orange to orange-red in color, opening at maturity and soon deciduous; the peduncle remaining attached to the branchlet occasionally with a few basal scales from the cone.

CONE SCALES—Wide (2 cm), thick, the apophysis raised, strongly pyramidal to protuberant, with a prominent transverse keel; umbo poorly defined due to the continuous growth of the cone.

SEEDS—Wingless; pale yellow when first shed, later becoming brown; 10–15 mm long, the seed coat thick and hard, the endosperm white. The seeds are gathered by rural families together with seeds of P. *cembroides* and sold locally in the markets as piñones. As the cones begin to mature,

small flocks of parrots search out the trees and pry open the cone scales to obtain the seeds for food.

WOOD—The small trees are so limby and bushy that the wood is used locally only for fuel.

DISTRIBUTION—P. *nelsoni* has a limited distribution in the Sierra Madre Oriental (Fig. 3.24). It has been collected in Nuevo León near the villages of San Lorenzo, Aramberri, Galeana and Doctor Arroyo; in Tamaulipas near the villages of Miquihuana, Palmillas and Tula; in San Luis Potosí near the village of Las Tablas; in

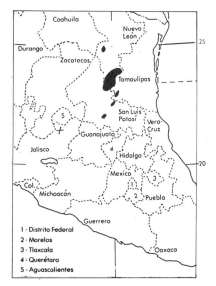

Fig. 3.24. Distribution of P. *nelsoni*.

Coahuila it was reported in the Montañas del Carmen.

HABITAT—The arid and semi-arid foothills and mesas of the Sierra Madre Oriental. Most sizable populations are found in a broad area centered around the very high (∿ 3,600 m) mountain, Peña Nevada, near the junction of the states San Luis Potosí, Nuevo León and Tamaulipas. Its altitudinal range is generally 1,800–3,100 m; however, I found a number of trees growing at 3,200 m on the dry, southwestern slopes of Peña Nevada, near the very small village of Valle Hermosa. Soils are rocky-gravelly limestone. Associated species are *P. cembroides*, *P. johannis* and *Juniperus* spp. Annual rainfall in the area ranges from 300–600 mm and occurs during the summer months. The coldest months are December and January with temperatures that drop to freezing at the higher altitudes (2,500–3,000 m).

WHERE TO FIND *P. nelsoni*—While many of the collection areas for this taxon are very isolated, there is one area that is quite accessible in the state of Tamaulipas near the border of San Luis Potosí. The most direct approach is south from Cd. Victoria on Highway 101. Go to the village of Juamave, ∿ 60 km and continue southward toward the village of Tula. About 15 km before reaching Tula, look for small pines on both sides of the highway, growing in a dense stand of *Juniperus* spp., *Quercus* spp. and *P. cembroides*.

NOTES AND COMMENTS—*P. nelsoni* is very different from the nut pines that comprise the Cembroides group. It appears to better fit into the group of four pines that I have designated subsection Pinceana, the large-cone nut pines. It is readily separated in the field from all the other nut pines by its stout, curved, persistent peduncle, grayish white bark, connate leaves and persistent leaf sheath. Also its oleoresin is quite different from the Cembroides group of pines; it generally has a high percentage of β-pinene in comparison to generally low percentages of this terpene in the Cembroides group. Shaw pointed out the peculiarity of continuous shoot and conelet growth in this species; however, I have not been able to find an explanation for this.

Although the species is not endangered, I believe it should certainly be considered rare.

Pinus rzedowskii Madrigal et Caballero

Pino, Ocote

THE TREE—A medium-size pine 30–50 cm in diameter and 20–25 m high. The crown of mature trees is generally open and irregularly branched. In young trees the branches are arranged in regularly spaced whorls and the form is pyramidal.

BARK—On young trees thin, smooth, grayish green. On large, mature trees it is thick and rough with deep horizontal and longitudinal fissures dividing the bark into rectangular plates that are rough, scaly and dark brown.

BRANCHLETS—Slender, ashy gray, rather rough. However, bases of the leaf bracts are not decurrent; the leaves are borne along the entire branchlet.

LEAVES—Flexible, slender, in groups of 3–4 and 5, mostly 4; 6–10 cm long, the edges finely serrate; stomata on the ventral surfaces only; resin canals 2–3, occasionally 4, external on the dorsal surface with occasionally 1 external on a ventral surface; fibrovascular bundle single. The fascicle sheaths form a rosette of recurved scales and are later deciduous.

CONELETS—Erect on peduncles 1.5–2.0 cm long; scales thick, wide and recurved.

CONES—Oblong, tapering slightly, symmetrical, pendent, borne singly and in pairs; 10–15 cm long and 6–9 cm wide when open; yellowish brown to lustrous ochre color when mature, ripening in the fall and soon deciduous; the peduncle 1.5–3.0 cm long, falling with the cone.

P. rzedowskii Tree   Bark   Branchlet, cone, conelet, and leaves

Thanks to Biól. X. Madrigal Sánchez.

CONE SCALES–Thick, hard, stiff, 15–22 mm wide; the apophysis subpyramidal with a prominent, horizontal keel, the apex acutely angled; umbo dorsal, small, dark brown, depressed, with a very small, downward-curved prickle. The apophyses and the umbo usually bear a small drop of clear amber resin.

SEEDS—Dark brown to mottled; 4.0–4.5 mm wide, 8–10 mm long with an articulate wing 20–32 mm long and 8–11 mm wide; brown with darker brown striations. Cotyledons 9–14, mostly 10, 11 and 12.

WOOD—Moderately hard, the heartwood lustrous pale brown, sapwood creamy white, not very resinous. The species is so rare and difficult to find that it is not used commercially.

DISTRIBUTION—This species is found only in the Sierra Madre del Sur, municipality of Coalcomán, State of Michoacán, Mexico (Fig. 3.25). Only three small populations have been reported, one on Cerro de Chiqueritas, another on Cerro Ocotoso, and a third at Puerto del Pinabete.

HABITAT—The three small stands of *P. rzedowskii* occur on steep, very rocky limestone soils. At two sites the trees were growing between large limestone boulders. At the third site there were very few large boulders and the pines were making much better growth.

All populations were growing at elevations of 2,040–2,300 m; rainfall in the area is

Fig. 3.25. Distribution of *P. rzedowskii*.

1 - Distrito Federal
2 - Morelos
3 - Tlaxcala
4 - Querétaro
5 - Aguascalientes

estimated to be 1,500 mm annually, almost all occurring during the period June–October; temperature is estimated to range from a minimum of –5° C to a maximum of 30° C in April just prior to the rainy season. On the best site, Puerto del Pinabete, the species was associated with *P. pseudostrobus*, *P. herrerai*, *P. michoacana* and *P. oocarpa*. At Cerro Chiqueritas and Cerro Octoso, both very rocky sites, no other pines were found with the small populations of *P. rzedowskii*.

WHERE TO FIND *P. rzedowskii*—From Mexico City drive due west on Highway 15 to Morelia, capital of Michoacán State. At Morelia continue west to the city of Uruapan; at Uruapan turn south on

Highway 37 to the small town of Nueva Italia. There turn west again to the town of Apatzingan, then go south again to the village of Aguililla. From Aguililla a narrow dirt road leads westward to the village of Dos Aguas. There a guide will be needed in order to locate the small, isolated stands of *P. rzedowskii*. The trip to Dos Aguas should be undertaken only during the dry season (November–March) and only in a vehicle with high clearance.

NOTES AND COMMENTS—This is a newly described (Sanchez, X. M. and Deloya, M. C. 1969) and very strange species since it possesses many characters that are commonly associated with either the Haploxylon or Diploxylon pine groups. In fact, taxonomists are puzzled regarding its correct status within the present classification system of the genus *Pinus* and may need to describe a new subdivision of the genus, possibly between the subgenus Haploxylon and the subgenus Diploxylon, in order to accommodate the unusual combination of characters.

In addition to its unusual qualities, the species has the unfortunate distinction of being extremely rare. The three small groups of pines in Michoacán are the only known populations in Mexico. Only one other Mexican pine is more rare and endangered viz. *P. maximartinezii*.

Since *P. rzedowskii* was described in 1969, additional information has been obtained regarding anatomy of the wood and analyses of xylem oleoresin. In 1979 a single wood specimen was taken from a tree in the group of pines at Puerto del Pinabete. At the same time and at the same location, samples of xylem oleoresin were also collected for analysis. From the wood sample only a single slide was obtained that clearly showed the cell walls of a ray tracheid—these were smooth (a character generally associated with the walls of ray tracheids found in the Haploxylon group of pines). Analysis of the resin samples from 15 trees showed the turpentine to consist of two major components, (α-pinene—70% Limonene—18%) plus a number of minor components (β-pinene—4%), Mycrene—2%, Δ^3 carene—1%, β-caryophyllene—2%.) Most of the Mexican Hard Pines have turpentine with high percentages of α-pinene and low percentages of β-pinene. Only a few of the Mexican and Central American pines have a high percentage of Limonene, and those few include species from both the Hard Pines and Soft Pines.

In all three small groups of pines totaling $\sim$ 30 ha, most of the mature trees had large fire scars and many trees were dead—evidence of repeated ground fires. In addition very little reproduction was noted, and it was difficult to find young trees under 12 cm in diameter. It is entirely possible then, that during the long dry season, this species could be wiped out completely by a severe fire. It is hoped that the Mexican government will take note of this rare and endangered species and, as soon as possible, take the necessary steps to ensure its survival.

DIPLOXYLON OR HARD PINES

As pointed out earlier, subgenus Diploxylon embraces the pines having needles with two fibrovascular bundles. In the classification system used here, the Diploxylon group is divided into eight sections. These are listed in Table 3.5 along with some of their significant morphological characteristics.

Table 3.5.   Morphological characteristics of the Diploxylon group.

Section	Leaves per fascicle, growth habit, sheath description	Cone description	Bases of leaf bracts
Leiophyllae	3–5, erect to pendent, deciduous	Small, 5–8cm long	Decurrent
Ponderosae	3–6 (7), erect, persistent	Small to medium, 6–17 cm long	Decurrent
Montezumae	3–6 (7), erect to drooping, persistent	Small to large, 6–30 cm long	Decurrent
Pseudostrobus	5 (6–7), drooping to almost pendent, persistent	Small to medium, 6–18 cm long	Not decurrent
Serotinae	2–5, erect to pendent, persistent	Small to medium, 3–14 cm long	Decurrent
Teocote	3–5, erect, persistent	Small, 2–8 cm long	Decurrent
Carribaea	3–4, erect, persistent	Small to medium, 5–12 cm long	Decurrent
Macrocarpae	3, erect, persistent	Very large, 20–35 cm long	Decurrent

Section Leiophyllae

I have placed three species in this section since two are closely related, *P. leiophylla* and *P. chihuahuana*, and all have deciduous fascicle sheaths, an unusual character for diploxylon pines. Listed here are some of their significant morphological characteristics (Table 3.6).

Table 3.6.   Morphological characteristics of Species in Section Leiophyllae.

Species	Leaves per fascicle and growth habit	Years for cone to mature	Cone length, cm, persistence
P. leiophylla	5, slender, erect	3	5–8, persistent
P. chihuahuana	3, thick, erect	3	4–7, persistent
P. lumholtzii	3, thick, absolutely pendent	2	4–7, deciduous

Pinus leiophylla Schl. and Cham.

Ocote, Pino, Pino Chino

THE TREE—A large pine 20–30 m high, occasionally reaching 35 m and 35–80 cm diameter; the crown rather open and irregularly rounded, the branches large and mostly horizontal, irregularly spaced on the trunk.

BARK—On mature trees very thick, rough with deep longitudinal and horizontal fissures that divide the bark into irregular, geometric shapes, grayish brown plates. On young trees the bark is thin, reddish and scaly.

BRANCHLETS—Slender, rather smooth, with thin, reddish scales; bases of the leaf bracts are decurrent.

LEAVES—Mostly in fascicles of 5, rarely 4 or 6; from 8–15 cm long, slender, flexible but not drooping, the margins finely serrate; stomata present on dorsal and ventral surfaces; resin canals mostly 2, occasionally 1, 3 and 4, medial, occasionally 1 or 2 internal; outer walls of the endoderm cells are thickened; fibrovascular bundles 2, contiguous, occasionally merged into one. Fascicle sheaths are 10–15 mm long, pale brownish yellow and soon deciduous.

CONELETS—First-year conelets small, rose or pink with a tint of purple, borne singly or in clusters of 2–5, subglobose on long stout peduncles; the small scales with an erect, persistent prickle that curves upward. The second-year conelets are larger and greenish brown in color.

CONES—Mature in the third year, fairly symmetrical, subglobose to conical, 5–8 cm long; borne singly and most often in groups of 2, 3 and 4 on stout peduncles 5–10 mm long; reflexed. They open gradually over a long period and are persistent for 2–3 years after the seeds have fallen.

CONE SCALES—Rather small, thin but stiff and strong, not flexible; the apophysis flat but somewhat thickened along the apical margin; the umbo dorsal, generally flat to depressed or very slightly raised, clearly showing the period of growth during the first two seasons, particularly on the unopened green cones; bearing a sharp, upward-curved prickle usually deciduous after the first year.

SEEDS—Small, somewhat triangular; 4–5 mm long, the wing 10–12 mm long, articularte; about 85,000 seeds/kg; cotyledons 5, 6 and 7, mostly 6.

WOOD—Rather dense, hard, heavy, very resinous, the heartwood pale brown; used for general construction, railway ties and, of course, for fuelwood.

DISTRIBUTION—This species has a very wide range extending from northwestern Mexico, southward along the Sierra Madre Occidental into Oaxaca (Fig. 3.26). It occurs in the states of Chihuahua, Sinaloa, Durango, Nayarit, Colima, Zacatecas, Jalisco, Micohoacán, Mexico, Hidalgo, Puebla, Tlaxcala, Morelos, Veracruz and Oaxaca. Its range does not extend beyond the Isthmus of Tehuantepec.

HABITAT—*Pinus leiophylla* appears to grow best in temperate to temperate-warmer climates, on deep, well-drained soils with annual rainfall of 600–1,000 mm. It is found most often at altitudes ranging from 2,200–2,800 m; however, it has been collected in Morelos at 1,600 m and at 3,000 m on the slopes of the two snow-capped volcanoes, Ixtaccihuatl and Popocatepetl. Over most of its range temperatures may drop to freezing during the coldest winter months, December and January.

WHERE TO FIND *P. leiophylla*—With its very wide distribution, small populations can often be found as roadside trees on many of the major Mexican highways. An easy and interesting collecting trip from Mexico City would be to drive from the city eastward on Highway 150 toward Puebla. A few kilometers out of the city look for a turn off to the right on Highway 115; continue on this highway for 15–20 km, looking carefully for a turn off on the left to the town of Amecameca. This is one of the few instances when I can say "you can't miss it" because the two immense, picturesque, snow-capped mountains, Ixtaccihuatl and Popocatepetl, dominate the landscape. At Amecameca look for a good road that leads directly to the mountains and winds slowly up the slopes through pine and fir forests to a saddle between the two peaks. *Pinus*

Cones, seeds, and leaves

P. leiophylla Tree Bark

Adventitious branchlets on the trunk, characteristic of this species.

Fig. 3.26. Distribution of *P. leiophylla*.

leiophylla will be found much lower (2,000–3,000 m) mingled with *P. montezema, P. pseudostrobus, P. teocote, Cupressus lusitanica* and *Quercus* spp.

NOTES AND COMMENTS—This taxon, though far from rare, is one of Mexico's very unusual Hard Pines. The slender, flexible leaves in groups of 5 and the deciduous sheaths are, superficially, similar to the white or Soft Pines. The characteristic epicormic shoots on the trunk and the ability to sprout from the stump are also unusual qualities in the group of Hard Pines. This species and the closely related *Pinus chihuahuana* are the only Mexican and Central American pines with cones requiring 3 years to mature.

The trees produce large crops of cones and in many areas reproduction is very good. However, cones are susceptible to the fungus *Caeoma conigenum*, and the greatly enlarged, orange-yellow cones are a rather common sight wherever there are large populations of *P. leiophylla*. This species is also one of Mexico's largest producers of pine resin. It is also one of the pines most susceptible to attacks of the Mexican bark beetle (*Dendroctonus mexicanus* Hopkins). Literally thousands of hectares of *P. leiophylla* were killed in 1949 and 1950 by the beetle in the Amecameca-Tlalmanalco area near Mexico City. Young pines (2–3 years old) have shown considerable ability to survive ground fires. Even though the stem and top may be completely destroyed by fire, many young trees sprout from the root collar, the young sprouts emerging from a thickened area in the root just below the surface of the ground. This ability to survive ground fires could be a very important asset in any reforestation project in Mexico, since ground fires during the long dry season are numerous and practically impossible to control.

One final note on this interesting species; I have collected and observed it over its entire range and found the tallest, best-formed trees in Chihuahua and Durango. In the southern states along the Volcanic Axis or Great Cross Range (roughly about 19° N latitude), the trees generally were not so tall and much more limby and crooked. In 1947 and 1948, E. E. M. Loock collected seed of *P. leiophylla* over most of its range for planting in South Africa. He too noted the differences in size and form of the trees. In his notes Loock also mentioned that seed from this species was obtained in 1911 and 1917 and a number of stands were planted in eastern South Africa. He states (1950), "The trees grew fairly rapidly from the beginning, but were mostly of a rather crooked form." Later, regarding other plantations of this same species he notes (op. cit.), "The tendency towards crookedness is evident everywhere."

Pinus chihuahuana Engelm.

Chihuahua Pine, Ocote, Pino Prieto, Pino Chino

THE TREE—Medium-size, 15–25 m high and 40–60 cm in diameter; the branches horizontal, irregularly spaced on the trunk forming an open, uneven, rounded crown.

BARK—Thick, rough, dark brown to almost black, divided by wide, deep, vertical fissures into irregular, longitudinal plates.

BRANCHLETS—Rather stiff, reddish, smooth at first, later becoming rough and scaly; bases of leaf bracts are decurrent.

LEAVES—In fascicles of 3, occasionally 4 and 5, borne in clusters at the ends of the branchlets; 5–15 cm long, about 1 mm thick, stiff, the margins finely serrate; stomata on dorsal and ventral surfaces, resin canals 4–7, medial, occasionally 1 or 2 internal; exterior walls of the endodermal cells thickened, fibrovascular bundles 2, contiguous but distinct; the sheaths are pale brown and

P. chihuahuana Tree   Bark   Cones, seeds, conelet, and leaves

early deciduous.

CONELETS—Borne singly or in groups of 2–5 on long (10–12 mm) stout peduncles; subglobose, the scales wide and bearing a conspicuous prickle.

CONES—Long-ovoid, symmetrical; 4–7 cm long, persistent and reflexed on strong peduncles 7–12 mm long, bright yellowish green before maturing, then becoming dark brown. Like *P. leiophylla* the cones require 3 years to mature (clearly shown by the concentric umbo on the mature, unopened cone), opening slowly and remaining on the branchlets for as much as 2–3 years.

CONE SCALES—Not thick, but stiff and hard, thickened a little along the apical margin, apophysis flat to very slightly raised; the umbo "double," i.e. concentric (one within another) dorsal, grayish, slightly raised, bearing a small semi-persistent prickle.

SEEDS—Very small; 3–4 mm long, the wing 7–10 mm long, articulate, 85,000–88,000 seeds/kg.

WOOD—Rather soft, not strong, resinous, sawn into construction timbers along with other associated pines.

DISTRIBUTION—In the Sierra Madre Occidental of northwestern Mexico, in the states of Chihuahua, Sonora, Durango, Zacatecas with a few small populations occurring in Mayarit and Jalisco (Fig. 3.27). Its range also extends across the border into the United States in southeastern Arizona and the southwestern corner of New Mexico.

HABITAT—*P. chihuahuana* grows at 1,600–2,600 m altitude on lower slopes of the Sierra Madre Occidental. Soils are generally shallow and sandy to rocky. In some of the broader valleys and more gentle slopes, the soil may be deeper and the trees are usually of much better form. In the northern part of its range, the climate is temperate to cold with average annual temperature ranging from 10–18° C and annual rainfall of about 250–600 mm. Snow and frosts are frequent during the winter months (November–February), and the hottest months are June and July when most of the rainfall occurs. Further south in Durango and Zacatecas the climate is

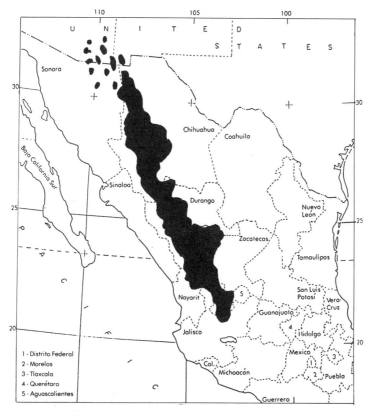

Fig. 3.27.   Distribution of *P. chihuahuana*.

slightly warmer with higher rainfall (500–650 mm). Over most of its range associated pine species are *Pinus engelmanni, Pinus lumholtzii, P. cembroides, Pinus teocote, Pinus arizonica, P. leiophylla,* and *P. oocarpa.*

WHERE TO FIND *P. chihuahuana*—Cross the U.S.-Mexico border at El Paso and drive south from Cd. Juárez on Highway MEX 45 to the village of El Sueco (about 200 km). There turn right onto Highway 10; drive due west to the town of Buenaventura (about 100 km). Look for the pines along this highway and along the highway to the village of Ignacio Zaragosa, about 40 km west of Buenaventura. At the city of Durango, take Highway 40 west to El Salto (about 90 km). In that area, and along the highway are many *P. chihuahuana* trees. However, in this area its range overlaps that of *P. leiophylla,* so care must be taken not to confuse the two species.

NOTES AND COMMENTS—This species does not form dense forests, rather it is often found in small open groups and as isolated individuals. Since the pine forests of western and northwestern Mexico have been intensively cut during the past 40–50 years, it is difficult to find large, mixed stands of the different pine species that formed the typical associations of this species. The best trees (tallest with excellent form) were observed in Chihuahua and northern Durango on rather moist sites. A number of botanists consider this taxon to be a variety of *P. leiophylla;* however, it is fairly easily distinguished from *P. leiophylla* by its much thicker and stiffer leaves borne 3 in a fascicle. At the southern limits of its range, it is not too difficult to find trees with leaves that are intermediate in thickness and numbering 3, 4 and 5 per fascicle, indicating probable hybridization of the two closely related species.

Pinus lumholtzii Robins. & Fern.

Pino Triste, Pino Amarillo, Ocote, Weeping Pine

THE TREE—A medium-size tree 10–20 m high with diameter 25–50 cm; the crown open and irregularly rounded, the branches horizontal to drooping.

BARK—On old, mature trees, dark grayish brown, thick, rough, divided into long, irregular, scaly plates by deep longitudinal and transverse fissures. On young trees the bark is thin, scaly and reddish brown.

BRANCHLETS—Slender, flexible and smooth when very young, later becoming scaly and rough since bases of the leaf bracts are decurrent.

LEAVES—Borne in fascicles of 3, very rarely 2 or 4, grouped at the ends of the branchlets; thick, flexible, absolutely pendent, 15–30 cm long, occasionally up to 43 cm; pale to yellowish green color, the margins finely serrate, stomata on the dorsal and ventral surfaces; resin canals 4–10 medial and internal; fibrovascular bundles 2, contiguous, occasionally merged into one; sheaths long (about 30 mm), pale brown and soon deciduous.

CONELETS—Solitary on stout, scaly peduncles (10 mm), subglobose, with lustrous brown scales that terminate in a small prickle pointed toward the apex of the conelet.

CONES—Conical to long-ovoid; 4–7 cm long, symmetrical, light brown, solitary, reflexed on stout peduncles 1.0–1.5 cm long that fall with the cone; opening at maturity and soon deciduous. Unlike *P. leiophylla* and *P. chihuahuana,* the cones of *P. lumholtzii* require only 2 years to mature.

CONE SCALES—Thin, rather flexible; apophysis flat to slightly raised; umbo dorsal, wide, depressed or flattened to slightly raised, bearing a small, deciduous prickle.

SEEDS—Very small, dark brown, 4–5 mm long, the wing articulate, 10–13 mm long.

WOOD—Heavy, hard though not very

| *P. lumholtzii* Tree | Bark | Cones and seeds | Branchlet with cone and pendent leaves typical of this species |

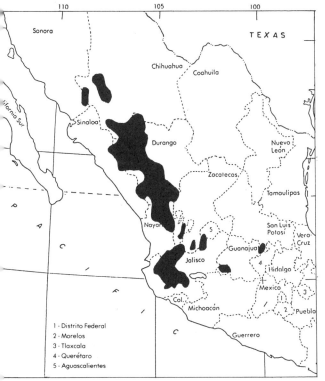

Fig. 3.28.   Distribution of *P. lumholtzii.*

1 - Distrito Federal
2 - Morelos
3 - Tlaxcala
4 - Querétaro
5 - Aguascalientes

resinous; trees are logged commercially along with associated pine species, the lumber being sold for general construction. Locally it is cut for firewood, posts and hewn timbers.

DISTRIBUTION—*P. lumholtzii* has a wide range along the Sierra Madre Occidental, extending from Chihuahua in the north, southeastward into the states of Durango,

Sinaloa, Sonora, Zacatecas, Nayarit, Jalisco, Aguascaliente and Guanajuato (Fig. 3.28).

HABITAT—The altitudinal range of this species is generally 1,600–2,400 m along the foothills and slopes of the mountains. Although it makes its best growth under temperate to warmer conditions with good rainfall, it also grows on dry, rocky slopes with very low rainfall. Average annual temperature over most of its range is about 12–15° C, and annual rainfall is 500–600 mm. At the higher altitudes frost and snow occur during the months of December and January, while the warmest months are May and June. Associated pine species are *P. chihuahuana, P. leiophylla, P. arizonica, P. teocote, P. oocarpa* var. *trifoliata, P. engelmanii* and *P. cembroides.* Despite heavy cutting in this entire area, small populations of this species can still be found particularly in inaccessible areas on the Pacific slopes of the mountains where rainfall is higher.

WHERE TO FIND *P. lumholtzii*—Drive to the city of Durango and take Highway 40 west to the town of El Salto. Along the highway at about 2,000 m look for the species as isolated trees or in small groups of pines. At El Salto find a guide familiar with the trails leading out into the surrounding mountains. The species is not rare and collections can easily be made in the area. However, exploring on the rocky unpaved roads or trails should be done only during the dry winter months and only with a high-clearance vehicle.

NOTES AND COMMENTS—Prof. Martínez (1948), the noted Mexican botanist, found considerable differences in the length of leaves and form of cone scales in this species. Specimens from the southern part of its range had longer, more flexible leaves than some collections made near Tepehuanes (north of Durango). Those leaves were short, thick and stiff—superficially very similar to the leaves of *P. chihuahuana*. Specimens that I collected west of El Salto in the state of Sinaloa (on the Pacific slopes) all had long, flexible, pendent leaves and cones with a thin, flat apophysis and umbo flat to depressed. East of El Salto on the eastern slopes of the Sierra Madre Occidental, I collected specimens with much shorter, pendent leaves, cones with apophyses slightly raised and the umbo raised and curved upward toward the apex of the cone. After examining the different cones and needles, Prof. Martínez (pers. comm.) suggested the possibility of hybridization with *P. chihuahuana*.

While not an outstanding timber-producing species, this taxon, with its pendent leaves, makes a very attractive tree as an ornamental or specimen plant for estate landscaping.

Section Ponderosae

Although *P. ponderosa* does not occur in Mexico, the five species listed here are included in this section because all are closely related to *P. ponderosa*. In fact with one exception, *P. arizonica* var. *stormiae*, all have been crossed with *P. ponderosa* at the Institute of Forest Genetics, Placerville, California. Three of the species are tall, well-formed trees, one (*P. engelmannii*) is medium-size ($\sim$ 20 m tall) and one, var. *stormiae* is a small (10–20 m tall), limby tree. Four of the species occur in the northwestern Sierra Madre Occidental while var. *stormiae* is found only in the northern Sierra Madre Oriental. Table 3.7 lists some of the species' important morphological features.

Table 3.7. Morphological features of Species in Section Ponderosae.

Species	Leaves per fascicle and length, cm	Cones length, cm	Umbo prickle	Cotyledon number
P. jeffreyi	3, 22–28	13–17	Persistent, recurved	10 (8–11)
P. arizonica	3 (4–5), 12–22	6–9	Persistent, recurved	8 (7–9)
P. arizonica var. *stormiae*	3 (4–5), 20–30	7–10	Persistent, not recurved	Not known
P. engelmannii	3 (4), 25–35	10–15	Persistent, not recurved	8 and 9
P. durangensis	6 (5–7), 12–20	7–10	Persistent, recurved	Not known

Pinus jeffreyi Grev. & Balf.

Jeffrey Pine, Western Yellow Pine, Pine Negro, Pino

THE TREE—A large pine 40–50 m high, with a straight, clear trunk often up to 1 m in diameter. The lower branches are large and somewhat drooping, the upper branches more ascending; in old, mature trees the crown becomes somewhat rounded, in younger trees it is pyramidal.

BARK—In mature trees the bark is divided by deep longitudinal and horizontal fissures into large, irregular plates almost brick red in color. In young trees the bark, though not plated, is still quite thick and rough.

BRANCHLETS—Thick, stiff, glaucous, bases of the leaf bracts decurrent.

LEAVES—In fascicles of 3, rarely 2; pale grayish green, 22–28 cm long, 1.7 mm wide, stiff, erect; stomata present on the dorsal and ventral surfaces; resin canals 2–5, medial, endoderm cells with thickened exterior walls; fibrovascular bundles 2, clearly distinct. Fascicle sheaths pale brown 12–15 mm long, not deciduous.

CONELETS–About 2 cm wide and 3 cm long, a very light pale brown; the small scales armed with erect, sharp, persistent prickles. They are borne singly and in pairs on a thick, reflexed, scaly peduncle about 2 cm long.

CONES—Ovoid, symmetrical, erect to slightly reflexed; 13–17 cm long; yellowish brown; borne singly and in pairs on a very short (0.5–1.0 cm) stout peduncle that remains attached to the branchlet with a few basal cone scales when the cone falls. The cone is not persistent but falls to the ground soon after it matures.

CONE SCALES—Hard, stiff; a lustrous tawny yellow color; apophyses raised, rhomboidal with a prominent horizontal keel; the umbo ashy gray, slightly raised and armed with a sharp, persistent, recurved prickle.

SEED—10—12 mm long; the wing brown, articulate, 25–30 mm long. Seeds average 8,800/kg; cotyledon number varies from 8 to 11 but are mostly 10.

WOOD—Of excellent quality, hard, strong, yellowish; in the United States the trees are logged with Ponderosa Pine and the lumber sold without being separated. In Baja California Norte, the trees are sawn for sale as lumber and construction timbers.

DISTRIBUTION—*P. jeffreyi* is primarily a pine of California, its range covering the entire length of the state and extending into Baja California Norte, Mexico (Fig. 3.29). The southern limit of *P. jeffreyi* in the U.S. occurs in the Laguna Mountains, San Diego County, California. About 60 km south in the Sierra de Juárez of Baja California Norte, the species occurs again a few kilometers east of the village Ojos Negros. Its range then continues southward along the Sierra de Juárez to San Matías Pass. There is about a 50 km disjunction at the pass, and its range then continues along the Sierra San Pedro Mártir to about 30°–39′ N latitude.

HABITAT—In Mexico the species grows at 1,500–3,000 m altitude along the rocky ridges, basins and arroyos of the Sierra de Juárez and San Pedro Mártir in Baja California Norte. Annual rainfall is 300–500 mm at lower elevations and ∿ 600 mm at the higher elevations where snowfall often occurs during the coldest winter months of December, January and February. The hottest and driest months are June–August. Associated pines in Mexico are *P. coulteri, P. contorta* subsp. *murrayana, P. lambertiana, P. quadrifolia* and *P. juarezensis.*

WHERE TO FIND *P. jeffreyi*—Collections of this species can easily be made in the U.S.

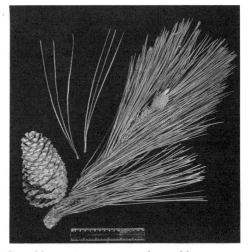

P. jeffreyi Tree   Bark   Branchlet, mature cone, conelet, and leaves

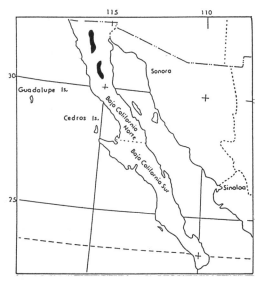

Fig. 3.29. Distribution of *P. jeffreyi*.

in Cleveland National Forest. The Laguna Mountains are quite accessible along California Highway 79, and the pines occur there as roadside trees. However, if collections are desired in Baja California Norte, an interesting trip would be to drive to Ensenada, Baja California and then plan a trip to Laguna Hanson, high in the Sierra de Juárez. It might be best to inquire at the Centro Experimento Forestal Mexicano in Ensenada for help in obtaining a guide. However, if that is not possible the trip can be made in a high-clearance, 4-wheel-drive vehicle. At Ensenada take Highway MEX 3 southeast for about 34 km to the village of El Gato. There inquire about the turn off to the left, to the villages of El Tecolote, La Choya and to Laguna Hanson. Three or four kilometers before reaching the lake, *P. jeffreyi* trees will be found growing along the trail. Be sure to allow an entire day for the round trip, take a good supply of water and gasoline and check that the tires are in excellent condition. Do not plan to make the

return trip after dark.

Another interesting though longer trip would be to leave Ensenada early in the morning and drive down Highway MEX 3 for about 100 km to the town of Valle de Trinidad; continue on MEX 3 for about 10 km (just before arriving at Ejido San Matías) and look for a turn off on the right to the villages of El Burro, San Javier and San Francisco. Follow this winding trail for about 12–15 km into the hills and mountains of the Sierra San Pedro Mártir, and pines will be found growing along the trail. As mentioned before, use a 4-wheel-drive vehicle with good tires, a good supply of water and gasoline, and allow plenty of time for the trip. Do not plan to return after dark.

NOTES AND COMMENTS—For years foresters and botanists debated whether or not this taxon should be considered a variety of *Pinus ponderosa* or a separate species. Over much of its range in California it grows with *P. ponderosa*, and the two taxa are quite similar in many respects. However, chemical analyses of *P. jeffreyi* xylem oleoresin revealed that the turpentine consists almost entirely (90–95%) of heptane while that of *P. ponderosa* is generally lacking in this compound. The turpentine chemistry also provides a quick field identification of *P. jeffreyi*; on warm days the trunk gives off a distinct sweet (not resinous) odor often described as "like honey or vanilla or maybe pineapple."

In the field, examination of the leaves with a hand lens will reveal that in *P. jeffreyi* the stomata are joined in a continuous line by the waxy deposits between the stomatal openings. In *P. ponderosa* this is not the case. One final note on field identification; grasp an open cone in the bare hand. The upright prickles on cone scales of *P. ponderosa* are decidedly prickly; the recurved cone scale prickles of *P. jeffreyi* are not prickly at all.

Pinus arizonica Engelm.

Arizona Pine, Yellow Pine, Pino

THE TREE—These pines have tall, straight trunks attaining heights of 30–35 m and diameters up to 1 m. Branches are thick and strong, the lower ones somewhat drooping, the upper branches ascending; the crown is thick and rounded in mature trees; young trees have a thick pyramidal crown.

BARK—On old mature trees it is thick, with deep fissures forming large, irregular, reddish brown, scaly plates. In young trees it is reddish brown, rough and scaly.

BRANCHLETS—Stout, stiff, grayish brown, scaly; bases of the leaf bracts are decurrent.

LEAVES—Borne in fascicles of 3, occasionally 4 and 5, thick, stiff, erect, 12–22 cm long, growing in clusters at the ends of the branchlets. Stomata are present on the dorsal and ventral surfaces, margins are finely serrate; resin canals 6–10, medial; exterior walls of the endoderm thickened, vascular bundles two, quite distinct. Fascicle sheaths brown, persistent, about 15 mm long.

CONELETS—Borne singly and in twos and threes on short stout peduncles; scales of the conelets bear a minute, sharp prickle.

CONES—Ovoid to conical, symmetrical, erect to slightly reflexed, 6–9 cm long, borne singly and in twos and threes on short, stout, peduncles; reddish brown; opening when mature and soon deciduous. When the cone falls, the peduncle with a few basal cone scales remains attached to the branchlet.

CONE SCALES—Hard, stiff; about 12–14 mm wide, the apical margin rounded and smooth, the apophyses raised to subpyramidal, transversely keeled; the umbo dorsal, not protuberant, ashy gray and bearing a persistent, sharp, recurved prickle.

SEED—Dark brown, oval, about 6 mm long; the wing articulate, 20–25 mm long and 8–9 mm wide; average number of seed/kg is about 28,000; cotyledons number 7–9, mostly 8.

WOOD—Light, strong, pale yellow, of excellent quality; the trees are logged commercially with associated pines and sawn into boards and timbers for construction purposes.

DISTRIBUTION—*Pinus arizonica* occurs in Mexico along the Sierra Madre Occidental in northeastern Sonora, western Chihuahua, eastern Sinaloa and Durango (Fig. 3.30). It also occurs in the United States in southeastern Arizona and southwestern New Mexico.

HABITAT—This species grows at altitudes ranging from 2,000–2,800 m. Rainfall in the mountains of Sonora and Chihuahua averages about 500–600 mm annually, with

P. arizonica Tree   Bark   Cones and leaves

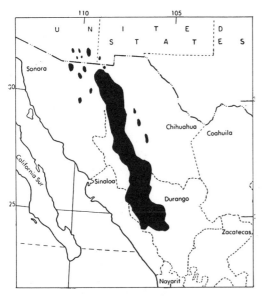

Fig. 3.30. Distribution of *P. arizonica.*

tions in the more accessible regions. Sizable stands can still be found in some of the isolated and inaccessible valleys.

WHERE TO FIND *P. arizonica*—If driving into western Mexico, then cross the border at El Paso and drive south on MEX 45 to the city of Chihuahua (about 385 km); there take Highway MEX 16 west to the town of La Junta. At La Junta ask for directions to Cascada de Basaseachic (Basaseachic waterfall) and the villages of Yepachic, Tres Amigos and Ocampo. That area is mountainous and specimens can be collected from roadside trees. Also in that area I found a number of stands of the species about 10 km west of the town Madera. For collections in this area it would be wise to use a high-clearance vehicle with a good supply of gasoline and water, and tires in very good condition.

NOTES AND COMMENTS—Many botanists and taxonomists consider *P. arizonica* to be a variety of *P. ponderosa.* The two species are indeed closely related and quite similar. For field identification the following notes will be helpful: *Pinus arizonica* has mostly 3 leaves (occasionally 4 and 5) per fascicle with 6–10 resin canals; *P. ponderosa* has 2–3 leaves/fascicle with 2–6 resin canals. In *P. arizonica* the cone scales have small recurved prickles while scales of *P. ponderosa* have large, strong, erect prickles. With a sharp razor blade and 10x hand lens, it is possible to make a quick count of the resin canals.

approximately 30% falling during the winter months of December–February when snow and sleet are fairly common. Further south in the state of Durango annual rainfall increases to about 650 mm, and the winter months are not as cold although frosts are common during December, January and February. The trees make their best growth on deep, well-drained soils of the more level valleys and mesas. *Pinus arizonica* at one time formed extensive forests in the area; however, intensive logging has left only small scattered populations.

Pinus arizonica var. *stormiae* Mart.

Pino Real, Pino Blanco

THE TREE—This is a small to medium-size pine 10–20 m high with branches that grow well down the trunk; the lower branches large, horizontal to drooping often extending almost to the ground, upper branches are horizontal to slightly ascending. The crown is low, often dense and rounded. Young trees are pyramidal in form with rather open crown.

BARK—On old, mature trees the bark becomes thick and deeply fissured forming large, irregular, scaly plates dark brown to dark reddish brown. In young trees the bark is rough and scaly but not plated as in old trees.

BRANCHLETS—Thick, stiff, strong, scaly; reddish brown; the bases of the leaf bracts decurrent.

LEAVES—Mostly in fascicles of 3 but often 4 and 5; 20–30 cm long, thick, stiff, the

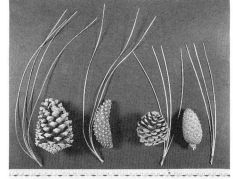

Cones and leaves; *P. arizonica* var. *stormiae* on the left, *P. arizonica* on the right.

P. arizonica var. *stormiae* Tree   Bark

margins finely serrate, stomata on the dorsal and ventral surfaces; resin canals 3–8, mostly 3–5, medial; exterior walls of the endoderm cells thickened, fibrovascular bundles 2, close together but distinct; fascicle sheaths brown at first, later becoming dark brown to black, not deciduous.

CONELETS—Borne in groups of 2–4, occasionally 5, on short, stout, erect, very scaly peduncles; the tiny scales of the conelet bearing a minute, erect, sharp prickle.

CONES—Long-ovoid, erect to slightly reflexed, slightly curved to symmetrical; dark brown; 7–10 cm long, borne in groups of 2–4, occasionally 5, on short (6–10 mm) stout peduncles. When the cone falls, the peduncle remains with a few basal scales attached to the branch. They mature in November–December and the seeds are soon released; however, the cones remain attached to the branches for several months.

CONE SCALES—Hard and stiff, the apophyses raised to pyramidal, generally reflexed with a strong transverse keel; the umbo raised, ashy gray and bearing a small persistent prickle generally not recurved.

SEED—About 6 cm long, brown, with an articulate wing 20–22 mm long and about 8 mm wide. Seeds are about the same size as *P. arizonica* seed and probably average about the same number per kilogram, i.e. 28,000.

WOOD—Light, pale yellowish color of only fair quality (very knotty). I saw it being sawn into rough boards and timbers at a small sawmill near Galeana, Nuevo León. Since the trees are generally quite limby, they are often cut for firewood and hewn timbers for mines and local construction.

DISTRIBUTION—Variety *stormiae* is found in the states of Coahuila, Nuevo León, in the southwestern corner of Tamaulipas near the town of Miquihuana and in a few isolated, small populations in San Luis Potosí (Fig. 3.31).

HABITAT—This variety grows on the dry western and southwestern slopes and mesas of the Sierra Madre Oriental at elevations of 1,900–3,000 m. At the lower alti-

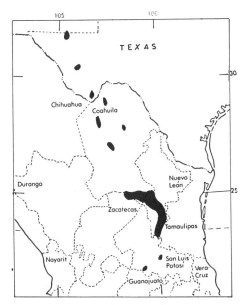

Fig. 3.31. Distribution of *P. arizonica* var. *stormiae*.

tude, annual rainfall is 400–500 mm, and at 3,000 m it increases to 500–700 mm. Frosts are common during the winter months of December, January and February, and at 3,000 m snow and sleet are fairly common. These pines generally grow in open pure stands; however, most of the forests have long been cut over and the remaining trees are found as individuals and small, scattered groups. I observed a few small stands on a fairly level mesa at 2,000 m near Galeana, and a sizable population growing in the foothills north of Miquihuana at 3,000 m.

WHERE TO FIND var. *stormiae*—If driving south to Mexico, cross the border at Laredo and take Highway MEX 85 south to Monterrey. Go through Monterrey and continue south on MEX 85 to the city of Linares (about 125 km). At Linares turn right onto Highway MEX 60. This very winding road will take you directly up into the Sierra Madre Oriental for about 40 km. Look carefully on the right for a narrow paved road to the town of Galeana. If you cross the border at Laredo early in the morning, you can reach Galeana in the afternoon. There is a small hotel in the town and you can spend the following day exploring the area around the town. Var. *stormiae* can be collected from roadside trees along the road into Galeana. There are very large, scattered trees growing near the base of Cerro Potosí, a few kilometers northwest of Galeana. Also, just south of Galeana there are scattered trees along Highway 61.

NOTES AND COMMENTS—A number of taxonomists and botanists consider *P. arizonica* var. *stormiae* a variety of *Pinus ponderosa* viz. *P. ponderosa* var. *arizonica*. It is interesting to note that the southeastern-most range of *P. ponderosa* apparently extends along the Guadalupe Mountains into the Big Bend National Park of western Texas. A small, isolated population of pines was found in the Chisos Mountains which form the "elbow" of the Big Bend area along the Rio Grande, and a few specimens were collected from three trees (G. Morgensen, pers. comm., 1984). Leaves per fascicle numbered 3 (80%, 25%, 40%), 4 (17%, 62%, 59%) and 5 (0%, 2%, 13%). Cones varied considerably in size and scale morphology, most having the reflexed, pyramidal apophysis typical of var. *stormiae*. Needle length varied from 16–26 cm. The range of var. *stormiae* does extend northward in Coahuila as small, widely scattered populations along the Sierra de la Encantada and approaches the Chisos Mountains in the Big Bend area of Texas. *Pinus arizonica* var. *stormiae* is certainly closely related to *P. ponderosa*, and I expect the collections cited here are indeed var. *stormiae* at about the northern limit of its range viz. the Big Bend area of Texas.

From many individuals and small groups observed in the Galeana and Miquihuana area, I found this taxon quite variable with regard to needle length, cone size and cone scale morphology. On a number of occasions I noted the possibility of hybridization with *P. estevezi*; however, I have no concrete evidence to support that view.

Pinus engelmannii Carr.

Pino Real, Apache Pine, Arizona Long Leaf Pine

THE TREE—A medium-size pine up to 25 m high and 70–80 cm in diameter; branches are large, thick and mostly horizontal forming an open, rounded crown. Young trees have an open, pyramidal crown.

BARK—On mature trees dark brown, rough, scaly, divided into long narrow plates by dark, shallow fissures. In young trees the bark is rough, scaly and furrowed but not formed into plates.

BRANCHLETS—Thick, stiff; the bark brown and rough; bases of the leaf bracts prominent, very rough, scaly and decurrent.

LEAVES—In fascicles of 3 and 4 (mostly 3), occasionally 5, grouped at the ends of the

P. engelmanni Tree   Bark   Cones, seeds, and leaves

branchlets, 25–35 cm long, thick (about 1.5 mm wide) stiff, erect, the margins serrate; stomata present on the dorsal and ventral surfaces, resin canals 4–13, usually 5–8; exterior walls of the endoderm slightly thickened, fibrovascular bundles 2, close together but distinct. Fascicle sheaths very scaly, dark brown to almost black, occasionally sticky, 20–25 mm long, not deciduous.

CONELETS—Long-ovoid, purple color, in groups of 2–5 on stout peduncles; scales thick and bearing a minute, erect prickle.

CONES—Asymmetrical, 10–15 cm long, slightly curved, long-connate, lustrous yellowish brown; hard, heavy; borne in groups of 2–4 on strong peduncles 5–10 mm long that are almost hidden under the basal scales. They ripen during the winter months and remain closed for some time; after opening they remain attached to the branchlet for some time (less than a year), and when they fall, the peduncle with a few basal scales remains attached to the branch.

CONE SCALES—Hard, strong, apophyses raised, pyramidal to protuberant, recurved, transversely keeled; umbo dorsal, small, gray, bearing a small, sharp, persistent prickle.

SEED—Small; dark brown; 5–8 mm long, the seed wing articulate, 20–25 mm long. They average 22,000/kg; cotyledons number 8–10, mostly 8 and 9.

WOOD—Soft, pale yellow, sawn along with associated pines into lumber and construction timbers. Locally it is also used for firewood, mine timbers and home construction.

DISTRIBUTION—*Pinus engelmannii* has a wide range in the northwestern Sierra Madre Occidental (Fig. 3.32). A few small, isolated populations occur in southeastern Arizona and in the extreme southwestern corner of New Mexico. Its range then extends southward into northeastern Sonora, western Chihuahua, western Durango, eastern Sinaloa along the border with Durango and terminates in southern Zacatecas. It has been reported in the state

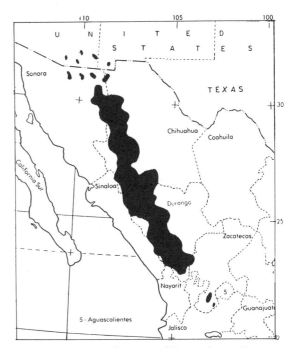

Fig. 3.32. Distribution of *P. engelmannii.*

of Aguascalientes, but I was not able to find it there.

HABITAT—Over its range the species is found growing under a variety of conditions from cool, moist valleys to high mesas and dry to arid slopes and ridges. In general, though, it grows at altitudes from 2,000–2,500 m on the drier slopes of the mountains; climate is cold-temperate and rainfall over its range varies from 400–500 mm in the north to 650 mm on the Pacific slopes of southern Durango and Sinaloa. Snow, sleet and frosts are common in the mountains of Sonora and Chihuahua during the coldest months—December, January and February. Further south in Durango, winter snows are less frequent; however, severe frosts continue during the winter particularly at altitudes above 2,000 m. Although the species grows on many different sites, its best growth is made on deep, well-drained soils of the high valleys and mesas.

WHERE TO FIND *P. engelmannii*—Since this species is often associated with *P. arizonica, P. durangensis* and *P. cooperi,* suggested collection areas for those species would also be appropriate for this taxon. Another suggestion; if you are in the Durango area, drive to the village of El Nayar (only a few kilometers from Durango) and find a guide who could take you on a trail into the nearby Sierra de Nayar. *Pinus engelmannii* grows there with *P. cooperi, P. teocote* and *P. leiophylla.*

NOTES AND COMMENTS—Field identification of this species should not be difficult since the lustrous, yellowish brown cones with protuberant, recurved apophyses are not found in any associated pines. The common name Arizona Longleaf Pine was applied because the long needles are similar to those of *P. palustris.* It is reported that 2-year-old seedlings are very similar to the 2–3-year seedlings of *P. palustris;* however, they do not develop the characteristic "grass stage" of *P. palustris.*

Pinus engelmannii var. *blancoi* Mart.

In 1948 Prof. Martínez described this variety and noted that it is closely related to *P. engelmannii.* He felt, however, that differences between leaves and cones from the two taxa warranted the description as a new variety. I collected and studied *P. engelmannii* in the mountains near Durango and found what seemed to me to be normal variations in the leaves (some longer or shorter or more slender) and cones (the apophyses more or less protuberant) and believe these variations are not of sufficient magnitude to warrant the description of a new variety. More detailed morphological studies and particularly chemical analyses of turpentine samples from the two taxa may, in the future, reveal highly significant differences. For the present I have not made a distinction between the two taxa.

Pinus durangensis Mart.

Ocote, Pino Blanco, Pino

THE TREE—This pine has a fine, straight, clear trunk reaching heights of 30–40 m and diameters of 50–80 cm. The crown is rounded and compact in mature trees with branches drooping to horizontal. Young trees have a thick crown and pyramidal form.

BARK—Rough, dark brown, divided by shallow vertical and horizontal fissures into rather long, narrow, scaly plates.

BRANCHLETS—Thick, stiff, erect, rough and scaly; bases of the leaf bracts are decurrent.

LEAVES—In fascicles of 6, often 5 or 7

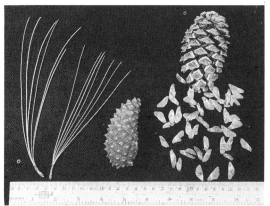

P. durangensis Tree   Bark   Cones, seeds, and leaves

and rarely 8, medium thick (0.6–0.9 mm), 15–20 cm long, stiff, erect, the margins finely serrate; stomata present on the dorsal and ventral surfaces; resin canals 2–3, occasionally 4, medial; exterior walls of the endoderm thickened, fibrovascular bundles 2, contiguous but distinct. Fascicle sheaths persistent; brown; scaly; 15–18 mm long.

CONELETS—Borne singly or in groups of 2, 3 and 4 on short, stout peduncles; the small scales thick and bearing a sharp, erect prickle.

CONES—Slightly curved, long ovoid, 7–10 cm long, reddish brown color, usually in groups of 2 and 3 on short, stout peduncles 5–8 mm long (mature cones appear sessile). They ripen in December and January, open when mature, and are semi-persistent for a number of months. When the cones fall the peduncle with a few basal cone scales remains attached to the branch.

CONE SCALES—Stiff, hard, strong, the apophysis raised, subpyramidal, transversely keeled, slightly reflexed; the umbo dorsal, raised, ashy gray, with sharp, often recurved, persistent prickle.

SEED—Small, grayish in color, roughly triangular; 5–7 mm long with an articulate wing 12–15 mm long and 5–7 mm wide. Seeds are about the same size as *P. arizonica* seed and probably average near the same number per kilogram, i.e. about 24,200.

WOOD—Light, soft, yellowish color, of good quality, sawn commercially into lumber and timbers for general construc-

tion. Of course, it is also cut locally for firewood.

DISTRIBUTION—*P. durangensis* is found in the northwestern ranges of the Sierra Madre Occidental in Chihuahua, Sonora, Durango, and in eastern Sinaloa near the Durango border (Fig. 3.33).

HABITAT—The species grows at 2,000–2,500 m altitude in a temperate-cold climate. At this altitude, annual rainfall is about 600 mm in Durango; frosts and occasional snow and sleet occur during the coldest months, December and January. Formerly *P. durangensis* formed extensive pure forests in Durango and southern

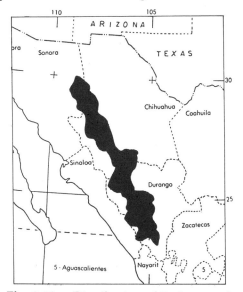

Fig. 3.33. Distribution of *P. durangensis*.

Chihuahua; however, intensive logging over the years has left only scattered, open stands over most of its range. Small, pure groups of fine, mature trees can still be found in high, very inaccessible valleys and ridges.

WHERE TO FIND— *P. durangensis*— Driving to Mexico from the east, cross the border at Laredo. Drive south to Monterrey and take MEX 40 to Saltillo, Torreon, and the city of Durango (about 2 days, once you cross the border). If driving down from the west, cross the border at El Paso and drive south on MEX 45 to Chihuahua, Hidalgo del Parral and to Durango. These are long drives through mostly hot desert country. In any event, the objective is Highway MEX 40 from Durango to Mazatlan. Where the highway crosses the Sierra Madre Occidental, the road is very winding and the mountains are spectacular. West of the old sawmill town, El Salto, look for the species on side roads into the mountains. Parking on narrow, winding Highway 40 can be difficult and very dangerous.

NOTES AND COMMENTS—Botanists and taxonomists have variously described this taxon as closely related to *P. ponderosa*, or more closely related to *P. montezumae*. From my own collections and observations in Chihuahua and Durango, I agree with Prof. Martínez that it should be given specific rank and I have placed it in section Ponderosae.

Pinus durangensis forma *quinquefoliata* Mart.

Prof. Martínez (1948) described this taxon as a form of *P. durangensis.*

Over most of its range, *P. durangensis* is often found growing with a closely related species, *P. arizonica*. Probably the two species cross naturally and produce offspring with some cones and needles that are intermediate between those of the parents. I collected and observed *P. durangensis* in Chihuahua and Durango and found many examples of what I considered normal variation in the leaves (some thicker or more slender, others longer or shorter) and cones (some smaller or larger). Given the probability of natural hybridization and the normal variation of needle and cone morphology, I believe the differences noted by Martínez (needles in fascicles of 5 rarely 6, cones slightly smaller) do not justify description of a new form.

Section Montezumae

Trees in this section are generally tall and well-formed. The bark on young trees is rough and scaly and bases of the leaf bracts are decurrent leaving the branchlets rough and scaly. Section Montezumae is divided into three subsections, and these are listed in Table 3.8 with some of their important botanical features.

Table 3.8. Morphological characteristics of Section Montezumae.

Subsection	Leaves per fascicle	Cone length, cm	Cone scales	Fascicle sheath length, cm
Montezumae	5–7	6–15	Thin, flexible to hard, thick, stiff	1.0–2.5
Rudis	3, 4, 5 (6–7)	8–15	Thin, flexible to medium stiff	1.0–2.0
Michoacana	5–6	15–30	Thick, hard, stiff	2.0–4.0

Subsection Montezumae

Four species and one variety are included in this group. These are listed in Table 3.9 along with some of their distinguishing characters.

Table 3.9. Characteristics of Species in Subsection Montezumae.

Species	Leaf length, cm, habit	Cone length, cm	Cone scales
P. cooperi	8–10, thick, stiff, erect	6–10	Thin, flexible
P. montezumae	15–25, erect to drooping	12–15	Thick, hard, stiff
P. montezumae var. lindleyi	20–30, slender, drooping	12–15	Thin, medium stiff
P. martinezii	20–28, thick, erect	8–13	Hard, stiff
P. douglasiana	20–30, stiff, erect	7–10	Stiff, hard, strong

Pinus cooperi Blanco

Pino Amarillo, Pino Chino, Ocote

THE TREE—A well-formed pine that reaches heights of 30–35 m and diameters of 50–80 cm. Old, mature trees have large, thick, pendent branches and generally a pyramidal, rather open crown. Young trees have a thick, bushy crown.

BARK—On mature trees the bark is rough, thick reddish brown to brown with narrow, shallow vertical and horizontal fissures that form polygonal and hexagon-like scaly plates.

BRANCHLETS—Thick, stiff; the bark rough, brown and scaly; bases of the leaf bracts are prominent and decurrent.

LEAVES—In fascicles of 5, rarely 4; thick, stiff, erect, usually 8–10 cm long though occasionally 14 cm, the margins finely serrate. Stomata present on the dorsal and ven-

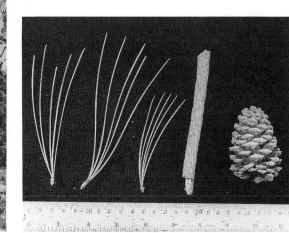

P. cooperi Tree   Bark   Cones, leaves, branchlet section

tral surfaces; resin canals 3–7, medial, exterior walls of the endoderm thickened, fibrovascular bundles 2, contiguous but distinct. The leaves grow in groups at the ends of the branchlets; fascicle sheaths are scaly, brown, about 10 cm long and not deciduous.

CONELETS—Solitary and in pairs, borne on stout, scaly peduncles; the scales pointed and bearing a minute curved prickle.

CONES—Almost symmetrical, ovoid, slightly curved, 6–10 cm long, about 6 cm wide when open, light reddish brown; borne singly and in pairs on short (5 mm), stout peduncles that accompany the cone when it falls. The cones open when mature and are semi-persistent.

CONE SCALES—Thin, flexible, the apophyses flat to slightly raised, transversely keeled, the apical margin rounded and somewhat thickened; the umbo dorsal, slightly raised, bearing a small, recurved, persistent prickle.

SEED—Small, 5–7 mm long; brown, with an articulate wing 12–20 mm long and 5–8 mm wide.

WOOD—Light, strong, the sapwood yellow and heartwood pinkish brown. Trees are cut along with associated pines and sawn into lumber and timbers for general construction purposes.

DISTRIBUTION—*P. cooperi* occurs in the state of Durango and just across the eastern border of Sinaloa (Fig. 3.34). Some writers show it occurring in southwestern Chihuahua. Although I did not find it in that

Fig. 3.34. Distribution of *P. cooperi*.

area, there are probably small scattered populations that extend beyond the northwestern border of Durango into Chihuahua.

HABITAT—*P. cooperi* grows at 2,400–2,800 m altitude. Rainfall varies from 500 to 600 mm annually, occasionally more if there is unusually heavy snowfall during the winter months of December, January and February. The species once formed extensive pure stands in the mountains, mesas and valleys north, south and west of El Salto. However, heavy cutting has left only occasional small scattered stands of trees in the area around El Salto. There still are, however, "pockets" of fine trees in the inaccessible valleys and ridges west of El Salto.

WHERE TO FIND *P. cooperi*—Drive to the city of Durango and take MEX 40 west toward the town of El Salto. Just before reaching El Salto look for the village of Coyotes. There are two trails that turn off the highway here, one north to the villages Santo Domingo, Ajitas and San Luis. Another trail turns southward toward the villages Cebollas, Cruz and Palo Gordo. Trees can be found on both trails; however, a high-clearance vehicle is needed with good tires and it would be best to hire a guide at Coyotes or El Salto. In any event, only attempt the trip during the dry season.

NOTES AND COMMENTS—This species is often found growing with *P. durangensis*, *P. arizonica*, *P. leiophylla* and *P. chihuahuana*. It is not difficult to separate *P. leiophylla* and *P. chihuahuana* from the other taxa; however, *P. cooperi* is related to *P. durangensis* and *P. arizonica*, and in the field it is often difficult to separate one from another. Closer study of the bark, cones and leaves will, however, distinguish one from another. Table 3.10 lists the more outstanding differences.

Table 3.10. Distinguishing features of *P. arizonica*, *P. durangensis*, and *P. cooperi*.

Species	Bark	Leaves	Cones	Cone scales
P. arizonica	Thick, large reddish-brown plates	In fascicles of 3, occasionally 4 and 5; 12–18cm long. Resin canals 5–10	Ovoid, yellowish-brown, about 6cm long. The peduncle does not fall with the cone	Hard, strong; apophyses raised, umbo large with a recurved persistent prickle
P. durangensis	Plates neither as large as above nor as thick	In fascicles of 6, occasionally 5 and 7; 15–20cm long. Resin canals 2–3, occasionally 4	Long-ovoid, 7–10cm long, reddish-brown, the peduncle does not fall with the cone	Stiff, hard; apophyses raised, the umbo with a persistent prickle
P. cooperi	Plates much smaller, more hexagonal in form, thinner	In fascicles of 5; usually 6–10cm long. Resin canals 3, 4, and 5, usually 4 and 5	Lustrous, reddish-brown 6–10cm long, the peduncle generally falls with the cone	Thin, flexible —not hard and stiff. Apophyses flat to slightly raised; umbo small to flat, with a persistent prickle

Pinus lutea var. *ornelasi* Mart.

Prof. Martínez (1948) described *P. lutea* var. *ornelasi,* pointing out that it differed from the species in its thicker bark, somewhat longer leaves, cones rather larger, clustered and less lustrous, and the peduncle did not fall with the cone. He noted too that cone scales were thicker and the wood lighter colored.

I collected and observed *P. cooperi* in Durango and found what I felt to be normal variations in bark thickness, cone size and needle length for the species. Accordingly I have not recognized *P. lutea* var. *ornelasi* as a distinct variety. Perhaps more intensive field and laboratory studies will reveal differences that clearly justify the varietal status. Comparative analyses of turpentine from the oleoresins of these taxa would be very helpful in this respect.

Pinus montezumae Lamb.

Pino, Ocote, Montezuma Pine

THE TREE—This is a large, very fine pine, 20–35 m high and 50–80 cm in diameter; occasionally it may reach a height of 40 m and diameter of 1 m. The branches are large, mostly horizontal, forming a thick, rounded crown. Young trees have a dense pyramidal crown.

BARK—On mature trees thick, dark grayish brown, divided by deep vertical and horizontal fissures into rough, scaly plates. In young trees the bark is reddish brown, rough and scaly.

BRANCHLETS—Thick, stiff, scaly and rough; reddish brown; bases of the leaf bracts are prominent and decurrent.

LEAVES—Mostly in fascicles of 5, occasionally 4 or 6, variable from thick and erect to slender and slightly drooping, 15–25 cm long, occasionally 30 cm; the margins finely serrate; stomata present on the dorsal and ventral surfaces; resin canals 2–6, usually 4 or 5, medial; exterior walls of the endoderm thickened, fibrovascular bundles 2, contiguous but distinct. Fascicle sheaths brown, about 15 mm long, persistent.

CONELETS—Ovoid-conical, the scales thick and bearing a small erect prickle, in groups of 2 or 3 on stiff, scaly, erect peduncles.

CONES—Like the leaves, cones are also variable, from long-ovoid to ovoid or conoid. They are usually slightly curved, 12–15 cm long and 7–10 cm wide when open. Light brown and often lustrous, they are borne in groups of 2 and 3 on short (about 10 mm), stout peduncles that remain attached to the branchlet with a few basal cone scales when the cone falls. The cones open at maturity (during the winter months) and are deciduous.

CONE SCALES—Thick, hard, stiff, the apophyses raised to subpyramidal, transversely keeled; the umbo dorsal, slightly raised, grayish brown, bearing a small prickle that is usually deciduous.

SEED—Small, dark brown, 6–7 mm long with an articulate seed wing about 20 mm long and 7 mm wide; cotyledons number 6, 7 and 8, mostly 6 and 7.

WOOD—Sapwood yellowish white, the heartwood light brown; hard, heavy and resinous; widely used for lumber and general construction.

DISTRIBUTION—*P. montezumae* is found primarily in the mountains of the Great Cross Range of Mexico; however, its range extends northward along the Sierra Madre Oriental and far southward into Guatemala (Fig. 3.35). In Mexico it has been reported in the states of Nuevo León, Coahuila, Tamaulipas, Hidalgo, Tlaxcala, Puebla, Veracruz, Mexico, Morelos, the Federal District, Michoacán, Jalisco, Guerrero, Oaxaca and Chiapas. In Guatemala it is found in the departments of Huehuetenango, Quiché, San Marcos, Quezal-

P. montezumae Tree   Bark   Cones, seeds, and leaves

tenango, Totonicapán, Sololá, Chimaltenango, Guatemala and Jalapa.

HABITAT—Over its range *P. montezumae* grows under a variety of conditions ranging from warm-temperate to cold-temperate and altitudes from 2,000 (rarely less) to 3,200 m. Rainfall over its range also varies from 800 to 1,000 mm or more annually. At the higher altitudes snow, sleet and frosts occur during the winter months, while most of the rain occurs during June–September. I found the best trees growing on the high mesas and valleys of the Great Cross Range of mountains that extend across Mexico from Perote and Orizaba peak (Cerro Orizaba) on the east, to Toluca (Nevada de Toluca and of course "Popo" and "Sleeping Lady" (Popocatepetl and Ixtaccihuatl), Morelia, Uruapan and into the forests of Michoacán westward toward Coalcomán. Very fine trees were also found growing under similar conditions and elevations in Chiapas south of San Cristobal de las Casas and in Guatemala along the mountains eastward from San Marcos (15° N latitude) to Quezaltenango, Sololá, Chimaltenango and the town of San José Pinula. The species attains its best development on well-drained soils of the high mesas and lower slopes of the mountains. Although it also grows on dry to arid sites, under those conditions growth is slow and the trees are often low and very branchy.

WHERE TO FIND *P. montezumae*—If you are in Mexico City, collections could be made very easily by driving west from the city on Av. Reforma. Ask anyone for directions to the Federal Park, Desert of the Lions (Desierto de Los Leones). Reforma Avenue becomes Highway MEX 15 to Toluca; just follow this avenue-highway for about 8–10 km as it winds upward out of the valley and into the park. When the highway enters the forest, immediately begin to look for a space to turn off. Traffic in the area is formidable, and it is difficult to find a place to park. Once that problem is solved, exploring the park becomes fairly simple since a network of paths and trails wind through the entire forest. *P. montezumae* can be found growing alongside the highway and along most of the trails.

Another very interesting area for collecting *P. montezumae* is the snow-capped mountain, Nevada de Toluca. Follow Highway MEX 15 from Mexico City to Toluca (about 50 km). There turn left on Highway MEX 55, drive for about 15 km and ask for directions to the Nevada de Toluca, only a few kilometers from the highway. It might be wise to inquire in Toluca for a guide, but that is not absolutely necessary since the road up the mountain is kept in fair condition. Use a high-clearance vehicle and take a good supply of gasoline. This is a very picturesque area and the trail passes directly through open forests of pines. *P. montezumae* will be found growing with *P. rudis*, *P. leiophylla* and *P. pseudostrobus*.

Much further south in Chiapas, there are

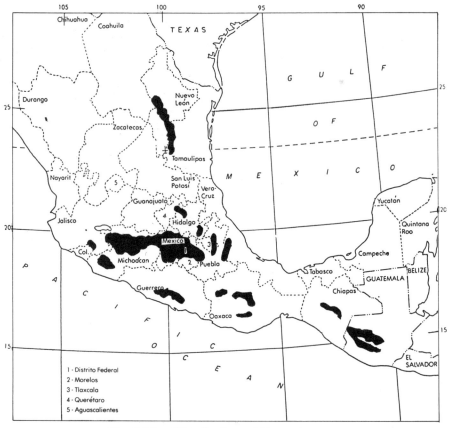

Fig. 3.35. Distribution of *P. montezumae*.

fine stands of *P. montezumae* along Highway MEX 190. From San Cristobal de Las Casas drive south for about 100 km. The species can be found growing in open forests and fields along the highway.

If you continue south and drive into Guatemala, follow the Pan-American Highway (CA 1 in Guatemala) for about 170 km south to a major crossroads near the city of Quezaltenango (south) and Totonicapán (north). *P. montezumae* can be found along the roads and trails in that area, often as roadside trees. Further east on CA 1 toward the city of Sololá, the species also occurs as roadside trees often growing with *P. pseudostrobus, P. oaxacana, P. nubicola* and *P. rudis.*

NOTES AND COMMENTS—Many writers have stressed the variability of this species, particularly the morphology of its cones and leaves. Identification is also made more difficult by the presence of intermediate forms between this species and *P. pseudostrobus,* another 5-needle species. The

two taxa often grow together in mixed stands, and populations of fertile hybrids are not uncommon. In Mexico I found these particularly evident in mixed *P. montezumae* and *P. pseudostrobus* forests in the Zitacuaro, Uruapan, and Patzcuaro area. Apparently *P. montezumae* also crosses naturally with two closely related species *P. rudis* and *P. hartwegii.* I found many presumed hybrids between these taxa in the mountains between Saltillo and Galeana in the states of Coahuila and Nuevo León. In Hidalgo I also found *P. montezumae* growing with *P. michoacana* and among the trees a number of intermediate forms. The two species are closely related and I believe that hybridization between the two taxa also occurs naturally. How then to distinguish the different species in the field? Most of the species (*P. rudis, P. hartwegii, P. michoacana*) can be readily separated from *P. montezumae* by combinations of cone and leaf characters. *P. pseudostrobus* is more difficult. I have found one character that enables me to separate the Pseudostrobus group of pines from the Montezumae group; viz, the character of the bark on the branchlets, the stem of young trees (3–8 years) and the upper trunk of mature trees. In *P. montezumae* the bark will be rough and scaly; in *P. pseudostrobus* it will be smooth. On the branchlets and stems of young trees, bases of the leaf bracts are decurrent in the Montezumae group, leaving the surface rough, and bark formation follows quickly. In the Psuedostrobus group, bases of the leaf bracts are not decurrent but soon become submerged and, in effect, disappear into the young bark leaving the surface smooth, and so it remains for several years. In very old, slow-growing trees of both groups it is often difficult to observe this character, but if young reproduction and young trees can be found nearby it will not be difficult to separate the two taxa. One other character is helpful in separating *P. montezumae* and *P. pseudostrobus*. I have never found a "grass stage" in young *P. pseudostrobus* seedlings, while in *P. montezumae* a "grass stage" in the seedlings is usual. "Grass stage" can be described as what happens to the growth of young seedlings during their first 5 years. In *P. montezumae* (and a number of other species) height growth of the young pine above

ground is very slow, generally from 15–30 cm. However, a thick, dense growth of leaves is formed at ground level that apparently protects the young stem and bud from fire damage. Below ground a tremendous taproot develops during that period, and following this, rapid growth of the stem (and bark formation) takes place.

In *P. pseudostrobus* the young seedlings, under good growing conditions, make very rapid height growth during the first 5 years without any "grass stage" whatever, and the bark remains thin and very smooth. There are other differences between the two species that aid in their identification; *P. montezumae* cones are generally larger than cones of *P. pseudostrobus*; cone scales of *P. pseudostrobus* are thinner and more flexible, and leaves are generally more slender and drooping than those of *P. montezumae*. However, in areas where the two species intergrade, these differences often disappear and it is difficult to determine where one species disappears and another begins. At that point the smooth bark of young *P. pseudostrobus* trees contrasting so markedly with the rough, scaly bark of branchlets and young trees *P. montezumae*, becomes the most reliable means of identification.

Pinus montezumae forma *macrocarpa* Mart.

In describing forma *macrocarpa*, Prof. Martínez (1948) pointed out that it is similar to *P. montezumae* but the cones are longer and the cone scales more fragile and reflexed than those of *P. montezumae*. He reported collections from Michoacán, Morelos, Mexico (state), Tlaxcala, Hidalgo, Veracruz, Guerrero and Chiapas.

I found this taxon at most of the locations cited by Martínez (Tlaxcala and Guerrero were the exceptions) and in addition observed it in Guatemala near the highway from Chichicastenango to Quiché at about kilometer 150. At most locations only occasional trees were found, generally in association with *P. montezumae* and *P. michoacana*.

An interesting exception to the "occasional tree occurrence" was a small stand of trees found north of Uruapan, Michoacán, near the small, isolated village of Sevina. These were mostly large, mature pines from 50 to 100 cm in diameter with only two species present, *P. montezumae* and *P. michoacana*. Intermingled with the two species were many pines (about the same size) bearing cones and needles that graded almost imperceptibly from one species into another. Among those were many trees that might be identified as forma *macrocarpa*.

I took resin samples from the trunks of 10 of those taxa. Subsequent analyses of the turpentine showed that it consisted of 96% α-pinene with small amounts of camphene

(1%), β-phellandrene and p-cymene. *P. montezumae* turpentine that I collected in Michoacán is almost identical to the above analysis. In Michoacán I also collected resin (stem) from *P. michoacana* var. *cornuta.* Analysis of its turpentine revealed that it is almost identical with the analyses of *P. montezumae* and forma *macrocarpa* (minor differences were the presence of small amounts of β-caryophellene and α-terpineol).

From these findings and from my collections and field observations, I believe that forma *macrocarpa* represents an intermediate form between *P. montezumae* and *P. michoacana* var. *cornuta.* Further morphological and chemical (turpentine analyses) studies may reveal more significant differences between the three taxa that would justify elevating forma *macrocarpa* to varietal status.

Pinus montezumae var. lindleyi Loudon.

Ocote, Pino, Lindley Pine

THE TREE—A large tree up to 30 m high and 50–70 cm in diameter, the lower branches horizontal to drooping, upper branches horizontal to ascending; the crown rather dense and rounded.

BARK—On old trees, grayish brown to dark brown; divided into scaly plates by narrow, shallow fissures. On young trees the bark is rough, reddish brown but not formed into plates.

BRANCHLETS—Stiff, the bark reddish brown, rough and scaly; bases of the leaf bracts prominent and decurrent.

LEAVES—In fascicles of 5, slender, flexible, 20–30 cm long generally somewhat drooping, the margins finely serrate; stomata present on the dorsal and ventral surfaces; resin canals 2–5, medial, occasionally 1 internal; exterior walls of the endoderm thickened, fibrovascular bundles 2, close together but distinct. Fascicle sheaths about 25 mm long, pale brown and persistent.

CONELETS—Ovate, the scales narrow, pointed with a small weak prickle; they are solitary or in clusters of 2–3 on short, stout peduncles.

CONES—Long-ovoid, 12–15 cm long, pale brown, slightly curved, tapering toward the apex, mostly solitary and in pairs on short (10 mm), stout peduncles that remain with a few basal scales attached to the branch when the cone falls. The cones mature during the winter months, shed their seed almost immediately and are soon deciduous.

CONE SCALES—Thin, rather stiff but not as stiff as in the species; the apophyses almost flat to slightly raised, subpyramidal with a weak transverse keel; the umbo dorsal, dark, flat to slightly raised, bearing a small, persistent prickle.

SEED—Small, about 6 mm long with an articulate wing about 20 mm long.

WOOD—Sapwood creamy white; the heartwood pale brown, hard, heavy and resinous. The trees are cut and sawn into lumber along with *P. montezumae*, *P. pseudostrobus* and *P. leiophylla.*

DISTRIBUTION—Var. *lindleyi* has been reported from the states of Jalisco, Michoacán, Mexico, Hidalgo, Puebla, Veracruz, Morelos, Guerrero and Chiapas (Fig. 3.36). In Guatemala I found it in the departments of Quiché, San Marcos, Quezaltenango, Sololá, Chimaltenango and Guatemala.

HABITAT—In Mexico I found the best trees growing on mountain slopes and valleys of the Great Cross Range that extends in an east-west (approximately) line from Colima on the Pacific Coast to the volcanic peaks of Perote and Orizaba near the Gulf of Mexico. Annual rainfall along these mountain ranges varies from 800 to 1,000 mm. Frosts and occasional snowfalls occur during December, January and February. Most of the rain falls during the

P. *montezumae* var. *lindleyi* Tree   Bark   Branchlet, cone, and leaves

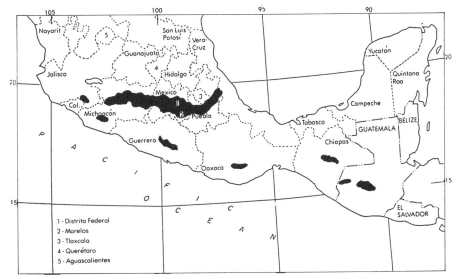

Fig. 3.36. Distribution of *P. montezumae* var. *lindleyi*.

summer months of June–September; April, May and June are the warmest months. Var. *lindleyi* grows at 2,000–3,200 m altitude usually in association with *P. montezumae, P. pseudostrobus, P. teocote, P. leiophylla* and *P. michoacana*. It makes its best growth on deep, well-drained soils of the high mountain slopes, mesas and valleys in both Mexico and Guatemala.

WHERE TO FIND var. *lindleyi*—In Mexico I found very fine trees in the area west of Uruapan in the state of Michoacán about a day's drive from Mexico City. In Uruapan, find a guide who can take you to see the well-known volcano, Paricutín. The road to the volcano is gravelled and in good condi-

tion. Look carefully along the road for the trees; I found two small, pure stands of the variety growing alongside the road. In the same area (actually within a few kilometers) this variety can also be found on the slopes of Mt. Tancítaro. Your guide could take you there during the same trip.

In Guatemala I found var. *lindleyi* at kilometer 168 on Highway CA 1, Department of Sololá. You must turn west onto a narrow trail for about 1 km, find a place to park and slowly climb (because the altitude here is about 3,200 m) the slope on the right. On the ridge I found the variety growing with *P. montezumae, P. rudis, P. ayacahuite, P. Donnell-Smithii* and a magnificent stand of *Cupressus* sp.

I also found some unusually fine trees near Highway 5 west of the city Quezaltenango at about kilometer 220. The trees were growing on the slopes of a steep arroyo and the soil was a deep red clay-loam. The site was shady and moist and the trees were as fine as any I saw on the trip; one tree measured 1 m in diameter and about 40 m in height.

NOTES AND COMMENTS—Some botanists believe that var. *lindleyi* does not differ enough in its morphology from that of *P. montezumae* to warrant its classification as a variety; others believe that it does. I agree with the latter even though identification is difficult. I have found that a process of elimination works well in the field when trying to separate the three taxa, *P. montezumae*, var. *lindleyi* and *P. pseudostrobus*. First, look carefully at the branchlets and/or stems of young trees; if they are fairly smooth, not scaly and rough, then put the specimens aside because you have *P. pseudostrobus* or one of the species that form a part of the Pseudostrobus group. At this point *P. montezumae* and var. *lindleyi* can usually be separated by the characteristics shown in Table 3.11.

I found it interesting to note that throughout its range in Mexico, *P. montezumae* var. *lindleyi* is often found growing with *P. montezumae* and *P. pseudostrobus*. This, with the intermediate morphology of its leaves and cones, suggests the possibility of hybrid origin of the variety, although I believe the answer may be far more complex than that. It would, though, be interesting to make extensive plantings of seed from var. *lindleyi* collected in Michoacán, Mexico and in Guatemala and to compare seedling growth and leaf morphology with those of seedlings from typical *P. montezumae* and *P. pseudostrobus*.

It would be interesting and helpful, too, to compare var. *lindleyi* seedlings with seedlings produced from a *P. montezumae* × *P. pseudostrobus*. That cross has been made at the Institute of Forest Genetics, Placerville, California. Unfortunately there are doubts concerning identification of the *P. montezumae* parent.

One final note on var. *lindleyi* may be helpful; in Michoacán I collected resin from this taxon and analysis reveals significant differences between its turpentine and that of *P. montezumae*. Typical *P. montezumae* turpentine has very high levels of α-pinene with myrcene mostly absent. Var. *lindleyi* turpentine had much lower levels of α-pinene and myrcene is consistently present at high levels. Turpentine from *P. pseudostrobus* is more similar to that of var. *lindleyi*; in both taxa myrcene is consistently present and at about the same levels. These comparisons may not hold up very well, though, since I had resin samples from only 5 trees of var. *lindleyi*. Many more samples taken over its entire range would give a strong base for comparison of the three taxa.

Table 3.11. Distinguishing characteristics of *P. montezumae* and *P. montezumae* var. *lindleyi*.

Species	Cones	Cone scales	Leaves
P. montezumae	More ovate, not long and tapered	Stiff, strong; the apophyses raised to pyramidal; the umbo raised, bearing a small, deciduous prickle	Generally thick and stiff; erect though sometimes slender and drooping
P. montezumae var. *lindleyi*	Long-ovoid, tapering to the apex of the cone	Thin, not so strong; apophyses flat; the umbo flat or slightly raised, the prickle very small and persistent	Always slender and some-what drooping, not erect or stiff

Pinus martinezii Larsen

Pino, Ocote

THE TREE—A medium-size pine reaching a height of about 25 m and 50–60 cm diameter, the lower branches thick and horizontal to drooping, the upper branches somewhat ascending forming a rounded crown.

BARK—On mature trees grayish brown, thick, divided into longitudinal plates by deep, vertical fissures. In young trees the bark is brown, thick, scaly and rough.

BRANCHLETS—Thick, stiff; the bark brown, rough and scaly; bases of the leaf bracts are decurrent.

LEAVES—In fascicles of 5, 6 and 7, rarely 8, mostly 6; thick, stiff, erect; the dorsal surface dark green and ventral surfaces glaucous; 20–28 cm long, mostly about 23 cm; the margins finely serrate, stomata present on the dorsal and ventral surfaces; resin canals 3, medial; exterior walls of the endoderm thickened, fibrovascular bundles 2, close together but distinct. Fascicle sheath 1.5–2.0 cm long, dark brown to almost black; not resinous; persistent.

CONELETS—Light brown, the scales thick and bearing a small weak prickle; they are borne on stout, erect, scaly peduncles.

CONES—Ovoid-conical, subsymmetrical, slightly curved, 8–13 cm long, 5–7 cm wide; brown; borne singly and in pairs on stout peduncles 10–15 mm long that remain attached to the branchlet with a few basal cone scales when the cone falls. The cones are not serotinous but open during the winter months soon after they mature and are then deciduous.

CONE SCALES—Hard, stiff; the apophyses slightly raised to subpyramidal, lightly horizontally keeled, the apical margin rounded; umbo dorsal, slightly raised, ashy gray, bearing a small, weak prickle that is soon deciduous.

SEED—About 6 mm long and 4 mm wide; brown with dark spots; the seed wing articulate, 12–15 m long; about 48,000 seeds/kg.

WOOD—Hard, heavy, resinous, yellowish white; the trees are cut along with *P. montezumae*, *P. pseudostrobus* and *P. leiophylla* and sold for lumber and construction timbers.

DISTRIBUTION—Larsen reported *P. martinezii* as occurring only in the state of Michoacán near the city of Uruapan (Fig. 3.37). More recently this taxon has been collected in Jalisco in the Sierra de Manatlán in the area of Cuautitlán. In Michoacán two additional populations have been reported at Tres Equinas near the town of Paracho.

HABITAT—I found this species at the site reported by Larsen (1964) growing on a poor soil of mostly loose volcanic ash, clay and stone, at 2,300 m altitude. Rainfall in the area varies from 800 to 1,000 mm annually

P. martinezii Tree   Bark

Leaves and cones

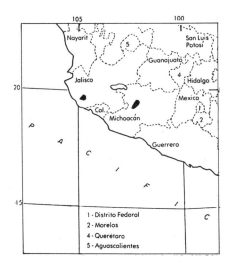

Fig. 3.37. Distribution of *P. martinezii*.

though occasional snowfalls may increase this total. Frosts are frequent during the winter months of December, January and February. Most rainfall occurs during June–September; the warmest months are April, May and June. Trees were growing in an open stand mingled with *P. montezumae, P. pseudostrobus, P. teocote* and *P. leiophylla* and, despite the rocky site, were making good growth and were very well formed.

WHERE TO FIND *P. martinezii*—Apparently the range of this species is very limited. The stand cited by Larsen is very

accessible since Highway 37 north from Uruapan is paved and one needs only to drive north of the city "between km markers 45 and 48". The population of trees is east of the highway and less than .25 km from the road. No trail leads there though.

NOTES AND COMMENTS—My observations indicate that *P. martinezii* is not closely related to *P. pseudostrobus* (bases of the leaf bracts *are* decurrent in *P. martinezii*). However, it does appear to be intermediate between *P. montezumae* and *P. michoacana*. Prof. Martínez (1948) described *P. michoacana* var. *quevedoi* as having 6 leaves in a fascicle, 28–39 cm long. The leaves and cones are also different from those of *P. montezumae*. In *P. martinezii* leaves are mostly 6 in a fascicle, thick, stiff and erect; cones are ovoid-conical (pointed toward the apex) and the prickle is weak and deciduous; the fascicle sheath is dark brown to almost black though not resinous. In *P. montezumae*, leaves are not so thick and stiff and are mostly in fascicles of 5. The sheaths are light brown and the cones are ovoid. In general, the dark green, stiff, erect leaves in groups of 6 give the *P. martinezii* trees a very different appearance from these of *P. montezumae*. I found *P. martinezii* to be an interesting species and one that should be considered rare and possibly endangered.

Pinus douglasiana Mart.

Pino, Ocote

THE TREE—A large pine reaching a height of 30–35 m and diameter of 50–75 cm. The crown is generally rounded and dense with the lower branches horizontal and upper branches slightly ascending. Young trees have a rather dense, pyramidal crown.

BARK—On mature trees, dark reddish brown, rough, scaly and divided into large, irregular plates. In young trees the bark is reddish brown varying from rough and scaly to smooth.

BRANCHLETS—Rather slender, often somewhat drooping. I have found many

trees with branchlets that are rough and scaly and other trees with smooth branchlets and bases of the leaf bracts not decurrent.

LEAVES—Often yellowish green, in fascicles of 5, thick and erect, 20–30 cm long, the margins serrate. Stomata are present on the dorsal and ventral surfaces; resin canals 3, medial; hypoderm irregularly developed, extending at some points completely across the chlorenchyma to the endoderm; cells of the endoderm with thickened outer walls, fibrovascular bundles 2. Fascicle sheaths are persistent, brown and not resinous.

P. douglasiana Tree   Bark

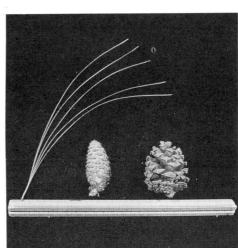

Cones and leaves

CONELETS—Ovoid with scales that terminate in a small prickle; borne singly and in groups of 2–5 on stout, scaly peduncles.

CONES—Reddish brown, 7–10 cm long, ovate, almost symmetrical; borne on stout, oblique peduncles 1–2 cm long that remain attached to the cone when it falls. They ripen during the winter months, open at maturity and are soon deciduous.

CONE SCALES—Stiff, strong, 10–12 mm wide, the apical margin irregularly rounded, apophyses slightly raised to subpyramidal, transversely keeled; the umbo raised and armed with a small, deciduous prickle.

SEED—Dark brown, small, 4–5 mm long with an articulate wing about 25 mm long; cotyledons 6–9, mostly 7–8.

WOOD—Fairly strong, rather soft, creamy to pale yellow in color; not very resinous though tapped for resin along with *P. oocarpa* in mixed stands. It is cut for timber along with associated pines *P. pseudostrobus*, *P. michoacana* and *P. michoacana* var. *cornuta*.

DISTRIBUTION—*P. douglasiana* occurs primarily in the mountains of Mexico's Great Cross Range; however, its range extends northward along the Sierra Madre Occidental and southward along the Sierra Madre del Sur (Fig. 3.38). It has been reported in the states of Sonora, Chihuahua, Durango, Sinaloa, Nayarit, Jalisco, Michoacán, Mexico, Guerrero and Oaxaca.

HABITAT—*P. douglasiana* grows at 1,500–

Fig. 3.38. Distribution of *P. douglasiana*.

2,500 m altitude in warm to temperate areas with annual rainfall averaging about 1,000 mm. At the higher elevations frosts are common during the winter months. I found the best trees growing on rather moist sites near Uruapan, Michoacán. Associated pines are often *P. pseudostrobus*, *P. maximinoi*, *P. michoacana* and *P. herrerai*.

WHERE TO FIND *P. douglasiana*—From Mexico City drive west on Highway 15 to Morelia. Then take the highway to

Patzcuaro and on to Uruapan. There inquire for directions to the Federal Forest Experiment Station at Barranca Cupatítzio. The director at the Station can show you very fine stands of this species. Another very interesting collection area can be reached by driving south from Uruapan to Neuva Italia. There turn west to Apatzingán and then south to the town of Aguililla. Arrange for a guide there to take you to the village of Dos Aguas. This is an isolated, densely forested area, and the trip should be attempted only with a competent guide and 4-wheel-drive vehicle equipped with excellent tires, extra gasoline and water. There are many winding, criss-crossing logging trails, so all collecting should be completed well before sunset. *P. douglasiana* can be found growing along the trails along with *P. pseudostrobus, P. maximinoi, P. michoacana* and *P. herrerai.*

NOTES AND COMMENTS—Martínez (1948) placed this species in his Section V Pseudostrobus and considered it a "connecting link" between his Section V Pseudostrobus and Section VI Montezumae. I collected specimens from trees in Valle de Bravo, Mexico state, that had slender, smooth branchlets with bases of the leaf bracts not decurrent; in Michoacán I found trees with both rough, scaly branchlets and smooth branchlets. Farther west in Jalisco I found trees of this species with rough, scaly branchlets, the bases of the leaf bracts clearly decurrent. Although *P. douglasiana* resembles *P. maximinoi* in the internal morphology of its leaves (in both taxa the hypoderm often forms extensions across the chlorenchyma to the endoderm), I believe the thick, stiff needles and predominantly rough, scaly branchlets with decurrent bases of the leaf bracts indicate a closer relationship with Section Montezumae. Chemical analysis of its turpentine reveals a remarkable similarity to that of *P. montezumae* (both taxa have very high levels of α-pinene viz. 80–90% and very low to absent Myrcene). Turpentine of *P. pseudostrobus* has high levels of α-pinene and fairly high levels of Myrcene ($\sim$ 40%). In the field the thick, stiff needles and generally rough, scaly branchlets readily separate this taxon from *P. maximinoi* and *P. pseudostrobus*. Its cone, with the oblique peduncle, is quite different from cones of *P. montezumae.*

Subsection Rudis

Three species comprise this group. Some of their distinguishing characteristics are listed in Table 3.12.

Table 3.12. Characteristics of Species in Subsection Rudis.

Species	Leaves per fascicle and length, cm	Cone color and length, cm
P. rudis	5; 10–17	Dark brown to purple, 10–15
P. Donnel-Smithii	5–6; 15–22	Dark brown, 10–13
P. hartwegii	3, 4, and 5, 8–16	Dark purple, 8–10

Pinus rudis Endl.

Pino, Ocote

THE TREE—A tall, well-formed pine 20–30 m high and 40–70 cm diameter; the lower branches horizontal to drooping, the upper branches ascending forming a thick, rounded crown.

BARK—Thick, light grayish brown, divided into scaly plates by horizontal and vertical fissures. On young trees the bark is rough and scaly though not plated.

BRANCHLETS—Thick, stiff, scaly and

P. rudis Trees   Bark   Cones, seeds, and leaves

rough; bases of the leaf bracts are decurrent.

LEAVES—Generally in fascicles of 5, rarely 4 or 6; thick, stiff, erect, slightly curved, 10–15 cm long, mostly about 14 cm; the margins coarsely serrate; stomata on the dorsal and ventral surfaces; resin canals 3–5, occasionally 6, medial; exterior walls of the endoderm are thickened, fibrovascular bundles 2, contiguous but distinct. Fascicle sheaths persistent, 15–20 mm long, dark brown.

CONELETS—Resinous, oblong, light reddish purple on short, thick, scaly peduncles.

CONES—Long-ovoid, almost symmetrical, slightly curved, mostly erect, 10–15 cm long, mostly about 12 cm; dark brown to almost purple-brown in color; borne in pairs or groups of 3 and 4 on short (about 10 mm), thick peduncles that remain with a few basal cone scales attached to the branchlet when the cone falls. They open at maturity during the winter months and are semi-persistent.

CONE SCALES—Thin, flexible, the apophyses slightly raised but not protuberant, transversely keeled, the apical margin rounded; the umbo dorsal, slightly raised and bearing a small, weak prickle.

SEED—Small, dark, about 5 mm long, with a narrow, articulate wing 13 mm long. Cotyledons number 5 or 6.

WOOD—Hard, strong, resinous, yellowish white; the trees are cut along with associated pine species, *P. ayachuite* var. *brachyptera*, *P. montezumae* and *P. hartwegii*,

and sold for lumber and construction timbers.

DISTRIBUTION—In Mexico the species has been reported in Nuevo León, Coahuila, Tamaulipas, Hidalgo, Puebla, Veracruz, Tlaxcala, the Federal District, Mexico, Colima, Michoacán, Nayarit, Jalisco, Guerrero, Oaxaca and Chiapas (Fig. 3.39). In Guatemala it has been found in the departments of Huehuetenango, San Marcos, Totonicapán, Quezaltenango, Sololá, Quiché, Chimaltenango and Guatemala. The species also occurs in Honduras on the high slopes of Cerro Santa Bárbara.

HABITAT—*P. rudis* is a pine of rather high elevations, generally growing at 2,200–3,300 m. Occasionally trees can be found at lower elevations and rarely above 3,300 m. It appears to be a conservative species and even over its very wide north-south range (northeastern Mexico to central Guatemala) characters of the cones, foliage and bark remain quite constant.

Over its entire range the species appears to grow best under cool to cold-temperate conditions with annual rainfall of 1,000 mm or more. The best trees that I found were growing on well-drained, sandy-gravelly slopes, often of volcanic origin, at 2,500–3,000 m. Trees were occasionally found at 2,000 m altitude or lower on drier sites, but growth was generally poor and the trees were low and branchy.

On high slopes of the mountains where *P. rudis* grows best, temperatures drop well

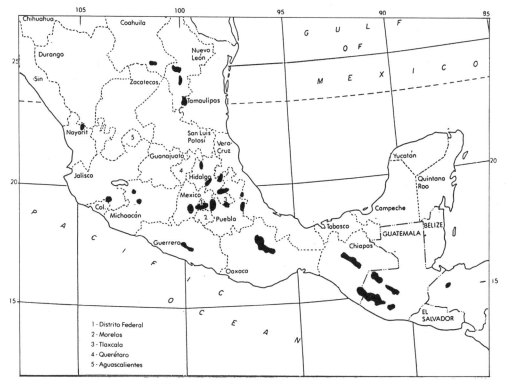

Fig. 3.39. Distribution of *P. rudis*.

below freezing, and snow and sleet are common during the winter months of November–February. In Mexico it is often found in association with *P. montezumae, P. hartwegii, P. ayacahuite* var. *brachyptera* (in northern Mexico), and *Abies* sp. In Guatemala I found it growing with *P. montezumae, P. hartwegii, P. Donnell-Smithii, P. ayacahuite, P. pseudostrobus, Abies* spp. and *Cupressus lusitanica*.

WHERE TO FIND *P. rudis*—I found the species growing on the upper slopes of a number of Mexico's very high mountains. In northeastern Mexico near Monterrey, an interesting collection trip would be to drive west to Saltillo, then south on Highway MEX 57 for about 120 km to the village of San Roberto, where a large Pemex station on the left indicates a turn off on Highway 60. Drive east about 28 km to a small, paved road that turns left to the town of Galeana. There is a small hotel at the town, so make arrangements for a guide to go with you the next day on a winding, steep, rocky trail up to the peak of Cerro Potosí, just a few kilometers from Galeana. *P. rudis* trees will be found at about 2,500 m altitude growing

in an open pure stand. Only attempt the trip with a guide and in a high-clearance vehicle. The trail is very rocky and narrow, so take an adequate supply of gasoline and water and tires that are in excellent condition. Of course, be sure to return well before sunset.

Further south near Mexico City, another very fine collection area is on the upper slopes of the Nevada de Toluca. Drive west from Mexico City on Highway 15 to the city of Toluca. There inquire for directions to the snow-capped mountain, Nevada de Toluca, only a few kilometers from the city. Since the road up the mountain is generally in good condition, a guide is probably not needed here. Follow the road up the slopes to about 3,000 m altitude. *P. rudis* will be found growing with *P. montezumae* and *P. hartwegii*.

Nearer Mexico City the species can be found on the slopes of the two famous snow-capped peaks, Popocatepetl and Ixtaccihuatl. Drive to the town of Amecameca and ask for directions to the road leading up the mountains. Follow the road up the mountain slopes to 2,800–3,000 m altitude. Here the species occurs as roadside trees often mingled with *P. montezumae, P. pseudostrobus, P. hartwegii* and *Abies religiosa.*

In Guatemala I found very fine trees northeast of Highway CA 1. At a major crossroads called Cuatro Caminos, turn northeastward on a paved road for about 15–20 km. *P. rudis* is found as roadside trees along this highway. Also on Highway CA 1 at kilometer 168 southwest of the highway, look for a high hill (3,000 m) at roadside with scattered pines on the summit. *P. rudis* forms part of this open group of trees.

NOTES AND COMMENTS—Some taxonomists and botanists consider *P. rudis* synonymous with *P. montezumae.* From many field and laboratory observations, I believe that *P. rudis* should be given specific status.

The differences between the two taxa listed in Table 3.13 support this belief.

Table 3.13. Differences between *P. montezumae* and *P. rudis.*

Characteristic	*P. montezumae*	*P. rudis*
Leaves	15–25 (to 30) cm long, ∿ 0.7mm thick; erect to drooping, not incurved	10–15 (to 17) cm long ∿ 1.0–1.5mm thick; erect, stiff, incurved, not drooping
Cones	12–15cm long, mostly ovoid to long-ovoid; light brown to lustrous brown color; not resinous	12–15cm long, mostly long-ovoid, tapering toward the apex and the base; brownish-purple, often resinous
Cone scales	Thick, stiff, strong, apophysis raised, subpyramidal	Thin, flexible, not stiff, apophysis slightly raised, not subpyramidal
Cotyledons	6, 7, and 8, mostly 6 and 7	4, 5, 6, and 7, mostly 5 and 6
Habitat	*P. montezumae* is generally found at 1,700–3,000m (occasionally up to 3,400m)	*P. rudis* is found at 2,000–3,300m (up to 3,400m); in general, somewhat higher than *P. montezumae*
Turpentine chemistry	Very high levels of α-pinene (85–95%) with only minor amounts of other terpenes	Medium levels of α-pinene but also with medium levels of β-pinene and limonene

Pinus Donnell-Smithii Masters

Pino, Ocote

THE TREE—A medium-size pine up to 25 m high, the lower branches horizontal and upper branches ascending, the crown dense and somewhat pyramidal. In young trees the branches are ascending and the crown is dense and pyramidal.

BARK—In mature trees dark brown, thick, with deep longitudinal furrows that form rough, scaly ridges. In young trees the bark is brown, rough and scaly.

BRANCHLETS—Thick, stiff, upright, brown; bases of the leaf bracts are decurrent.

LEAVES—In fascicles of 5, 6 and occasionally 7; stiff, erect, 1.0–1.25 mm thick and 15–22 cm long (occasionally 25); stomata present on the dorsal and ventral surfaces, the margins finely serrate; resin canals 1–5, medial, in many leaves resin canals are absent; fibrovascular bundles 2 and quite distinct. Fascicle sheaths pale brown, about 2 cm long, not deciduous.

CONELETS—Borne singly and in pairs on short, thick, stout, reflexed peduncles, the small conelets dark brown and cylindrical in form.

CONES—Dark brown, almost symmetrical, oblong-ovoid, 10–13 cm long, borne singly and in pairs on thick, stiff, reflexed peduncles about 10 mm long. They

P. Donnell-Smithii Tree   Bark   Branchlet, cones, and leaves   Tree showing form of crown
Thanks to Willy Mittak.

mature during the winter months, open soon afterward and are semi-persistent. When the cones fall, the stout peduncle generally remains attached to the branchlet but seldom do any basal cone scales remain attached to the peduncle.

CONE SCALES—Rather thin and somewhat stiff; the apophyses slightly raised to subpyramidal, occasionally almost flat, transversely keeled; the umbo dorsal, clearly defined, slightly raised, usually dark and bearing a stout, persistent prickle.

SEED—Grayish brown, spotted; about 6 mm long, vaguely triangular; the seed wing articulate, 17–22 mm long, 7–9 mm wide and a very pale, translucent brown.

WOOD—Hard, heavy, resinous, pale yellowish white. I found it only occasionally cut for firewood.

DISTRIBUTION—*P. Donnell-Smithii* has been reported only in Guatemala in the departments of Quezaltenango, Totonicapán, Chimaltenango, Sololá, Sacatepequez, El Quiché and Guatemala (Fig. 3.40). Possibly it also occurs in San Marcos on the high slopes of Volcán Tacana and in Huehuetenango. I have not found the species in Mexico.

HABITAT—The species grows at 3,000–3,700 m on slopes of the very high mountains in Guatemala. Frosts, snow and sleet are quite common at those elevations particularly during December, January and February. Although weather stations are not maintained consistently at those alti-

Fig. 3.40. Distribution of *P. Donnell-Smithii.*

tudes, annual rainfall is estimated at 1,000–2,000 mm; soils are deep, well-drained, with a very high percentage of volcanic ash. Associated pines are *P. hartwegii, P. rudis* and occasionally *P. ayacahuite.*

WHERE TO FIND *P. Donnell-Smithii*—I found this species growing in the Maria Tecun mountains in the department of Totonicapán at altitudes of 3,100–3,300 m. It has also been collected on the slopes of Volcán de Fuego and Volcán de Agua at about 3,700 m. Directions for reaching those areas are already given under *P. hartwegii.* Still another collection area, and one that is more accessible, can be found by driving west from Guatemala City on Highway CA 1 to kilometer 168. At that point, a narrow trail turns left off the highway; follow this for about 2 km then climb the steep slope on the right. High up on the ridge at about 3,200 m are scattered pines; *P. Donnell-Smithii* will be found there mingled with *P. hartwegii* and *P. rudis*.

NOTES AND COMMENTS—*P. Donnell-Smithii* was described by Masters in 1891 from a specimen collected in Guatemala on the slopes of Volcán de Agua at about 3,700 m. Later botanists listed it with a number of species as synonymous with *P. montezumae*. Based on my own field observations and collections, I believe that this taxon is quite different from *P. montezumae* and merits classification as a separate species. *P.*

Donnell-Smithii is closely related to *P. hartwegii* and *P. rudis* and at times it is difficult to separate the three taxa in the field. Table 3.14 will be helpful in that regard.

One final note on this interesting species; in describing a specimen collected on Volcán de Agua, Guatemala, J. Donnell Smith (1891), pointed out that resin canals were very few to completely absent. W. L. Mittak (pers. comm.) also found many needles without resin canals in specimens that he collected in the Sta. Maria Tecun Mountains, department of Totonicapán, Guatemala.

Table 3.14. Distinguishing characteristics of *P. Donnell-Smithii*, *P. hartwegii*, and *P. rudis*.

Species	Bark	Leaves	Cones	Cone scales
P. Donnell-Smithii	Dark brown, deeply furrowed but not formed into plates	Stiff, 15–22cm long, 1.0–1.25mm wide; in fascicles of 5 & 6, occasionally 7; resin canals 1–5, medial; often absent	Dark brown oblong–ovoid, 10–13cm long, reflexed on thick peduncles that remain on the branch without basal cone scales when the cone falls	Apophyses slightly raised to sub-pyramidal; the umbo also slightly raised with a persistent stout prickle
P. hartwegii	Reddish-brown, large, scaly plates formed by narrow horizontal and vertical fissures	Thick, stiff 1.5mm wide, erect, 10–16cm long, in fascicles of 3 and often 4 and 5; resin canals 2–12 medial, occasionally 1 or 2 internal	Purple to almost black, ∿10cm long, ovoid, generally erect, the peduncle remains on the branchlet with basal cone scales when the cone falls	Apophyses flat; the umbo flat to depressed, the very small prickle early deciduous
P. rudis	Grayish-brown; small, thick, geometrically-shaped plates	In fascicles of 4 and 5; thick, 1.0–1.5mm wide, erect, 10–15cm long, curved inward, in small groups at the ends of the branchlets; resin canals 3–6, medial	Dark, purplish, 10–15cm, long-ovoid, tapering to the apex of the cone; the peduncle remaining attached to the branchlet with a few basal cone scales when the cone falls	Apophyses flat to slightly raised; the umbo flat to slightly raised, the prickle, small and soon deciduous

Pinus hartwegii Lindl.

Hartweg Pine, Pino, Ocote

THE TREE—A large pine 20–30 m high and up to 1 m in diameter; in mature trees the lower branches are large, thick and drooping, higher in the crown they are horizontal to slightly ascending forming a thick, rounded crown. Young trees have a pyramidal form with a dense crown.

BARK—On old, mature trees, reddish brown, thick and divided by narrow, vertical and horizontal fissures into large, flat, scaly plates. Young trees have rough, furrowed bark but it is not divided into plates.

BRANCHLETS—Thick, stiff, erect, rough and brown; bases of the leaf bracts are prominent and decurrent.

LEAVES—Generally in fascicles of 3 but often in fascicles of 4 and 5; thick, stiff, erect, 8–16 cm long, occasionally 5–8 cm, borne in groups or clusters at the ends of the branchlets. Margins of the leaves are finely serrate, stomata present on the dorsal and ventral surfaces; resin canals variable in number from 3 to 12, usually 6 or 7, medial with occasionally 1 or 2 internal; exterior walls of the endoderm are thin, occasionally slightly thickened, fibrovascular bundles 2, very close together, distinct and often with a number of contiguous re-enforcing cells. Fascicle sheaths are persistent, brown and 10–15 mm long.

CONELETS—Oblong-ovoid, dark purple color, in clusters of 2–6 on stout, scaly peduncles.

CONES—Long-ovoid, almost symmetrical, slightly curved, generally about 8–10 cm long, though occasionally up to 17 cm (Nevada de Colima); borne in pairs and groups of 3, 4 and 5 on very short (5–10 mm), stout peduncles almost hidden by basal scales of the cone. The cones have a distinctive dark purple, almost black color, open when mature during the winter months and are semi-persistent; when they fall the peduncle with a few basal cone scales remains attached to the branchlet.

CONE SCALES—Thin,weak, flexible, the apophyses flattened, transversely keeled; the umbo dorsal, flat to depressed, very dark, the small prickle fragile but persistent.

SEED—Almost black, about 5 mm long, the seed wing articulate, pale brown, 10–11 mm long, cotyledons number 5–6, mostly 5.

WOOD—Hard, heavy, resinous, the sapwood yellowish white, heartwood light brown. Since this species grows at very high elevations it has not been logged as intensively as those species found at lower, more accessible levels. Still, as the pine forests diminish, the loggers are reaching even these high-altitude forests. The trees are cut and sawn into lumber and timbers for construction along with *P. montezumae, P. leiophylla, P. rudis* and *P. pseudostrobus* (these species all found at lower elevations).

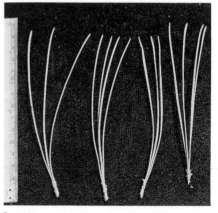

P. *hartwegii* Tree   Bark   Cones and seeds   Leaves

DISTRIBUTION—In Mexico, *P. hartwegii* has been reported growing in Nuevo León, Tamaulipas, Hidalgo, Puebla, Veracruz, Tlaxcala, Mexico, the Federal District, Morelos, Colima, Michoacán, Jalisco, Oaxaca and Chiapas. In Guatemala it has been reported in the departments of Huehuetenango, Totonicapán, Quezaltenango, Quiché, Sololá, San Marcos, Chimaltenango, Sacatepequez and Gautemala (Fig. 3.41). It has also been reported to occur in Honduras on Cerro Santa Bárbara. This mountain attains a height of about 2,800 m and the specimen cited was collected at 2,750 m and described as follows: leaves 15–20 cm long, stiff, stout and in fascicles of 5; the 2 cones were 7–8 cm long, the apophyses dark brown; the umbo slightly raised and blackish. I believe those pines are probably *P. rudis,* not *P. hartwegii.* The species has also been reported as occurring in El Salvador. I was not able to find it in the collection area noted or on other mountain slopes along the El Salvador-Honduras border. There are still many relatively unexplored high mountains along the Honduras-El Salvador border and *P. hartwegii,* along with other

unreported species, may occur on those mountain peaks.

HABITAT—*P. hartwegii* grows at very high altitudes often forming pure forests at 3,000–3,700 m. On the high, snow-capped mountain peaks of Mexico, this species is the only pine to grow at timberline. At those elevations temperature falls below freezing every month and snowfall and sleet are common throughout the year. Apparently very strong winds accompany the snow and sleet storms since I found on a number of mountain peaks, large trees with their tops broken and shattered by the wind.

WHERE TO FIND *P. hartwegii*—This species grows on the snow-capped mountains of Mexico, Nevada de Colima, Cerro Potosí, Peña Nevada, Popocatepetl, Ixtaccihuatl, Nevada de Toluca, La Malinche and Orizaba. In the preceding pages I have described how to reach Cerro Potosí, "Popo," "Sleeping Lady" and Nevada de Toluca. Still another collection area that is very accessible and not far from Mexico City is the "super highway" from Mexico City to Cuernavaca. At the highest point on the highway, near the village of Tres Cumbres, look for open stands of pines and

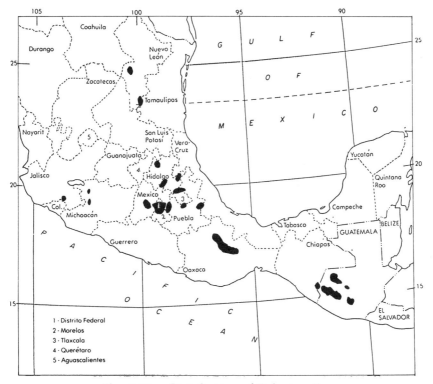

Fig. 3.41. Distribution of *P. hartwegii.*

grasslands along the highway. The pines will generally be *P. hartwegii* and *P. rudis* growing together. Also near Mexico City, the highway from Mexico City to Puebla passes through very high pine forests; near the village of Ajusco (about 3,200 m) look for open pine forests and grassland, the pines are mostly *P. hartwegii* and *P. rudis*. In Guatemala I collected the species near the city of Totonicapán in the Maria Tecun Mountains. A winding rocky trail leads eastward into very high mountains and a guide will be needed because of the many crisscrossing mountain trails. Attempt this trip only with a high-clearance vehicle, very good tires and a good supply of gasoline. Fairly extensive stands are also found on the high slopes of Volcán de Agua and Volcán de Fuego. From Guatemala City drive to the village of Atotenango, at that point you are about midway between the two volcanoes. Find a guide who can take you on a trail to the slopes of one or both volcanoes and be prepared for a long, hard climb on foot up to the forests at 3,500 m.

NOTES AND COMMENTS—I have always admired this pine because of its ability to survive in such a harsh environment. The ability to grow into a fine tree at an altitude of 3,500–3,700 m should be of value to tree breeders and silviculturists interested in reforesting high mountain slopes in many areas of the world. *P. hartwegii* is closely related to *P. rudis*, and I found evidence of hybridization where the two species overlap near the summit of Cerro Potosí, just below timberline on "Popo" and "Sleeping Lady" and high on the slopes of Nevada de Toluca.

Subsection Michoacana

This group is made up of a number of closely related taxa all easily recognized by their long, thick needles and a "grass stage" during the early growth of the seedlings. Table 3.15 lists distinguishing features of this group.

Table 3.15.   Characteristics of Species in Subsection Michoacana.

Species	Leaves per fascicle and length, cm	Cone length, cm	Fascicle sheath
P. michoacana	5; 25–35	20–30	Brown to black; resinous
P. michoacana var. *cornuta*	5; 25–30	15–30	Dark brown; resinous
P. michoacana var. *quevedoi*	6 (5); 20–35	20	Brown to black; resinous
P. michoacana forma *procera*	5; 30	23–27	Dark brown; resinous
P. michoacana forma *nayaritana*	5; 30–37	21	Dark brown; resinous

Pinus michoacana Mart.

Pino Lacio, Michoacán Pine

THE TREE—A large pine 20–30 m high and up to 1 m in diameter. When growing in a closed forest the trunk is generally straight and clear of branches up to a small, dense, rounded crown. In more open forests the branches are lower, drooping to horizontal, and the crown is pyramidal.

BARK—On mature trees the bark is formed in thick, brown, scaly plates; on young trees it is brown, rough and scaly but not plated.

BRANCHLETS—Rough, thick, stiff, the bark dark brown; bases of the leaf bracts are decurrent.

LEAVES—In fascicles of 5, rarely 6; 25–35 cm long, thick, fairly flexible, occasionally erect, more often slightly drooping; the margins finely serrate, stomata present on the dorsal and ventral surfaces; resin canals 3, occasionally 4, medial; fibrovascular bundles 2, distinct but close together; fascicle sheaths 20–30 mm long, dark brown, often almost black with a "sooty" appearance, often sticky and always persistent.

CONELETS—Oblong, often light purple; borne singly, in pairs and groups of three, the small scales thick and bearing a short, sharp prickle; the peduncles are thick, strong, erect and very scaly.

CONES—Oblong-ovate to oblong-cylindrical, almost symmetrical, straight to slightly curved, 20–30 cm long, light brown, borne mostly in twos and threes on very short (∼ 15 mm), barely visible peduncles that remain attached to the branchlet with a few basal cone scales when the cone falls. The cones open at maturity (December and January) and are semi-persistent after the seeds are shed.

CONE SCALES—Hard, strong, thick; the apophyses raised, pyramidal, (more so on the scales at the base of the cone) with a well-defined transverse keel; the umbo slightly depressed, ashy gray bearing a small, deciduous prickle.

SEEDS—Rather triangular in shape, 5–6 mm long and 3–4 mm wide with dark spots; the seed wing articulate, about 20 mm long and 8–9 mm wide, pale brown with darker striations. Cotyledons number 7–10, mostly 8 and 9.

WOOD—Yellowish white, the heartwood pale brown; hard, heavy, only moderately resinous; the trees are cut along with *P. montezumae, P. pseudostrobus, P. leiophylla* and *P. maximinoi* and sold for general construction purposes.

DISTRIBUTION—*P. michoacana* has quite a wide range, extending from central Mexico to central Guatemala (Fig. 3.42). In Mexico it is found in the states of Nayarit, Zacatecas, Jalisco, Colima, Michoacán, Hidalgo, Mexico, Puebla, Morelos,

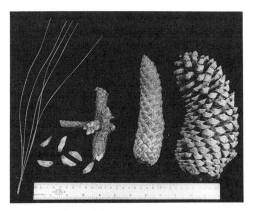

Cones, seeds, and leaves

P. michoacana Tree   Bark

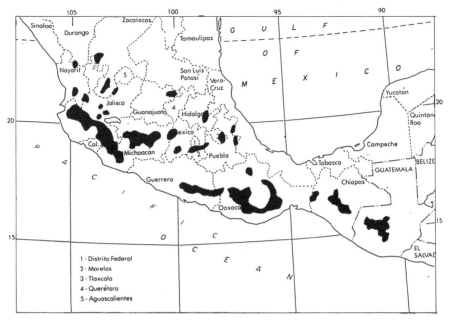

Fig. 3.42.   Distribution of *P. michoacana.*

Guanajuato, Tlaxcala, Guerrero, Oaxaca, Veracruz and Chiapas. In Guatemala I found it in the departments of Totonicapán, Quiché, Quezaltenango, Chimaltenango, Sacatepequez and Guatemala.

HABITAT—This species occurs in warm-temperate zones at altitudes that range from 1,500–2,500 m. I have collected specimens as high as 3,000 m, but the trees appear to make their best growth at about 2,000 m. I found very fine stands of *P. michoacana* growing in the forests of Michoacán with *P. montezumae, P. pseudostrobus, P. leiophylla, P. maximinoi* and *P. douglasiana.* Rainfall at the altitudes cited here (Michoacán and the volcanic axis) is about 1,000 mm annually; temperatures fall to freezing during the winter months (January is the coldest month) with occasional rain and snow. Most rainfall occurs during the summer months of June, July, August and September; the hottest month is May. Further south in Chiapas and Guatemala, the climate is slightly warmer though the species is found at about the same elevations. Most rainfall occurs during the summer months June, July, August and September and varies from 1,000 to 1,500 mm annually. I found the species often growing with *P. montezumae, P. oocarpa* var. *ochoterenai, P. oaxacana* and *P. pseudostrobus.*

WHERE TO FIND *P. michoacana*—In Mexico the species is fairly common and collections can be made easily from roadside trees in the area near the city of Uruapan, Michoacán. I found fine trees north of the city on Highway 37 toward the town of Cherán. Nearer Mexico City take a relatively short drive to the city of Pachuca, then go northeast on Highway 105 for about 20 km to a narrow paved road on the right that leads to the town of Huasca. Before reaching Huasca the road passes through a small pine forest known as "El Ocotal". Here I found fine *P. michoacana* trees at altitudes of 2,300 m, growing with *P. montezumae* and *P. teocote.* A number of these trees had leaves in fascicles of 5, 6 and 7 and a few trees had cones that were intermediate between *P. montezumae* and *P. michoacana.*

Another very interesting collection area is the volcano Cofre de Perote in Veracruz State. This is about the easternmost occurrence of the species in Mexico. Drive to the city of Puebla and take Highway 140 east toward Jalapa. About 55 km before reaching Jalapa, look for the volcano off to the right. I found very fine pines growing low on the slopes and within walking distance of the highway. In Guatemala the species is not difficult to find in some areas. Fine, typical trees were found at roadside on Highway CA 1, km 57 east from Guatemala City. This was a small, pure stand of young trees with fine reproduction. It was interesting to note that pollen was being shed by the trees on the first of May. I also found many trees along Highway 15 from Sololá to Chicicastenango, north of the town Los Encuentros.

NOTES AND COMMENTS—This species is not difficult to identify in the field since the unusually long, straight (in one variety, curved) cones and very long leaves are very distinctive. Anyone who has seen *Pinus palustris* (Long-Leaf Pine) in the southeastern United States will be amazed at the similar growth form of the two species,

particularly in the young trees about 8–10 years old. *P. michoacana* is closely related to *P. montezumae,* and I found what appeared to be hybrid trees where the populations overlap in an area near the town of Cherán, Michoacán and near Huasca, Hidalgo. The pronounced "grass stage" in young trees of *P. michoacana, P. montezumae* and *P. palustris* is an interesting example of a similar adaptation (perhaps to ground fires) by three different species of pines, two of the species closely related. I do not know of any attempts to cross *P. michoacana* with *P. palustris,* but this would make a very interesting experiment and one that, if successful, might shed light on the evolutionary history of these pines.

Pinus michoacana forma *tumida* Mart.

This taxon was described in 1948 by Prof. Matínez as having cones 17 cm long and scales with a prominent, rounded apophysis. He noted that it had been observed in Oaxaca (the type collected at Telixtlahuaca), Guerrero and Chiapas.

NOTES AND COMMENTS In collecting *P. michoacana* and its varieties and forms, I

have found many cones that resemble the cones described above. I believe these forms are part of recurring, variable populations that intergrade into the species, varieties and forms recognized here. The characters described above do not, in my opinion, justify a separate classification for this taxon.

Pinus michoacana var. *corunta* Mart.

Pino Blanco, Ocote Escobeton, Pino Prieto

THE TREE—A fine, well-formed pine 20–30 m high and 50–75 cm in diameter, the lower branches long, somewhat drooping, the upper branches ascending forming a dense rounded crown. In young trees the crown is open and pyramidal.

BARK—Dark grayish brown, in thick, almost geometrical plates formed by vertical and horizontal fissures. In young trees the bark is also rough, brown but not plated.

BRANCHLETS—Thick, stout, stiff, very rough and scaly, dark brown, bases of the leaf bracts are decurrent.

LEAVES—In fascicles of 5 rarely 6; 25–30

cm long, occasionally longer, thick (occasionally slender) flexible, slightly drooping, the margins finely serrate, stomata present on the dorsal and ventral surfaces; resin canals 3 and 4 occasionally 5, mostly medial (occasionally 1 internal), exterior walls of the endoderm thickened; fibrovascular bundles 2, quite distinct; fascicle sheaths persistent, about 30 mm long, dark brown, often resinous.

CONELETS—Reddish purple, long-cylindrical, the small scales thick with a small pointed prickle; they are borne singly, in pairs and groups of 3 and 4 on stout, scaly

P. michoacana var. *cornuta* Tree   Bark   Branchlet, cones, and leaves

peduncles.

CONES—Long, 15–30 cm, mostly about 20 cm, tapering toward the apex, asymmetrical, curved, occasionally almost straight, reflexed, yellowish brown; borne singly, in pairs and groups of 3–4 on short (about 10 mm), stout peduncles that generally remain attached to the cone when it falls. The cones ripen during the winter months, open when mature and are semipersistent after the seeds are shed.

CONE SCALES—Stiff, strong, hard, slightly resinous; the apophyses raised to pyramidal, particularly on the upper side of the cone, transversely keeled; the umbo often grayish brown, raised, bearing a small, persistent, recurved prickle.

SEEDS—Somewhat triangular in shape, 6–7 mm long, the seed wing articulate, about 25 mm long. Cotyledons are mostly 8.

WOOD—Creamy white, the heartwood light brown, hard and heavy, only moderately resinous; trees are cut and sawn along with associated species, *P. montezumae*, *P. pseudostrobus*, *P. michoacana* and *P. douglasiana*.

DISTRIBUTION—Var. *cornuta* has a wide range quite similar to that of *P. michoacana* (Fig. 3.43). In Mexico it occurs in the states of Nayarit, Zacatecas, Guanajuato, Jalisco, Colima, Michoacán, Mexico, Hidalgo, Morelos, Puebla, Veracruz, Oaxaca, Guemeno and Chiapas. In Guatemala I found it growing with *P. michoacana* in the departments of Totonicapán, Quiché, Quezaltenango, Chimaltenango, Sacatepe-

quez and Guatemala.

HABITAT—The habitat description for *P. michoacana* also applies to var. *cornuta*. However, my observations indicate that var. *cornuta* is often found at somewhat lower elevations (1,500–2,000 m) than most populations of *P. michoacana*. I found the best populations along Mexico's Volcanic Axis, particularly in Michoacán mostly at 1,800–2,000 m altitude; rainfall and temperature conditions are about the same as those for the species.

WHERE TO FIND var. *cornuta*—As pointed out earlier, this variety is found growing throughout its range with *P. michoacana*. In the area around Uruapan, Michoacán, it can be found as roadside trees along many of the paved roads. In Guatemala I found many trees near the highway from Los Encuentros to Chichicastenango.

NOTES AND COMMENTS—A number of conservative botanists do not recognize this variety. Although *P. michoacana* and var. *cornuta* are indeed quite similar in many respects, I believe that the strongly curved cones of var. *cornuta* and the pyramidal apophyses with raised umbo bearing a recurved, persistent prickle (in *P. michoacana* the umbo is usually depressed and the prickle is weak and deciduous) justify its classification as a variety. Further confirming the validity of varietal status for var. *cornuta* was my finding of very significant differences between turpentine (from xylem oleoresin) of the two taxa. In *P.*

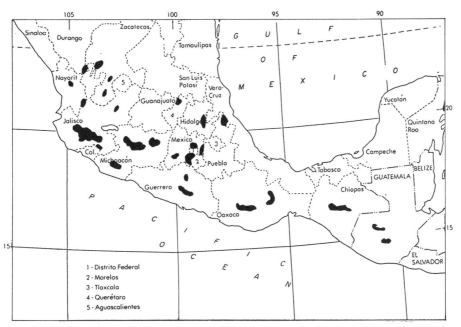

Fig. 3.43. Distribution of *P. michoacana* var. *cornuta.*

michoacana analysis revealed an average of 60% β-pinene (% of total turpentine) while in var. *cornuta* an average of only 3% β-pinene was obtained. Differences in α-pinene were also highly significant; in *P.* *michoacana* α-pinene averaged 35% while in var. *cornuta* it averaged 88%. Obviously these data are not helpful in field identification of the two taxa; however, they do add to our knowledge of the species and variety.

Pinus michoacana var. *quevedoi* Mart.

Pino, Ocote, Pino Blanco

THE TREE—A medium-size pine 15–25 m high, generally about 20 m, with a rather limby trunk 50–80 cm diameter, the branches large, horizontal to ascending, forming a dense rounded crown.

BARK—On old mature trees dark reddish brown, divided into rectangular, scaly plates by deep, almost black, horizontal and vertical fissures. On young trees the bark is dark reddish brown, rough and formed into ridges by vertical fissures.

BRANCHLETS—Dark brown, rough, scaly, thick and stiff; the bases of the leaf bracts decurrent.

LEAVES—In fascicles of 5–6, mostly 6, pale green, 20–35 cm long, thick, about 2 mm wide, stiff, mostly erect, occasionally slightly drooping, the margins finely ser-

rate; stomata on dorsal and ventral surfaces; resin canals 3–6, medial with occasionally one internal, exterior walls of the endoderm thickened; fibrovascular bundles 2, distinct. Sheaths are persistent, 3–4 cm long, dark brown to almost black and sticky.

CONELETS—Oblong-cylindrical, light purple, the small scales thick, pointed, bearing a small recurved prickle. They are borne singly or in pairs, and groups of 3 on short, stout, scaly peduncles.

CONES—Long-cylindrical, tapering slightly toward the apex of the cone; slightly curved, asymmetrical. Before maturing they are a pale yellowish green color. When mature they become light ochre to pale brown; about 20 cm long on short (10 mm), stout peduncles; they open when mature

P. michoacana **var.** *quevedoi* Tree   Bark   Cones, seeds, and leaves

(December and January) and are semi-persistent.

CONE SCALES—Thick, stiff, strong, the apophyses transversely keeled, pyramidal; the umbo dorsal, small, greenish gray, slightly raised and bearing a small, persistent, recurved prickle.

SEEDS—Somewhat triangular in shape, 7–8 mm long and about 6 mm wide, the seed wing articulate, generally pale brown and about 25 mm long.

WOOD—Hard, strong; the sapwood yellowish white, the heartwood pale brown. The trees are cut with *P. teocote*, *P. montezumae* and *P. michoacana* for construction timbers and fuelwood.

DISTRIBUTION—Prof. Martínez (1948) described this variety from a specimen collected in San Luis Potosí State, Mexico, and did not mention specimens from any other state. I found a few old trees on the mountain slopes near Zaragosa, S. L. Potosí, that fit Prof. Martínez' description, and on another trip found a few large trees growing near the village of Huasca, Hidalgo. Possibly its range is limited to the states of San Luis Potosí and Hidalgo (Fig. 3.44).

HABITAT—At both locations the trees were growing at 2,300 m altitude. In S. L. Potosí the site was a rocky, well-drained slope, and rainfall probably amounted to about 800–1,000 mm annually. Near Huasca, annual rainfall is about 1,000–1,5000 mm. At both locations frosts are common during the winter months, i.e. November through February. Most rainfall

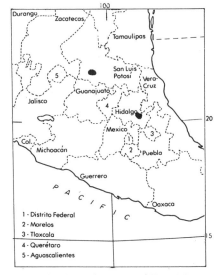

Fig. 3.44.   Distribution of *P. michoacana* var. *quevedoi*.

occurs during the summer months, June, July, August and September.

WHERE TO FIND var. *quevedoi*—The few trees that I found near the village of Huasca, Hidalgo are easily reached via Highway 105 northeast from Pachuca, the capital of Hidalgo. Drive for 20–25 km and look for a narrow paved road turning off to the right. Before reaching the village of Huasca (8 km) the road passes through a small pine forest. Var. *quevedoi* can be found growing with *P. teocote*, *P. montezumae* and *P. michoacana*.

NOTES AND COMMENTS—I am hesitant to list this taxon as a variety of *P. michoacana*.

However, the shorter cones (20 cm as compared to 25–30 cm in *P. michoacana*), the more pyramidal apophyses with recurved prickles and the very thick (up to 2 mm), often erect leaves in fascicles of 6 probably warrant its varietal status. Analysis of its turpentine would also be helpful and might reveal significant differences between the two taxa.

Pinus michoacana forma *procera* Mart.

Professor Martínez described forma *procera* in 1948 and noted that needles are 30 cm long and cones 23–27 cm long with unusually long (7 cm), wide (27 mm) scales, the apophysis slightly raised; the umbo large and erect and the apical margin with distinct projections. He reported that this taxon had been observed in Jalisco, Michoacán and Oaxaca.

NOTES AND COMMENTS—I collected cones of this type in Jalisco north of Guadalajara at 1,600 m altitude and observed trees with similar cones near Tancítaro, Michoacán at 1,150 m altitude. Stem oleoresin was collected at both locations. Subsequent analysis revealed that turpentine from the two populations was almost identical and, more importantly, quite different from turpentine of *P. michoacana* var. *cornuta* and significantly different from turpentine of *P. michoacana*. The turpentine of var. *cornuta* is ∿ 88% α-pinene with very small amounts of β-pinene and Limonene; *P. michoacana* turpentine is ∿ 35% α-pinene, 60% β-pinene and 2% Limonene; forma *procera* turpentine is ∿ 33% α-pinene, 40% β-pinene and 4% Limonene.

More extensive collections of cones, needles and turpentine may well indicate that this taxon should be raised to varietal status.

P. michoacana **forma** *procera* Tree   Bark

Branchlet, cones, and leaves

Pinus michoacana var. *cornuta* forma *nayaritana* Mart.

Prof. Martínez described this form in 1948 and stated that it differs from var. *cornuta* in its more slender leaves 30–37 cm long and dark brown cone, conical, tapering toward the apex and toward the base, ∿ 21 cm long; the scales more numerous, with the apophyses raised (7 mm) and reflexed, bearing a prominent umbo with a straight persistent prickle. He mentioned that collections were made only in the state of Nayarit, Mexico.

NOTES AND COMMENTS—Years ago I collected cones and needles from an occasional tree in Morelos and Michoacán that were similar to the description above. More recently (1987) Prof. J. Alberto de la Rosa showed me a small stand of trees near the town of Xalisco, Nayarit, that seemed to fit Martínez' description of forma *nayaritana*.

Cones were rather variable in size but similar to Martínez' description. Needles were not unusual except that there were a number of fascicles with 6 needles rather than the usual number of 5. Samples of oleoresin were taken and their subsequent analysis appears to place this taxon between *P. michoacana* and *P. michoacana* forma *procera*.

Analyses of turpentine from the three taxa are approximately as shown in the following table.

From these analyses forma *nayaritana* appears to be closely related to forma *procera*; however, more extensive collections should be made of oleoresin and cones and foliage in order to determine whether or not these observations warrant varietal classification of this taxon.

	% Turpentine		
	α-pinene	β-pinene	Limonene
P. michoacana	35	60	2
forma procera	33	40	4
forma nayaritana	58	27	6

Cone and seeds

P. michoacana var. cornuta forma nayaritana Tree

Bark

Branchlet, cone, and leaves

Section Pseudostrobus

Trees in this group are readily distinguished from the other diploxylon pines by their smooth branchlets (bases of the needle bracts are not decurrent), the smooth upper stem of mature trees, and smooth stems of young trees. The section is divided into two groups, Subsection Pseudostrobus and Subsection Oaxacana. The species included in Subsection Pseudostrobus generally do not have the light hydrocarbons Heptane, Octane and Nonane present in their turpentine while species in Subsection Oaxacana have relatively large amounts of Heptane and Nonane with Octane often absent or occasionally present in small amounts.

There are also important morphological differences between the two groups and a few of these are listed in Table 3.16.

Table 3.16. Differences between Pseudostrobus and Oaxacana subsections.

Subsection	Cone scales	Umbo
Pseudostrobus	Generally thin and flexible	Small, often flat to depressed except in *P. pseudostrobus* forma *protuberans*
Oaxacana	Thick, hard and stiff	Raised to prominent except in *P. nubicola*

Subsection Pseudostrobus

I have included two species and two forms in this group. They are listed in Table 3.17 with some of their important botanical characteristics.

Table 3.17. Characteristics of Species in Subsection Pseudostrobus.

Species	Cone length, cm; form	Cone scales	Peduncle
P. pseudostrobus	8–10; ovoid almost symmetrical	Thin, only medium hard and stiff	Short, stout not oblique
P. pseudostrobus forma *protuberans*	12–14; long ovoid, symmetrical	Thin, not hard and stiff	Short almost sessile, not oblique
P. pseudostrobus forma *megacarpa*	15–18; curved and tapering	Thin, flexible	Short, stout, not oblique
P. maximinoi	5–8; long ovate, oblique	Thin, flexible	Stout, very oblique

Pinus pseudostrobus Lindl.

Pino, Pino Blanco, Ocote

THE TREE—This is one of Mexico's finest pines reaching heights of 30–40 m and occasionally 45 m. I saw trees in Michoacán more than 1 m in diameter though most trees range from 40–80 cm in diameter. The trunk is usually straight and clear of branches for 20–30 m in the very large trees. Branches are mostly horizontal and in mature trees form a rounded crown. Young trees have a rather open, pyramidal form with widely spaced branches.

BARK—Mature trees have thick, dark

P. pseudostrobus Tree   Bark   Branchlet, cones, and leaves   Cone and seeds

brown bark divided by deep vertical fissures into rough, scaly plates. On the upper trunk near the top, the bark becomes smooth and reddish brown. In young trees the bark is smooth and reddish to gray-brown.

BRANCHLETS—Slender, slightly up-turned, smooth; bases of leaf bracts are not decurrent.

LEAVES—In fascicles of 5, mostly slender (about 0.7–0.9 mm thick) flexible, slightly drooping, 20–25 (to 30) cm long, the margins finely serrate, stomata present on the dorsal and ventral surfaces; resin canals 2–4 mostly 3, medial; exterior walls of the endoderm thickened, fibrovascular bundles 2, contiguous but distinct. Fascicle sheaths light to dark brown, 12–15 mm long, persistent.

CONELETS—Long-conical, the small scales thick with a small, erect prickle; borne singly and in groups of 2–3 on stiff, scaly peduncles.

CONES—Ovoid to long-ovoid, slightly curved, almost symmetrical, not reflexed, 8–10 cm long and 5–7 cm wide (open). Light brown, rather lustrous, borne singly and in twos and threes on short peduncles that, when the cone falls, generally remain attached to the branch with a few basal cone scales. The cones open when mature and are soon deciduous.

CONE SCALES—Thin, only medium hard, the apophyses slightly raised to flat and lightly transversely keeled; the umbo dorsal, small, occasionally depressed, not prominent, armed with a small weak, deciduous prickle.

SEED—Small, about 6 mm long, dark brown; the seed wing articulate, 20–23 mm long; cotyledons number 6–9, mostly 8.

WOOD—Light yellow color, fairly soft but strong and slightly resinous. The trees are logged and sawn into lumber along with *P. montezumae, P. douglasiana* and *P. leiophylla.* Lumber is of good quality and widely used for general construction. Locally it is cut for hewn timbers and firewood. The trees are also tapped for resin along with *P. oocarpa, P. montezumae* and *P. douglasiana.*

DISTRIBUTION—*P. pseudostrobus* is primarily a Mexican pine although its range extends southward into Guatemala (Fig. 3.45). In Mexico it is found in Jalisco and eastward along the mountains of the Great Cross Range in the states of Michoacán, Mexico, the Federal District, Morelos, Puebla, Hidalgo, Tlaxcala, Veracruz, Oaxaca, Guerrero and Chiapas. In Guatemala it has been found in the departments of Totonicapán, Quezaltenango, Sololá, Chimaltenango, Sacatepequez and Guatemala. Some botanists indicate collections of this taxon in Nuevo León but the trees I found there all had decurrent bases of the needle bracts and thus would not fall within the Pseudostrobus group.

HABITAT—This species is found on mountain slopes at elevations of 1,600–3,200 m. Over its range rainfall is quite variable but probably averages 800–1,500 mm annually. The largest trees were found

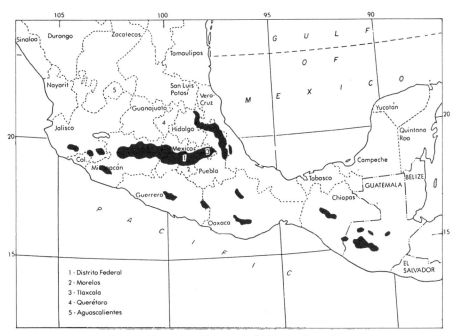

Fig. 3.45. Distribution of *P. pseudostrobus*.

at elevations of 2,000–2,400 m in western Michoacán. There they were growing on a deep volcanic soil with annual rainfall of about 1,500 mm. Over its range frost is common at the higher altitudes during December and January. At many locations in Mexico, associated species are *Abies* spp., *P. montezumae, P. douglasiana, P. michoacana, P. maximinoi* and *P. pringlei*. In southern Mexico (Oaxaca and Chiapas) *P. pseudostrobus* appears less frequently and its range ends in central Guatemala.

WHERE TO FIND *P. pseudostrobus*—Near Mexico City hire a taxi or take a bus west on Avenue Reforma to the Federal Park, Desierto de Las Leones (Reforma Avenue becomes Highway MEX 15 to Toluca). At the park there is a maze of hiking trails winding through the trees. *P. pseudostrobus* will be found growing with *P. montezumae, P. patula* and occasionally *P. ayacahuite* var. *veitchii* and *P. rudis*. If time permits, continue west on MEX 15 to Ciudad Hidalgo. About 30 km west of the city (still on MEX 15) look for very fine roadside trees. At Mil Cumbres these pines can be found in dense stands along the road.

Other very interesting areas to explore are the slopes of the twin volcanoes near Mexico City, Sleeping Lady (Ixtaccihuatl) and Popo (Popocatepetl). Drive east toward

Puebla but on the outskirts of Mexico City turn onto Highway MEX 115 toward Chalco and Amecameca. At Amecameca turn left toward the two snow-capped peaks that dominate the landscape. The road leads directly to the mountains and winds upward through forests of pine and fir. *P. pseudostrobus* will be fund growing along the road with *P. leiophylla, P. montezumae* and *P. rudis*.

NOTES AND COMMENTS—*P. pseudostrobus* and *P. montezumae* are often found growing together. Both species are 5-needled and a number of authors have mentioned that the two species probably hybridize readily under natural conditions. My own experience in the field confirms this viewpoint. About 6 km on a narrow trail above the village of Angangueo, Michoacán, I found a stand of trees that appeared to be natural hybrids between *P. montezumae* and *P. pseudostrobus*. The cones and foliage were definitely intermediate in their morphology. However, the upper trunk and branchlets were smooth. On another occasion I found a small, pure stand of trees growing near a logging road about 2 km from the village of Dos Aguas, Michoacán. Here, too, the cones and foliage possessed characters of both *P. montezumae* and *P. pseudostrobus*. Also at km 180 on

Highway MEX 15 from Zitacuaro to Morelia (near Mil Cumbres), I found many trees with large "montezumae-like" cones; however, the upper trunk and branchlets were smooth.

In any event, mature trees of both species are often magnificent specimens. Since they probably do hybridize naturally (they have been successfully crossed at the Institute for Forest Genetics, Placerville, California) it seems apparent that there is an opportunity here for the development of a "family" of outstanding hybrids.

Pinus pseudostrobus forma *protuberans* Mart.

Pino, Ocote

THE TREE—This pine has a very fine form, reaching heights of 20–30 m. The branches are large, horizontal to drooping and form a rather dense, rounded crown. Young trees have an open pyramidal crown with widely spaced branches.

BARK—Thick, rough, grayish brown and divided in uneven scaly plates. On mature trees bark on the upper trunk and branchlets is thin and smooth. In young trees the bark is smooth and grayish brown.

BRANCHLETS—Slender, somewhat drooping with the ends upturned, the bark smooth and pale greenish gray. Bases of the leaf bracts are not decurrent.

LEAVES—Borne in fascicles of 5, slender, flexible, slightly drooping, 20–25 cm long, the margins finely serrate and stomata present on the dorsal and ventral surfaces; resin canals number 2–4 and are mostly medial (Martínez (1948) mentioned a specimen from Ocampo, Michoacán with a single septal canal); exterior walls of the endoderm thickened and fibrovascular bundles 2, contiguous but distinct; fascicle sheaths brown, about 15 mm long and persistent.

CONELETS—Borne singly and in twos and threes, on stiff, scaly, erect peduncles.

CONES—Long-ovoid, symmetrical, 12–14 cm long, light lustrous brown color, borne mostly in twos and threes, almost sessile on short peduncles that generally fall with the cone. The cones open when mature and are deciduous.

CONE SCALES—Thin, not hard or strong; the apophyses flattened and the umbo projecting from the center as much as

P. *pseudostrubus* forma *protuberans* Tree   Bark   Branchlet, cone, and leaves   Cone and seeds

2–3 mm bearing a small, weak, early-deciduous prickle.

SEED—6–7 mm long, brown; the seed wing articulate, 20–22 mm long.

WOOD—Similar to that of *P. pseudostrobus*. Since forma *protuberans* grows with *P. pseudostrobus* over part of its range, the trees are cut along with *P. pseudostrobus* and *P. montezumae*.

DISTRIBUTION—Forma *protuberans* has been reported from the states of Jalisco, Michoacán, Mexico, Morelos, the Federal District and Oaxaca (Fig. 3.46). I also found a few trees near the town of Apulco (Hidalgo State) and Huauchinango (Puebla State). Thus the range of this taxon extends from Jalisco eastward along the Great Cross Range with some trees in Oaxaca.

HABITAT—Similar to that of *P. pseudostrobus*, though I never found it growing above 2,800 m altitude. Most trees were observed at 2,000–2,400 m. Associated species are often *P. pseudostrobus*, *P. montezumae*, *P. leiophylla*, *P. douglasiana*, *P. maximinoi* and *P. pseudostrobus* forma *megacarpa*.

WHERE TO FIND forma *Protuberans*—Drive west from Mexico City on Highway MEX 15. At km 183 from Toluca to Morelia, look for large roadside trees. Further west near the village of Sevina, Michoacán, I found a large population of trees at 2,500 m altitude growing with *P. montezumae*, *P. pseudostrobus* and *Quercus* sp.

NOTES AND COMMENTS—This taxon has an interesting taxonomic history. In 1857 B. Roezl & Cie. published a *Catalogue de Graines de Coniferes Mexicains* in which 82 new species of pines were described. In 1909 G. R. Shaw published *The Pines of Mexico* in which he presented the first systematic arrangement of the Mexican pines. In his book (pp. 2 & 3) Shaw listed Roezl's 82 Mexican pine species and opposite each name cited the judgment of each of three taxonomists (Carrière, Gordon and Parlatore) regarding the validity of that name (Roezl's). *Pinus protuberans* was one of those judged (No. 54 in the list). Both Carrière and Gordon

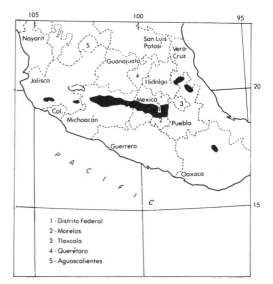

Fig. 3.46. Distribution of *P. pseudostrobus* forma *protuberans*.

agreed that *P. protuberans* was a valid name and Parlatore disagreed, referring the name to *P. pseudostrobus*. Of the three taxonomists, Shaw considered Parlatore the best qualified and apparently agreed with most of his determinations. In conclusion Shaw stated that "it may be safely assumed that there is, in the entire list of Roezl's Catalogue, not a single valid species, the six or seven Pines they represent having been described by previous authors under sixteen specific names." As an afterthought I counted Parlatore's referrals of other names (Roezl's) to *Pinus montezumae*; out of the total 82 names, Parlatore referred 45 to *P. montezumae*.

Forma *protuberans* clearly belongs in subsection Pseudostrobus and I believe is closely related to *P. pseudostrobus* and *P. pseudostrobus* forma *megacarpa*. The characteristic raised umbo on the flat apophyses makes this form fairly easy to recognize in the field. The chemistry of its turpentine is quite different from that of *P. pseudostrobus* (see my comments under forma *megacarpa*). This, along with the differences in cone morphology, has convinced me that this taxon should be given varietal status.

Pinus pseudostrobus forma *megacarpa* Loock.

Pino, Ocote

THE TREE—This pine occasionally attains heights of 30–40 m and diameters of 90–110 cm. It resembles *P. pseudostrobus* with its tall, clear trunk, horizontal branches and rounded crown.

BARK—On mature trees the bark is very thick, grayish brown and divided by deep vertical fissures into irregular scaly plates. On young trees the bark is pale brown and smooth.

BRANCHLETS—Slender, drooping, smooth greenish brown; bases of the leaf bracts are not decurrent.

LEAVES—Borne 5 in a fascicle, occasionally 6; 20–25 cm long, drooping, the margins finely serrate, stomata present on the dorsal and ventral surfaces; resin canals are 2–4, medial, exterior walls of the endoderm are thickened and fibrovascular bundles are 2, contiguous but distinct; fascicle sheaths are persistent, pale brown and about 15 mm long.

CONELETS—Borne singly and in twos and threes on erect scaly peduncles.

CONES—Oblong-conical, curved, rather oblique and tapering toward the apex. They are dull brown, 15–18 (to 20) cm long, not hard or heavy, borne singly and in pairs (mostly), on short, stiff peduncles that generally fall with the cone. The cones open when mature and are soon deciduous.

CONE SCALES—Thin, flexible, the apophyses flat to depressed with or without a small rounded umbo that bears a small, weak, early-deciduous prickle.

SEED—7–8 mm long, the seed wing articulate and about 24 mm long.

WOOD—Similar to that of *P. pseudostrobus*. The trees are felled along with *P. pseudostrobus*, *P. montezumae*, *P. maximinoi* and *P. douglasiana*. They are also tapped for turpentine along with associated pines.

DISTRIBUTION—Loock, who described this taxon in 1950, stated that he found it only on the mountains between Mil Cumbres, Monte Obscuro and Ciudad Hidalgo, all in Michoacán. However, I have found it in Durango west of El Salto, in Nuevo León above Horsetail Falls and at Chipinque Mesa, both just south of Monterrey (Fig. 3.47). I also collected it at Huauchinango, Puebla and west of Toluca (Mexico State) 15 km from the town of Zitácuaro and further west at km 182 on the same highway (MEX 15) as roadside trees. Much further south in Guatemala I found it near the town of Pachoc, department of Totonicapán. These were all scattered trees often associated with *P. montezumae*, *P. maximinoi* and *P. ayacahuite* (in Guatemala).

HABITAT—Forma *megacarpa* appears to grow best under temperate climate conditions. The best trees were found growing on moist, deep, well-drained soils on lower

P. pseudostrobus **forma**
megacarpa Tree

Bark

Branchlet, cones, seeds, and leaves

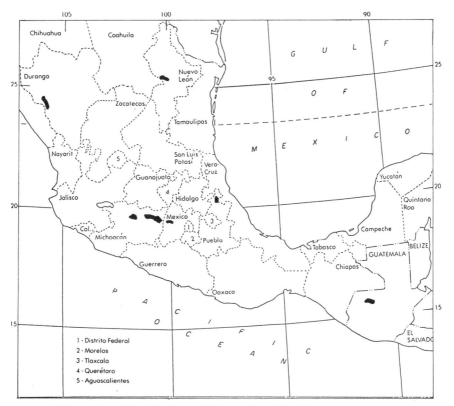

Fig. 3.47. Distribution of *P. pseudostrobus* forma *megacarpa*.

slopes of the mountains. It is not adapted to arid conditions and its altitudinal range is from 1,500–2,600 m. Rainfall probably averages at least 1,000 mm annually over most of its range.

WHERE TO FIND forma *megacarpa*—The most accessible trees were found along Highway MEX 15 east of Zitácuaro and on this same highway at km 182. These were all large roadside trees in groups of 3, 4 and 5 growing with *P. pseudostrobus* forma *protuberans* and *P. pseudostrobus*.

NOTES AND COMMENTS—This form can be distinguished from *P. pseudostrobus* and forma *protuberans* by its considerably larger cones (up to 18 cm long) with very thin, flexible scales and the flattened to appressed apophyses. Forma *megacarpa* appears to be closely related to forma

protuberans and *P. pseudostrobus*. There are, however, significant differences between the chemistry of its turpentine and that of *P. pseudostrobus* and forma *protuberans*. Very briefly, *P. pseudostrobus* turpentine is mostly α-pinene (80%) with a small amount of myrcene (11%). Turpentine of forma *megacarpa* is mostly α-pinene (53%) and Δ^3 carene/myrcene (40%). *P. pseudostrobus* forma *protuberans* has turpentine that is mostly α-pinene (47%) and Δ^3 carene (45%). It is clear that turpentine from both forma *megacarpa* and forma *protuberans* is quite different from that of *P. pseudostrobus*. If more extensive collections of turpentine, cones and needles confirm these differences then I believe that forma *megacarpa* and forma *protuberans* should be raised to varietal status.

Pinus maximinoi H. E. Moore

Pino, Ocote, Pino Canis

THE TREE—A very fine pine, tall, with a straight, clear trunk 20–35 m high and up to 1 m in diameter. Mature trees have mostly horizontal branches that form a fairly thick, rounded crown. Young trees have an open, pyramidal crown with the branches in regular, wide-spread whorls.

BARK—On old trees bark on the lower stem or trunk is rough and divided by deep horizontal and longitudinal fissures into large, grayish brown plates. On the upper stem or trunk the bark is smooth and grayish brown. Young trees have smooth grayish bark on the lower trunk for a number of years.

BRANCHLETS—Long, slender, flexible, somewhat pendent. Bases of the leaf bracts are not decurrent and soon become submerged into the bark, leaving the branchlets smooth rather than rough and scaly.

LEAVES—In groups of 5; 15–28 cm long, very slender 0.7–0.8 mm wide, drooping, the margins finely serrate; stomata are present on the dorsal and ventral surfaces; resin canals are medial, usually 3 but occasionally 2 or 4; hypoderm often forms deep intrusions into the chlorenchyma occasionally extending to the endoderm, exterior walls of the endoderm cells are thickened; fibrovascular bundles 2, contiguous but distinct; fascicle sheaths are persistent, 12–18 mm long and pale brown in color.

CONELETS—Subterminal, oblong; borne singly or in groups up to 4 or 5, the peduncles long and scaly; the scales are thick and bear a small, early-deciduous prickle.

CONES—Long-ovate, asymmetrical, oblique; 5–8 cm long, reddish brown, borne mostly in groups of 3 and 4 on slender, oblique (to the cone axis) peduncles, 10–15 mm long. The cones mature during the winter months and since they are neither serotinous nor persistent, the seeds are soon shed and the cones fall to the ground with the oblique peduncle still attached to the cone.

CONE SCALES—Thin, flexible, weak; the apophyses flat and lightly transversely keeled; umbo small, depressed, occasionally slightly raised with a small, weak, early-deciduous prickle.

SEED—Dark brown, almost black; small, 5–7 mm long and about 5 mm wide; the seed wing pale yellowish brown, articulate, 16–20 mm long and about 8 mm wide. Cotyledons 6, 7 and 8, mostly 7 and 8.

WOOD—Rather soft and light though strong, the sapwood pale yellowish white, the heartwood slightly darker. The species is logged along with associated *P. douglasiana, P. pseudostrobus* and *P. oocarpa*. It is also cut locally for firewood and hewn timbers for roof supports and doorways.

DISTRIBUTION—*P. maximinoi* has a wide distribution in Mexico, occurring in Sinaloa, Nayarit, Jalisco, Colima, Michoacán, Guerrero, Mexico, Morelos, Hidalgo,

P. maximinoi Tree

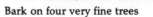

Bark on four very fine trees

Branchlet, cones, and leaves

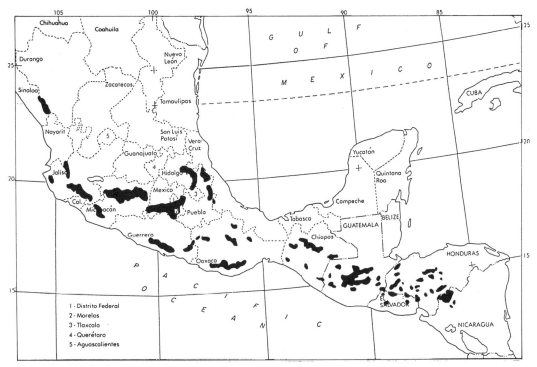

Fig. 3.48. Distribution of *P. maximinoi*.

Puebla, Tlaxcala, Veracruz, Oaxaca and Chiapas (Fig. 3.48). I also found it quite common in Guatemala and in scattered small stands in El Salvador, principally along the border with Honduras. In Honduras it is also found in scattered stands from the Guatemala-El Salvador border to the southwestern border with Nicaragua. In Nicaragua it occurs in a limited area near the northwestern border with Honduras.

HABITAT—*P. maximinoi* grows at elevations of 600–2,400 m; however, it makes its best growth at altitudes ranging from 800–1,500 m. I found the best stands growing under semi-tropical conditions, on well-drained soils with annual rainfall ranging from 1,000–2,000 mm. Associated pines are often *P. pseudostrobus, P. douglasiana, P. oocarpa, P. patula* var. *longepedunculata, P. herrerai* and *P. michoacana. P. maximinoi* is occasionally found on dry, steep slopes; however, under those conditions its growth and form are usually poor.

WHERE TO FIND *P. maximinoi*—Since the species is so widespread in Mexico, it is not difficult to find small groups of trees growing along many of the major highways. I found very fine roadside trees along

Highway 15 from Toluca to Morelia and southwest to Patzcuaro and Uruapan. If you are driving to Chiapas, there are fine trees along Highway 190 near San Cristobal de las Casas. South of San Cristobal de las Casas near the Guatemala border, there are groups of trees near the Federal Park, Lagos de Montebello.

In Guatemala I collected specimens from roadside trees along Highway CA-1 near Guatemala City. For a longer collecting trip in Guatemala, drive east from Guatemala City on Highway CA-9. Near El Progreso turn left on Highway 17 and go west and north to the town of San Jeronimo. Inquire for directions to the Federal Forest property only a few kilometers from San Jeronimo. There are very fine stands of *P. maximinoi* at this location.

In Honduras I found excellent stands of trees only a few kilometers east of Tegucigalpa on Highway 4. These were growing near the highway in the mountains before reaching the town of Zamorano.

In El Salvador scattered stands of trees were found near La Palma and Chalatenango near the Honduras border. In southern El Salvador small populations of trees were growing on the slopes of Volcán de Santa Ana, Volcán San Marcelino and Volcán de Izalco.

NOTES AND COMMENTS—*P. maximinoi* is one of the finest pines growing under tropical and semi-tropical conditions in Mexico and Central America. During the past few years extensive collections of seed have been made from selected provenances over most of its range. These collections have been planted by member organizations of CAMCORE (Central America & Mexico Coniferous Resources Cooperative) in Venezuela, Colombia, Brazil and South Africa. Preliminary observations of these plantings confirm that this taxon has great promise for planting under tropical and semi-tropical conditions in a number of countries.

Subsection Oaxacana

In his book Los Pinos Mexicanos, Martínez (1948) grouped the pines in nine seciones. Secion V. Pseudostrobus, included *P. tenuifolia* (now *P. maximinoi*), *P. douglasiana*, *P. pseudostrobus*, *P. pseudostrobus* forma *protuberans*, *P. pseudostrobus* forma *megacarpa*, *P. pseudostrobus* var. *coatepecensis*, *P. pseudostrobus* var. *estevezii*, *P. pseudostrobus* var. *apulcensis* and *P. pseudostrobus* var. *oaxacana*. On page 211 he postulates a close relationship between these taxa. Loock (1904) and Mirov (1967, page 559) agreed, in general, with Martínez' classification.

In his studies of the composition of pine turpentine Mirov (1958) found that the turpentine of *P. pseudostrobus* var. *oaxacana* differed remarkably from that of *P. pseudostrobus* (see page 245). Because of morphological and biochemical characteristics he elevated the variety to specific rank.

My own published studies of the morphological and chemical characteristics of this group (*P. maximinoi*, 1979; *P. estevezii*, 1982; *P. nubicola*, 1987) and unpublished turpentine analyses presented in this book, clearly indicate that *P. estevezii*, *P. pseudostrobus* var. *apulcensis*, *P. oaxacana*, *P. pseudostrobus* var. *coatepecensis* and *P. nubicola* are closely related, chemically and morphologically and are different chemically and morphologically from the remaining taxa in the Pseudostrobus group. In Section Pseudostrobus, I point out major chemical differences between the turpentine of these two groups. Also noted are major differences between the cones. Because of these relationships the taxa listed in Table 3.18 are grouped here in Subsection Oaxacana.

Table 3.18. Characteristics of Species in Subsection Oaxacana.

Species	Leaves per fascicle; length, cm	Cone length, cm	Umbo
P. estevezii	5; 20–30	10–13	Raised, prominent, with persistent, upcurved prickle
P. pseudostrobus var. *apulcensis*	5; 15–28	12–15	Prominent, thick, recurved toward base of cone, strong persistent prickle
P. oaxacana	5; 20–30	10–14	Large, prominent, erect
P. pseudostrobus var. *coatepecensis*	5; 20–30	6–9	Raised, recurved with a persistent prickle
P. nubicola	5–6; 25–43	10–15	Small, depressed with small prickle

Pinus estevezii (Mart.) Perry

Pino, Ocote

THE TREE—A small to medium-size pine 15–20 m tall and 75–100 cm in diameter; the crown thick and rounded with large, often low, horizontal branches. Young trees have a thick, bushy appearance often slightly pyramidal.

BARK—Mature trees have thick, scaly, reddish bark divided into longitudinal plates by deep vertical and horizontal fissures. In young trees the upper part of the stem is quite smooth.

BRANCHLETS—Grayish brown, smooth; bases of the leaf bracts are not decurrent and soon merge into the bark.

LEAVES—In fascicles of 5, bright green, 20–30 cm long, about 1 mm thick, stiff, the margins finely serrate; stomata present on dorsal and ventral surfaces, hypoderm irregular with many shallow penetrations into the chlorenchyma; resin canals 3–5, medial, endoderm with thickened outer cell walls; fibrovascular bundles 2, quite distinct; fascicle sheath about 20 mm long, persistent and pale brown.

CONELETS—Reddish purple; subterminal, erect; solitary or in groups of 2–4; scales are thick with a strong, upcurved prickle.

CONES—Yellowish brown to brown; 10–13 cm long and 7–8 cm wide when open; long-ovoid or conoid, asymmetric, often reflexed; opening at maturity, generally in December and January; borne on thick, strong peduncles about 1 cm long that remain attached to the branchlet with a few basal cone scales when the cone falls.

CONE SCALES—Hard, strong, 12–15 mm wide, the apex slightly rounded to pointed, apophysis subpyramidal with prominent transverse keel; the umbo raised, prominent, armed with a strong, persistent prickle most often curved upward.

SEEDS—Dark brown, 6–7 mm long with an articulate, brown wing about 25 mm long and 7–9 mm wide.

WOOD—The species occurs mostly as scattered trees or occasional small groups of trees and I found no evidence of logging for sawmills. I did find occasional trees cut for firewood and the wood appeared to be medium-hard, rather resinous, the heartwood pale brown.

DISTRIBUTION—This taxon has a rather limited range being found in northeastern Mexico only in the states of Coahuila, Neuvo León and Tamaulipas (Fig. 3.49).

HABITAT—*P. estevezii* grows at altitudes of 800–1,800 m on generally dry, rocky lower slopes and foothills of the mountains. Associated pines are often *P. cembroides* and *P. arizonica* var. *stormiae*. Rainfall averages 300–400 mm annually and occurs from June to September. During the dry winter months frosts occur in Novem-

P. estevezii Tree   Bark   Branchlet with cones, conelets, and leaves

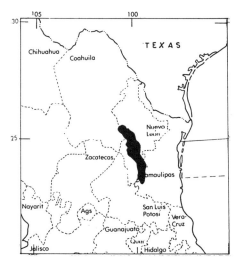

Fig. 3.49. Distribution of *P. estevezii*.

ber, December and January.

WHERE TO FIND *P. estevezii*—Drive south from Monterrey on Highway MEX 85 to Linares; turn right on Highway 60 to the town of Iturbide. Near Iturbide look for rather low pines growing singly and in small groups near the highway.

NOTES AND COMMENTS—Martínez (1948) originally descried this taxon as *P. pseudostrobus* var. *estevezii* and considered it a connecting link between his Section Pseudostrobus and Section Montezumae. In an effort to clarify these relationships, I collected samples of oleoresin from *P. estevezii*. Analysis of the turpentine showed it has an entirely different composition than that of *P. pseudostrobus* and *P. montezumae*. The latter two taxa have turpentine that is almost entirely α-pinene. In sharp contrast, *P. estevezii* consistently had high levels of Heptane and very consistent medium levels of Nonanae. These light hydrocarbons were not found in *P. montezumae* and only occasionally in *P. pseudostrobus* (rarely and in very small amounts). Despite the chemical differences noted here, the decurrent bases of leaf bracts definitely indicate a close relationship to the pseudostrobus group and I have placed it in Section Pseudostrobus, Subsection Oaxacana.

Pinus pseudostrobus var. *apulcensis* Mart.

Pino Chalmaite, Pino, Ocote

THE TREE—A very fine pine 20–30 m tall with diameters up to 90–100 cm. The branches are large, horizontal to drooping, forming a dense, rounded crown. Young trees have ascending branches in regular whorls and the crown is open and pyramidal.

BARK—On mature trees grayish brown, thick with deep longitudinal fissures. The upper trunk and small branches have smooth grayish brown bark. On young trees the bark is smooth and light brown.

BRANCHLETS—Greenish brown, slender, smooth, the ends upturned; bases of the leaf bracts are not decurrent.

LEAVES—In fascicles of 5, rarely 6; 15–28 cm long, slender, flexible, drooping, the margins finely serrate, stomata present on the dorsal and ventral surfaces; resin canals 3–4, mostly 3, medial, outer walls of the endodermal cells are thickened and fibrovascular bundles are 2, contiguous but distinct; fascicle sheaths are light brown, 15–20 mm long and persistent.

CONELETS—Subglobose, in pairs or in groups of 3, their small scales thick, pointed and bearing a sharp, stiff prickle. They are borne on thick, straight, scaly peduncles.

CONES—Widely ovoid to oblong-conical, very slightly curved and oblique, 12–15 cm long; lustrous yellowish brown to reddish brown, borne singly and in twos and threes on very stout peduncles ∿ 10–12 mm long. The cones appear sessile because the short peduncle is hidden by the wide basal cone scales. The cones open when mature (November and December) and are persistent for a few months. When they fall the stout peduncle remains with a few basal cone scales attached to the branch.

CONE SCALES—Strong, hard; up to 2 cm wide; the apophyses raised, recurved with a prominent transverse keel; the umbo prominent, thick, generally recurved

P. pseudostrobus　　　Bark　　　Branchlet, cones, conelets, and leaves
var. *apulcensis* Tree

toward the base of the cone and terminating in a strong, persistent prickle.

SEEDS—Dark brown; 6–8 mm long; the seed wing articulate, 30 mm long and 10–12 mm wide, pale brown with fine dark lines.

WOOD—Pale, creamy white, rather soft but of good quality, not very resinous. The trees that I found near Apulco were being cut along with *P. montezumae* and *P. pseudostrobus* for hewn timbers and firewood. I saw one pit-sawing operation where two men were sawing by hand large logs into 5/4″ boards—a slow and laborious process!

DISTRIBUTION—Martínez (1948) reported that var. *apulcensis* had been observed in Hidalgo, Puebla, Tlaxcala, Veracruz and the state of Mexico (Fig. 3.50).

HABITAT—Var. *apulcensis* grows on the lower slopes of the mountains at elevations of 1,800–2,200 m. At Apulco, Hidalgo, annual rainfall is about 1,000 mm. At slightly lower altitude near Huauchinango, Puebla, rainfall is considerably higher, nearer 1,500 mm annually. Climate is warm temperate with occasional frosts during the winter months. The trees that I observed in the Apulco-Huauchinango area were growing very well on fairly steep, moist, sandy to clayey soils. Associated pines were *P. montezumae, P. pseudostrobus, P. leiophylla* and *P. teocote.*

WHERE TO FIND var. *apulcensis*—From Mexico City drive northeast to Pachuca, the capital of Hidalgo, then east to Tulancingo. At about 12 km east of Tulancingo, look for a

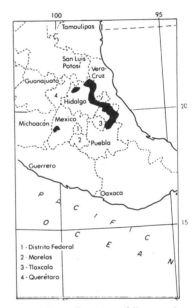

Fig. 3.50. Distribution of *P. pseudostrobus* var. *apulcensis.*

small road on the left that will take you to the villages of Metepec, Apulco and Agua Blanca. Very near Apulco look for small isolated groups of pines generally growing on the steep slopes of ravines, var. *apulcensis* will form a part of these small stands.

This entire area was once forested but population pressure for more land has left only small scattered populations of trees, among them *P. leiophylla, P. pseudostrobus, P. montezumae* and var. *apulcensis.*

NOTES AND COMMENTS—This taxon has a long and complicated taxonomic history and this is not the place for a complete review of its classification. Briefly though, it has now been classified by Stead & Styles (1984) as *P. pseudostrobus* subspecies *apulcensis*. I disagree with this and believe ssp. *apulcensis* should be restored to the rank of species as originally proposed by Lindley (1839). (Lindley described *P. apulcensis* from specimens collected by Hartweg at Apulco, Hidalgo). I collected samples of oleoresin from trees at Apulco and their turpentine chemistry clearly places them in Subsection Oaxacana with *P. estevezii, P. oaxacana* and *P. nubicola*—all species that have high percentages of light hydrocarbons in their turpentine. This is in marked contrast to the turpentine chemistry of the taxa included in Subsection Pseudostrobus. I am preparing a paper that will present these and other findings and will propose specific status for this taxon as originally described by Lindley.

Pinus oaxacana Mirov

Pino Chalmaite, Ocote

THE TREE—A large, well-formed pine 25–40 m high and up to 1 m in diameter. The trunk is fairly straight and clear, the branches mostly horizontal forming a rounded crown.

BARK—Thick, deeply fissured, dark grayish brown on old trees. On young trees the bark is light brown and smooth for a number of years. Even in old trees, bark on the upper stem is smooth and grayish brown.

BRANCHLETS—Slender, flexible, slightly ascending, the bark smooth and greenish brown; bases of the leaf bracts are not decurrent.

LEAVES—In fascicles of 5, occasionally 6; slender, 20–30 cm long, drooping but not pendent, the margins finely serrate; stomata present on the dorsal and ventral surfaces; resin canals generally 3, occasionally 4, medial; exterior walls of the endoderm cells thickened, fibrovascular bundles 2, contiguous but distinct; fascicle sheaths light brown, about 25 mm long and persistent.

CONELETS—Subterminal, solitary and in groups of 2, 3 and 4 on scaly peduncles; the small cone scales are thick, pointed and bear a small prickle.

CONES—Hard, 10–14 cm long, ovoid-long-ovoid, asymmetrical, generally reflexed; brown to yellowish brown; borne on a very short (5–10 mm) peduncle that remains attached to the branchlet with a few basal scales, when the cone falls. The cones

P. *oaxacana* Tree   Bark

Branchlet, cones, and leaves

open when mature and often remain attached to the branchlets for a number of months after the seed are dispersed.

CONE SCALES—Thick, stiff, hard; 12–20 mm wide, the apophyses with pronounced, unequal projections up to 20–22 mm long, transversely keeled; the umbo large, erect, hard with a small, deciduous prickle.

SEED—Dark brown, 7–10 mm long and about 6 mm wide with a light brown, articulate seed wing 20–25 mm long.

WOOD—The sapwood is creamy to yellowish white, and the heartwood is pale brown, strong and only moderately resinous. It is logged along with associated pines and cut locally for hewn timbers and large, hand-sawed cants that are sold in the local markets for home construction.

DISTRIBUTION—*P. oaxacana* has a fairly wide range, extending from central Mexico southward into Guatemala, El Salvador and Honduaras (Fig. 3.51). In Mexico it has been reported from the states of Mexico, Puebla, Veracruz, Guerrero, Oaxaca and Chiapas. In Guatemala I found it growing in small mixed stands with other pines along the central range of mountains extending from the border with Mexico, eastward to the border with El Salvador and Honduras. In Honduras and El Salvador it occurs along the mountain range that forms the border between the two countries.

HABITAT—This species grows at altitudes ranging from 1,500–3,200 m. It makes its best growth in temperate to warmer climates under rainfall averaging 1,500 mm annually. Although it will grow on steep, arid sites, it makes much better growth on deep, sandy–gravelly soils. While it appears best adapted to warm temperate conditions, I found trees growing at 3,100–3,200 m in the mountains near the village of Guajimalayas, Oaxaca. Two small trees were in flower there in February. Associated pines are often *P. maximinoi*, *P. rudis*, *P. pseudostrobus*, *P. patula* var. *longepedunculata*, *P. douglasiana*, *P. nubicola* and at higher altitudes, *P. ayacahuite*.

WHERE TO FIND *P. oaxacana*—To find a good stand of this species, drive from Mexico City to Puebla and follow Highway 150 east from Puebla for about 40 km to the intersection with Highway 140. Turn left onto 140 and drive about 40 km to the town of San Salvador el Seco. There turn right onto a paved road that passes through a small, almost pure stand of *P. oaxacana*. This stand ends abruptly just before reaching Superhighway 150. For more collections continue south on Highway 150 to Tehuacan and on to Oaxaca. This is a long, dry trip so count on at least four 4–5 h from Tehuacan to Oaxaca. In Oaxaca take Highway 190 east for 2–3 km, then turn left onto Highway 175 toward Tuxtepec. This road leads up into the high mountains north and east of Oaxaca city. Pines will be found along the road all the way to Ixtlán. Look for

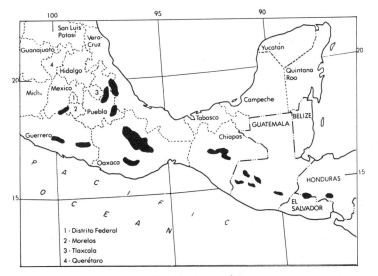

Fig. 3.51. Distribution of *P. oaxacana*.

P. oaxacana at elevations of 1,500–2,000 m. The species can be found at 3,000 m here, but the trees are widely scattered. At Ixtlán ask for a guide to go with you into the hills to the villages of Lachatao and Rancho Benito Juárez. A winding series of trails and roads can be followed down the mountains back to Oaxaca. This trip should be made only in a high-clearance vehicle during the dry season with a reliable guide and ample water and gasoline. Allow a full day from Ixtlán back to Oaxaca.

Further south in Chiapas I found very fine trees near the roads branching out from San Cristobal de Las Casas. Trees were also growing along Highway 190 south of San Cristobal de Las Casas near Teopisca.

In Guatemala the species can be found along Highway CA-1 to Chichicastenango, also on Highway 18 from Guatemala City to Jalapa. In El Salvador I collected the species near Highway 4 a few kilometers from the town of La Palma. In Honduras take Highway 7 south to Marcala. Look for signs to the town of Las Trancas. *P. oaxacana* can be found as roadside trees in this area.

NOTES AND COMMENTS—Although *P. oaxacana* is easily identified in the field by its cones with scales bearing an unusually prolonged apophysis, Styles & Stead (1984) recently concluded that this taxon should be classified as a subspecies of *P. pseudostrobus*. Mirov's (1958) description of this species along with his data on the unusual chemistry of its turpentine (quite different from that of *P. pseudostrobus*) very clearly justified its specific rank. Styles & Stead, however, did not feel that differences between turpentine chemistry of the two taxa were sufficiently clear to warrant specific rank. More recently (1987) I published gas chromatograph analyses of *P. oaxacana* turpentine taken from populations of trees in Mexico (Puebla, Oaxaca and Chiapas) and Guatemala. The results clearly confirm Mirov's findings, i.e. important differences between turpentine from this taxon and that of *P. pseudostrobus*. For this reason and the very pronounced differences between the cones of the two species, I have continued to use Mirov's name, *P. oaxacana*, for this taxon.

This species is one of five taxa forming Subsection Oaxacana. It crosses with *P. pseudostrobus* var. *coatepecensis*, *P. nubicola* and almost certainly with *P. pseudostrobus*.

P. oaxacana should grow well under subtropical conditions in other countries. Crosses between selected provenances of *P. pseudostrobus* and *P. oaxacana* should produce outstanding hybrids. I have seen many fine trees that appeared to be the progeny of natural crosses between these two taxa. Mirov thought that *P. oaxacana* also crossed naturally with *P. montezumae*. From my field observations I would certainly concur.

Pinus pseudostrobus var. *coatepecensis* Mart.

Pino, Ocote

THE TREE—A fine pine tree, 20–30 m high and up to 1 m in diameter, the branches large, horizontal to slightly drooping and the crown fairly dense and irregularly rounded. Young trees have an open pyramidal crown.

BARK—On large, mature trees it is grayish brown and deeply furrowed longitudinally forming long, scaly plates. Higher on the trunk near the top, it becomes smooth and brown. Young trees have smooth brown bark.

BRANCHLETS—Slender, smooth, greenish brown and slightly drooping; bases of the leaf bracts are widely spaced, nondecurrent and soon merging into the bark.

LEAVES—Borne in fascicles of 5, occasionally 6; 20–30 cm long, slender, drooping, the margins finely serrate; stomata present on ventral and dorsal surfaces; resin canals 2–3, medial, rarely with 1 or 2 external; exterior walls of the endoderm cells are thickened, fibrovascular bundles are 2 and quite distinct; fascicle

P. pseudostrobus **var.** *coatepecensis* Tree   Bark   Branchlet, cones, seeds, and leaves

sheaths are persistent, grayish brown and about 15 mm long.

CONELETS—Globose, solitary or in pairs, the small scales thick with a small, erect prickle. They are borne on short, stout, scaly peduncles.

CONES—Ovoid-long-ovoid, almost symmetrical, 6–9 cm long and about 5–6 cm wide when open. They are a lustrous brown color and borne on stout, slightly reflexed peduncles ∿ 10–12 mm long. They open when mature and remain attached to the branchlet for several months after the seed are shed. The peduncle with a few basal cone scales remains attached to the branch when the cone falls.

CONE SCALES—Hard, stiff, ∿ 1 cm wide, the apophysis raised to pyramidal with a prominent transverse keel; the umbo raised, slightly recurved and bearing a sharp persistent prickle.

SEED—Very small, ∿ 5 mm long and 4 mm wide; the seed wing articulate and ∿ 12 mm long and 7 mm wide; very pale brown.

WOOD—Very similar to the wood of *P. oaxacana*—not very resinous, strong and of good quality.

DISTRIBUTION—Prof. Martínez (1948) stated that it had been reported from the states of Veracruz and Oaxaca. I found it in those states and also in Chiapas and Guatemala (Fig. 3.52).

HABITAT—Var. *coatepecensis* grows at altitudes ranging from 1,600 to 2,300 m. Rainfall over most of its range is about 1,500 mm

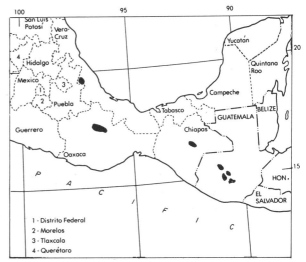

Fig. 3.52.   Distribution of *P. pseudostrobus* var. *coatepecensis*.

annually and climate varies from warm-temperate to temperate. I did not find this variety growing under dry–arid conditions or in pure stands. Rather, it was generally associated with *P. oaxacana, P. pseudostrobus, P. maiminoi, P. oocarpa, P. oorcarpa* var. *ochoterenai* and *P. patula* var. *longepdunculata*.

WHERE TO FIND var. *coatepecensis*— Drive from Mexico City to Puebla, there take Highway MEX 140 to Perote, Veracruz, and on to Jalapa, the capital of Veracruz. At Jalapa find a guide that can take you to the small village of Xico, only a few kilometers from Jalapa. There search the surrounding hills for small stands of pines. The forests in this area have been cut over for years for fuelwood and pines are now difficult to find.

In Oaxaca drive north from the city of Oaxaca toward Tuxtepec. At about 2,000 m altitude look for stands of *P. oaxacana*. Mingled with the pines are occasional trees of var. *coatepecensis*.

In Guatemala, north from Highway CA-1 to Chichicastenango, look for roadside trees at ∿ 2,100 m altitude. The trees were growing with *P. oaxacana* and *P. michoacana* var. *cornuta*. This variety can also be found in the area around Laguna de Atitlán, near the towns Panajakel and Tecpán at 2,100–2,200 m.

NOTES AND COMMENTS—Stead &

Styles (1984) concluded that the cone and needle morphology of *P. pseudostrobus* var. *coatepecensis* do not justify varietal status for this taxon.

The relatively small, ovoid-long-ovoid cones; the hard, lustrous brown cone scales with small recurved apophyses, umbo and sharp persistent prickle make identification of this taxon in the field fairly easy. I also collected samples of oleoresin from trees in Mexico and Guatemala and found that their turpentine chemistry is quite different from that of *P. pseudostrobus* and very similar to turpentine of *P. oaxacana*. For these reasons I have placed this taxon in Subsection Oaxacana.

Pinus nubicola Perry

Pino, Ocote

THE TREE—A very fine, well-formed pine 25–30 m tall with a diameter of 0.5–1 m; in mature trees the lower branches are large and horizontal, the upper branches slightly ascending forming a rounded, open crown. Young trees have an open, pyramidal crown with the young branches in evenly spaced whorls.

BARK—Grayish brown with shallow vertical and horizontal fissures that divide the bark into longitudinal, scaly plates. On the upper stem the bark is grayish brown and smooth; young trees have thin, smooth, grayish brown bark.

BRANCHLETS—Slender with smooth grayish green bark; bases of the leaf bracts are not decurrent.

LEAVES—In fascicles of 5–6, occasionally 7, rarely 8; 25–43 cm long, 0.6–1 mm wide, flexible, very drooping to almost pendent, the margins serrate; stomata on dorsal and ventral surfaces, hypoderm with many slight penetrations into the chlorenchyma; resin canals 3–4, medial with occasionally 1 internal; endoderm with outer cell walls thickened, vascular bundles 2, distinct; fascicle sheaths are persistent, 20–30 mm long, pale brown, not resinous.

CONELETS—Subterminal, ovate, the

small scales wide, pointed with a very small prickle. They are borne on long, erect, scaly peduncles.

CONES—Asymmetrical, ovoid-long-ovoid, 10–15 cm long, 8–10 cm wide when open; reflexed on stout peduncles that remain with a few basal cone scales attached to the branch when the cone falls. The cones are borne singly and in groups of 2–4. They open when mature and are soon deciduous.

CONE SCALES—Thick, stiff, 20–25 mm wide, the apex slightly angled, generally with distinct, unequal marginal projections; apophysis raised but not protuberant, transversely keeled; umbo ashy gray, about 2 mm long, the margins generally slightly depressed and bearing a small, persistent prickle.

SEED—Brown or spotted to mottled black, 5–7 mm by 4–5 mm with an articulate wing 20–25 mm long and 8–11 mm wide; cotyledons mostly 8–10.

WOOD—Of good quality; hard, not very resinous; the heartwood pale brown. The trees are cut with other associated pines and sawn into boards and timbers. Locally it is used for hand-hewn timbers and firewood.

DISTRIBUTION—This species ranges from southern Mexico into Guatemala, El

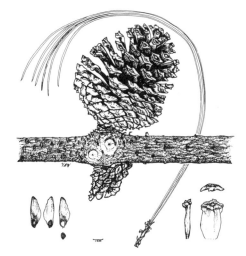

P. nubicola
Young tree with drooping
leaves typical of this species

Bark

Cone, branchlet, leaves, seed, and cone scale.
*Thanks to Ms. E. B. Schmidt. Journal of the Arnold
Arboretum, Vol. 68:447–459. Oct. 1987.*

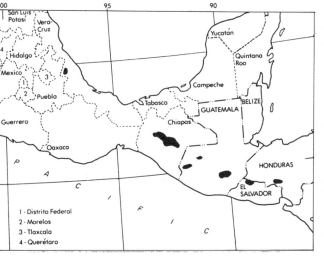

Fig. 3.53. Distribution of *P. nubicola*.

Salvador and Honduras (Fig. 3.53). In
Mexico I found it growing in Veracruz and
Chiapas (it probably also occurs in Oaxaca
along the northeastern escarpment of the
mountains). In Guatemala it occurs in the
departments of Quezaltenango, Sololá and
Jalapa; in El Salvador I found it only in the
department of Chalatenango; in Honduras,
the department of La Paz.

HABITAT—*P. nubicola* grows at 1,800–
2,400 m altitude on cool, moist mountain
slopes. Annual rainfall over its range
averages 1,000–1,500 mm with a dry season
from December to April. At the higher
elevations (2,200–2,400 m) frosts occasion-

ally occur during December and January.
Associated pines over much of its range are
*P. pseudostrobus, P. maximinoi, P. oaxacana, P.
montezumae, P. oocarpa* var. *ochoterenae, P.
tecunumanii* and *P. ayacahuite.* At many locations I found *Liquidambar styraciflua* mingled
with the pines.

WHERE TO FIND *P. nubicola*—Trees can
be found in Chiapas south of San Cristobal
de Las Casas on Highway 190 near the
village of Teopisca. They are some distance
from the road and will be found mingled
with other pines (*P. oaxacana, P. patula* var.
longepedunculata, P. ayachuite and *P. rudis*).

In Guatemala, east of Guatemala City,
look for a narrow, winding dirt road from
San José Pinula to Mataquescuintla. Trees
can be found near kilometer 35 at 2,300 m
altitude. Since there are many crossing trails
in the area, it would be helpful to obtain a
guide in San José Pinula.

NOTES AND COMMENTS—*P. nubicola*
with its slender, pruinose branchlets,
smooth-barked young trees and distinctive
turpentine chemistry readily falls into section Pseudostrobus, subsection Oaxacana
(a group of species that differ from typical *P.
pseudostrobus* in the morphology of their
cones and in the presence of heptane and
nonane, usually in high amounts, in their
turpentine). Although *P. nubicola* is closely
related to *P. oaxacana, P. estevezii* and var.
apulcensis, it is easily distinguished in the
field by its long, very drooping needles 5–6

(occasionally 7) in a fascicle and its large ovoid-long-ovoid cones with unusually wide, thick cone scales having unequal apical projections and a small depressed umbo.

Section Serotinae

Most of the pines in this group have serotinous cones with tenacious peduncles and many of the species have been successfully crossed at the Institute of Forest Genetics, Placerville, California. A few of the species are small, branchy trees and others are 40–50 m tall. Here Section Serotinae is divided into three subsections. These are listed in Table 3.19 with some of their important characteristics.

Table 3.19. Subsections of Section Serotinae.

Subsection	Leaves per fascicle; length, cm	Cone habit; length, cm	Peduncle habit; persistence
Contorta	2; 4–6	Not serotinous; 3–5	Sessile; not persistent
Patula	2–3 (4); 8–25	Serotinous (except var. *longepedunculata*), 5–14	Sessile; long persistent (except var. *longepedunculata*)
Oocarpa	3–5; 8–25	Serotinous (except var. *ochoterenai*); 3–10	Not sessile; long persistent (except var. *ochoterenai*)

Subsection Contorta

In Mexico and Central America this group is represented only by *P. contorta* ssp. *murrayana.*

Pinus contorta ssp. *murrayana* (Balf.) Critchfield

Lodgepole Pine, Pino

THE TREE—Medium size, 20–30 m high, the trunk generally straight and slender, 30–50 cm in diameter. The lower branches horizontal and often persistent, upper branches ascending; the crown narrow and pyramidal.

BARK—Thin, 0.5–0.8 cm thick, orange-brown, the surface covered with small, loose, thin scales.

BRANCHLETS—Slender, flexible, rather smooth, brown; bases of the leaf bracts are decurrent.

LEAVES—In fascicles of 2; 4–6 cm long, 1.5–1.8 mm wide, stiff, sharply pointed, the margins finely serrate; resin canals 2, medial; exterior walls of the endoderm thickened, vascular bundles 2, widely separated; fascicle sheaths are dark brown, persistent and about 3 mm long.

CONELETS—Small, pale brown, borne singly and in pairs on slender peduncles.

CONES—Ovoid-cylindric, lightweight, not hard or heavy; symmetrical, slightly reflexed, 3–5 cm long, borne singly and in

P. contorta ssp. *murrayana* Tree.
Thanks to Jack Duffield.

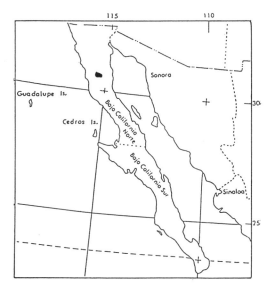

Fig. 3.54. Distribution of *P. contorta* ssp. *murrayana*.

pairs. The cones are a lustrous yellow-brown color, sessile and semi-persistent. Although the cones of *P. contorta*, ssp. *latifolia* are serotinous for many years, in ssp. *murrayana* the cones open when they reach maturity.

CONE SCALES—Flexible, not hard and stiff, apophysis raised, with a prominent transverse keel; the umbo dorsal and bearing a sharp, persistent prickle.

SEED—About 5 mm long with an articulate wing 8–12 mm long. There are about 257,000 seeds/kg and cotyledons number 3–4, mostly 4.

WOOD—Medium-hard, light, strong, of poor quality; in Baja California Norte it is logged and sold along with lumber from *P. jeffreyi*.

DISTRIBUTION—*P. contorta* is primarily a western Canadian, western U.S. species with the southern terminus of its range occurring as a small, disjunct population (ssp. *murrayana*) in the Sierra San Pedro Mártir, Baja California Norte, Mexico (Fig. 3.54).

HABITAT—In the Sierra San Pedro Mártir, Baja California Norte, *P. contorta* ssp. *murrayana* grows at 2,200–3,000 m altitude. It is found in open-scattered stands mingled with *P. jeffreyi*, *P. lambertiana* and *Abies concolor* (Gord. & Glend.) Lindl. along the rocky slopes, basins and arroyos of the mountains. Rainfall at these elevations is

about 600 mm annually, up to 30% occurring during the winter months from November to March. Snow and frosts are fairly common during December, January and February while the hottest and driest months are June, July and August.

WHERE TO FIND *P. contorta* ssp. *murrayana*—Drive to Baja California via Tijuana and take Highway MEX 1D to Ensenada. There take MEX 1 south to the town of Colonet (about 225 km from Tijuana). At Colonet fill up with gasoline and water and be sure all tires are in excellent condition. From Colonet continue south on MEX 1 for about 6 km. Look for a sign on the left to the village of San Telmo. Turn left off the highway onto a narrow road to San Telmo (about 6 km). Continue on the trail through the village heading due east. At about 11 km the road branches left and right. Take neither of those trails but continue straight ahead and look for signs pointing to Meling Ranch, Rancho Meling, about 15 km due east. At the Meling Ranch inquire about accommodations for the night and about a guide to go with you up into the national park (Parque Nacional Sierra San Pedro Mártir). From the Meling Ranch to the Observatory at the center of the park is about 30 km, and pines will be found growing along the road.

NOTES AND COMMENTS—*P. contorta* is a variable species and for many years foresters and botanists thought that there were two forms of Lodgepole Pine. One form, generally a small shrubby tree, grew at low elevations along the Pacific coast of Canada, Washington, Oregon and California. A second form, generally with good form and height, grew along the inland mountain ranges of western Canada and the northwestern U.S. at altitudes of 1,500–3,000 m.

In his book on the pines of Mexico, Martínez (1948) described this pine as *P. contorta* var. *latifolia* Engelm. However, Critchfield (1957), after making a detailed study of collections from the entire range of *P. contorta,* concluded that there are four groups which he classified as follows:

Coastal: *P. contorta* Doug. ex Loud. ssp. *contorta*

Mendocino white plains: *P. contorta* ssp. *bolanderi* (Parl.) stat. nov.

Sierra Nevada: *P. contorta* ssp. *murrayana* (Balf.) stat. nov.

Rocky Mountain: *P. contorta* ssp. *latifolia* (Engel. ex-Watson) stat. nov.

His study shows very clearly the pronounced differences between ssp. *latifolia* (Rocky Mountain group) and ssp. *murrayana* (Sierra Nevada group). Ssp. *murrayana* is characterized by its wide leaves and lightweight, symmetrical cones which open at maturity and are deciduous in a few years. Ssp. *latifolia* is characterized by its more narrow leaves and its heavy, asymmetrical, serotinous and long-persistent cones.

Subsection Patula

Four species and two varieties are included in this group. The cones of most are serotinous and sessile. The species and varieties are listed in Table 3.20 with some of their botanical characteristics.

Table 3.20. Characteristics of Species in Subsection Patula.

Species	Leaves: number per fascicle; length, cm	Cone serotiny; length, cm	Peduncle: sessile or not; tenacity
P. radiata var. *binata*	2–3; 8–15	Serotinous; 8–10	Almost sessile; very tenacious
P. muricata	2; 10–16	Serotinous; 5–7	Sessile; very tenacious
P. attenuata	3; 8–10	Serotinous; 8–12	Sessile; very tenacious
P. greggii	3; 10–15	Serotinous; 10–14	Sessile; very tenacious
P. patula	3; 15–25	Serotinous; 7–10	Sessile; very tenacious
P. patula var. *longepedunculata*	3–4; 15–25	Not serotinous; 5–8	Not Sessile; semi-persistent

Pinus radiata var. *binata* Lemm.

Monterrey Pine, Pino

THE TREE—A small to medium-size tree 10–25 m high, mostly 15–20 m, and 40–50 cm in diameter. (A few trees have been reported from Guadalupe Island with diameters of 112, 164 and 211 cm and heights of 27, 30 and 32 m.) Branches are thick, horizontal, often growing low on the trunk, irregularly spaced forming an open, irregular crown.

BARK—Rough, scaly, dark brown, divided into ridges by deep vertical and horizontal fissures.

BRANCHLETS — Slender, flexible, smooth; glaucous when very young but becoming brown and rough with age.

LEAVES—In fascicles of 2 and 3, mostly 2; bright green color; slender, erect, 8–15 cm long; stomata present on the dorsal and ventral surfaces; resin canals 2–5, occasionally more, medial, occasionally with 1 internal; exterior walls of the endoderm are not thickened, fibrovascular bundles 2, clearly separated; sheaths about 10 mm long, pale brown, persistent.

CONELETS—Dark purple, borne on stout peduncles, the scales bearing a small, sharp prickle.

CONES—Lustrous brown, hard, asymmetrical, ovoid-oblong-ovoid, oblique, 8–10 cm long; borne in pairs and groups of 3–5, reflexed on very short, stout peduncles (practically sessile), serotinous, remaining closed and attached to the branches for many years.

CONE SCALES—Hard, stiff; apophyses large, transversely keeled, pyramidal, rounded on the scales located at the base and upper side of the cone. On the lower side of the cone (abaxial), the apophyses are flat to slightly raised; the umbo small, slightly raised bearing a small, deciduous prickle.

SEED—Dark brown to almost black; 6–7 mm long and 4 mm wide, the seed wing articulate, 15–18 mm long; seed average about 103,000/kg and cotyledons number 6, 7 and 8, mostly 7 and 8.

WOOD—Light, soft, easily worked, used for firewood and hewn timbers for local construction (on Cedros Island).

DISTRIBUTION—In Mexico its range is very limited, occurring only on two small islands in the Pacific off the west coast of Baja California Norte; Guadalupe Island 250 km from the coast and Cedros Island 30 km off the coast (Fig. 3.55).

HABITAT—On Guadalupe Island the species grows at elevations of 300–1,100 m

P. radiata var. *binata* Tree. *Thanks to Biól. X. Madrigal Sánchez for this photograph taken on Cedros Island, Mexico.*

Cones collected from 10 trees on Cedros Island. Note variable shape and consistently rounded apophyses. *Thanks to Jack Duffield.*

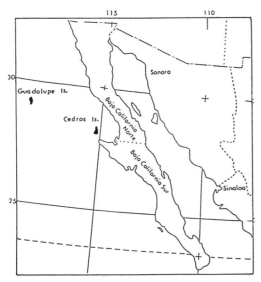

Fig. 3.55. Distribution of *P. radiata* var. *binata.*

at the northernmost point of the island. The population is very small, about 300–400 trees, possibly less and, due to the presence of goats, reproduction is scarce to non-existent. Since the island is of volcanic origin, the soil is derived from the ancient lava flows and is still very rocky. Frosts, snow and sleet occur during the winter months and heavy fogs and mist are common throughout the year. Prevailing winds are from the northwest and are very strong, often reaching gale force. Over most of the island rainfall appears to be limited, and dry to arid conditions prevail particularly at lower elevations. On Cedros Island the pines are found at elevations of 300–650 m. It has been suggested that this restricted range in altitude is caused by the maximum occurrence of fog over this belt. Cedros Island is not of volcanic origin but appears to have once been connected to the mainland. Its soils are rocky, mostly of sedimentary origin, and the mountains are steep with broken ridges and slopes dropping steeply to the sea. The climate is dry and arid; however, fogs and mists occur throughout the year and rainfall probably does not exceed 300 mm annually. Cedros Island is about 300 km southeast of Guadalupe Island and very near the mainland, and while the prevailing westerly winds are very strong, it does not experience the very cold winter storms that occur

on Guadalupe Island. Temperatures do drop to freezing during the winter months, and most rain occurs during June, July and August. No other pine species occur on the two islands.

WHERE TO FIND *P. radiata* var. *binata*—To collect the species in Mexico could become a fairly difficult project. A long drive must be taken down the peninsula to the city of Guerrero Negro with another drive south then northwest on the peninsula to the fishing village of Turtle Bay (Bahia Tortuga). There arrangements would have to be made for a reliable boat and crew for the trip to Cedros Island and the fishing village of Cedros. Once at the village of Cedros, it would be possible to collect specimens on the slopes of Cerro de Cedros that rises directly behind the village. A trip to Guadalupe Island would have to become a veritable expedition; this would likely be far too time-consuming.

NOTES AND COMMENTS—The pines growing on Cedros Island were, at one time, classified as a variety of *P. muricata* (*P. muricata* var. *cedrosensis*). Later studies indicated that the pines are more similar to *P. radiata* than to *P. muricata* and they are now classified as *P. radiata* var. *binata*. The pines on Guadalupe Island have often been classified as *P. radiata*; however, recent studies show that the trees possess a number of *P. muricata* characters as well as those generally associated with *P. radiata*. In summary, cones of typical *P. radiata* are somewhat larger than those found on Guadalupe and Cedros islands. Cones from trees on both islands are much smoother than those of *P. muricata*, i.e. the apophyses do not have such a pronounced spine as the cones of *P. muricata*. Needles from island trees are predominantly in groups of twos and threes. Typical *P. radiata* has needles mostly in threes and typical *P. muricata* has needles mostly in twos. Needles from the island pines have 2–5 resin canals whereas typical *radiata* needles usually have 2 or fewer resin canals. Finally, trees from Cedros Island flower much earlier than typical *P. muricata* trees and overlap the flowering period of the pines on Guadalupe Island. With these "shared characters" it seems logical to classify the pines from both islands as *P. radiata* var. *binata*.

From all reports it is clear that the population of pines on Guadalupe Island is approaching extinction. Except for a few shipwrecked sailors, goat hunters, an occasional army garrison and a small weather station, the island has been, and at present, remains uninhabited. However, more than 100 years ago goats were released, and in a few years had completely overrun the island. Their grazing has eliminated all reproduction of these rare pines, and unless steps are taken to eliminate or drastically reduce the goat population, the few remaining trees will disappear leaving no survivors.

The "other side" of this all-to-familiar goat-grazing story is: there are goats on Cedros Island too, but reproduction of the pines there does not appear to suffer as it has on Guadalupe Island. I am not clear why this is true; perhaps the goat population on Cedros Island is "controlled" by hunters from the town of Cedros and from the mainland. Also there could be minor but important differences in the resin chemistry of the needles, branchlets and seedlings that would make the Cedros Island pines less palatable to the goats than the Guadalupe pines. It would be interesting and not too difficult to check on both possibilities.

Pinus muricata D. Don

Bishop Pine, Prickle-cone Pine, Pino

THE TREE—A small, low irregularly branched tree 4–20 m high, the crown low, open and very irregular, the lower branches long and often touching the ground. Young trees have an open, pyramidal crown.

BARK—On the lower trunk thick with deep vertical fissures, the ridges covered with purplish brown scales. On young trees and the upper stem of mature trees, the bark is pale grayish brown and quite smooth.

BRANCHLETS—Rather thick and stiff, grayish brown, rough at first but becoming smoother as bases of the leaf bracts become submerged into the bark.

LEAVES—In fascicles of 2, thick, stiff, erect, borne in dense clusters at the ends of the branchlets; 10–16 cm long, the margins finely serrate; stomata present on the dorsal and ventral surfaces; resin canals are medial, the number ranging from 2–14 (average 7.6); fibrovascular bundles 2, clearly distinct; sheaths 10–12 mm long, pale brown, becoming much shorter (2–4 mm) with age until they appear almost deciduous.

CONELETS—In groups of 2–5 on thick, stiff, erect peduncles about 5 mm long; the conelets brown, the scales terminating in a minute, triangular, sharp, persistent prickle.

CONES—Borne singly and in groups of 2–5, ovoid-conical, 5–7 cm long; brown, slightly curved but often symmetrical; erect, sessile, serotinous and very tenacious, remaining attached to the branches and trunk for many years.

CONE SCALES—Hard, strong, stiff, apophyses on the dorsal or adaxial side of the cone protuberant with a pronounced umbo armed with a long, sharp, persistent, upcurved prickle or spine. Apophyses on the lower, abaxial side of the cone are flattened, the umbo armed with a small, persistent prickle.

SEEDS—Small, dark brown, almost triangular; 5–6 mm long, the wing articulate, 10–15 mm long, 5–6 mm wide. Seeds average about 103,000/kg and cotyledon number is mostly 5.

WOOD—Strong, hard, the heartwood pale brown and the sapwood creamy white. At "Cerro Colorado" northwest of San Vicente, there was evidence of some cutting for fuelwood.

DISTRIBUTION—*P. muricata* has a very limited range, occurring principally in small, scattered populations along the Pacific coast of California. In Mexico, Baja California Norte, two very small groups of

P. muricata Trees at Cerro Colorado   Crown of tree at Cañon   Bark
                                              San Vicente

Cones, seeds, and leaves

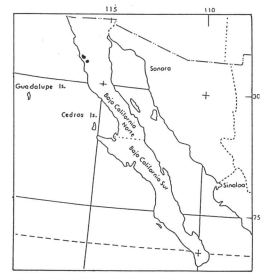

Fig. 3.56.   Distribution of *P. muricata*.

trees occur near the Pacific coast a few kilometers from San Vicente (Fig. 3.56).

HABITAT—The two Mexican populations of *P. muricata* grow very near the Pacific coast at altitudes of 30–50 m. One site, northwest from San Vicente, is a dry to arid, steep, south-facing slope of weathered volcanic igneous rock. The rocky, sandy soil is a rusty red color and the location is appropriately called "Cerro Colorado." No meterological data is available for this area; however, most rainfall probably occurs during the winter months and may amount to about 400 mm annually. June, July and August are the hottest months, and Decem-

ber and January are the coldest. Fog and mists often drift in from the Pacific and provide some moisture and protection from the sun.

The second population is located along the slopes of a small canyon, Arroyo San Vicente, about 10 km southwest of the town San Vicente and 5–6 km from the Pacific. The site is certainly dry to arid, the steep slopes are rocky to sandy and gravelly; here too there are no meterological data available and I estimated that annual rainfall might reach 500 mm. Temperature would be very high during the summer months and frosts probably occur during December and January. Mists and fogs do blow inland here from the Pacific. *P. muricata* was the only pine growing at both locations.

WHERE TO FIND *P. muricata*—The population at "Cerro Colorado" can be found near Highway MEX 1 north of San Vicente. Seven kilometers before reaching San Vicente look for a small paved road on the right; turn onto this and drive for 5–6 km; here the paved road ends and a good sand-gravel road continues. Follow this for another 5–6 km and look carefully on the right for scattered small pines growing on a steep slope that rises directly from the roadside.

Finding the second population is much more difficult. Jack Duffield and I were fortunate to have with us two members of Mexico's forestry staff in Ensenada (INIF) who could guide us to the small isolated population in Arroyo San Vicente. From "Cerro Colorado" we continued on the sandy road until we reached the Pacific. There we turned left on a sandy trail, crossed a dry stream bed and then followed a rough, muddy trail southward along the Pacific shoreline for 8–10 km. There we turned inland (eastward) along the edge of a deep arroyo for 5–6 km to the mouth of a small arroyo (Arroyo San Vicente). At that point one must go on foot up the arroyo for about 0.5 km; there we found a very small scattered population of *P. muricata*. We certainly would not have been able to find this isolated group of trees without the help of the INIF staff. Possibly there is a more accessible route from the town of San Vicente; however, we did not see any trail coming down the arroyo from that direction. In any event, this trip should only be attempted with a high-clearance, 4-wheel-drive vehicle, preferably during the dry season.

NOTES AND COMMENTS—It seems appropriate here to point out that this small, generally poorly-formed pine with a very limited distribution has attracted an unusual amount of attention from foresters, botanists, taxonomists, geneticists, paleo-botanists and others. It would require a separate publication to review the literature covering its synonymy, morphology, taxonomy, resin chemistry, isoenzyme studies, paleobotanical history and genetic

studies. Fortunately that has recently been done by C. I. Millar (1985) in her Ph.d dissertation entitled *Genetic Studies of Dissimilar Parapatric Populations in Northern Bishop Pine (Pinus muricata)*. This is not the place for a review of Millar's study; however, a number of her findings regarding the relationships of the Mexican populations to the California populations of *P. muricata* are pertinent and noted here.

P. muricata is a very variable species, morphologically, chemically and genetically. This variability has resulted in a confusing array of scientific names identifying new species, varieties and forms, with many of the descriptions valid and others not valid. Newer studies bringing to light new information have also produced newer names and different combinations of names. From her overview of the species Millar apparently believes there are three populations that differ significantly one from another; a northern group, a Channel Island group, and a southern group that includes the Baja California, San Vicente and Cerro Colorado populations.

Among the more important differences between the groups was Duffield's (1951) finding of an abrupt change in color of the needles. He found that near the south end of Sea Ranch, 27 km north of Ft. Ross, California, there is a change from green needles typical of all the populations south of Sea Ranch to "blue" needles typical of the populations north of Sea Ranch. Later research (Millar, 1985) also showed that at this same geographic point, there is an abrupt change in turpentine chemistry of the trees. North of Sea Ranch the turpentine is mostly α-pinene. South of Sea Ranch to Monterrey the major terpene is Δ^3 Carene. From Monterrey south to San Vicente, turpentine is mostly Sabinene. The northern group has needles with resin canals averaging 2–3. The Channel Islands' needles average 4–6 resin canals, and the southern group has needles with resin canals averaging about 8.

Differences in cone morphology also formed the basis for description of a new species, *Pinus remorata*. Cones of this species were smooth, symmetrical, and characteristic of the southern group—particularly the population found in Arroyo San

Vicente. Cones of the northern group were rough, asymmetrical, the apophyses elevated, protuberant with a raised umbo bearing a strong, persistent prickle. I found that many of the cones from the trees in Arroyo San Vicente are indeed quite smooth and symmetrical. However, many are asymmetrical with prominent apophyses and prickles. The trees did appear to be generally taller and straighter than the trees at Cerro Colorado. However, the low, bushy trees at Cerro Colorado all had rough, asymmetrical cones. Interestingly, resin samples that I took from trees at Cerro Colorado and Arroyo San Vicente had turpentine that was almost identical, the major terpene being Sabinene.

Millar pointed out that smooth cones were found in many populations of the northern group, also in the Channel Island group and in some populations of the southern group and thus preferred not to use the *Pinus remorata* epithet.

Needless to say there are other complex relationships between the three major groups particularly in the field of genetics. More detailed studies may indicate that a specific name is needed for the taxa in each group. For the present, however, I have followed Millar's suggestion and cite the "Cerro Colorado" and "Arroyo San Vicente" populations as *Pinus muricata*.

Pinus attenuata Lemm.

Pino De Piña, Chichonuda, Knob-cone Pine

THE TREE—A medium-size tree 15–20 m tall generally of rather poor form, the trunk often divided. Branches are often low and long on the lower part of the trunk; higher in the crown they are horizontal to ascending forming an irregularly rounded, rather open crown. Young trees are pyramidal in form with an open crown.

BARK—In young trees the bark is thin, smooth and a pale grayish brown color. In mature trees bark on the lower trunk is divided into small, roughly rectangular, thin, scaly plates; on the upper stem it is smooth grayish brown.

BRANCHLETS — Slender, flexible, smooth, grayish brown, bases of the leaf bracts are decurrent but the scars soon merge into the bark leaving the branchlet smooth.

LEAVES—In fascicles of 3 (rarely 2); thick (1.0–1.5 mm) stiff and erect, 8–10 cm long; stomata present on the dorsal and ventral surfaces; resin canals three, medial or occasionally internal; endoderm with thin cell walls, vascular bundles 2, clearly separated; fascicle sheaths brown and not deciduous.

CONELETS—Light brown, borne in clusters of 2–5 on stiff, erect peduncles 10 mm long; the small scales bearing a small, persistent, triangular prickle.

CONES—Asymmetrical, recurved, long-ovoid, pointed; lustrous light brownish yellow color; 8–12 cm long, borne in groups of 2–5; hard, strong, sessile, tenaciously persistent. The cones are serotinous, remaining attached and unopened, in nodal clusters on the branches and trunk for many years.

CONE SCALES—Very hard and stiff, those on the adaxial side of the cone have apophyses that are pyramidal to protuberant, transversely keeled; the umbo dorsal and bearing a stiff, sharp prickle. Scales on the abaxial side of the cone are much smaller with apophyses almost flat and the umbo depressed without a prickle.

SEED—Almost triangular in shape, dark brown, 5–7 mm long with an articulate wing 12–15 mm long, about 8 mm wide and pale brown in color; average number of seed/kg is 65,000. Cotyledons number 7–8, occasionally 6–9.

WOOD—Pale brown, light and soft, not strong; used occasionally for firewood.

DISTRIBUTION—*P. attenuata* occurs primarily in southwestern Oregon and in relatively small, scattered populations in northern and central California. In southern California it occurs only in a few very small, isolated stands. In Mexico the species is found only in Baja California Norte (Fig.

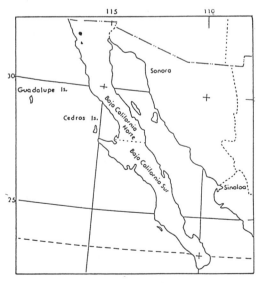

P. attenuata Tree   Bark   Cones and leaves

3.57). A number of small populations occur on the western and northern slopes of Cerro Miracielo a few miles north of Ensenada. Southeast of Ensenada (20 km) three stands were found at Cerro Los Pinos. I visited a small population of trees east of Ensenada in the foothills of the Sierra de Ulloa.

HABITAT—This species grows on the western slopes of the Sierra de Juárez at 250–1,200 m altitude. The site at Sierra de Ulloa was mostly rocky and the soil was a gravelly-sandy clay. Most rainfall occurs during the winter months and amounts to about 600 mm annually; the hottest months are June, July and August, the coldest

Fig. 3.57. Distribution of *P. attenuata*.

months are December and January. At higher elevations (1,500 m) in the Sierra de Juárez, snow and freezing temperatures occur during the winter months.

WHERE TO FIND *P. attenuata*—Driving to Baja California, one can cross the border to Tijuana and drive south to Ensenada. In Ensenada follow Calle Ruiz east out of the city directly onto a narrow, winding trail that leads up into the brush-covered hills. There are a number of turn offs and at one point a locked gate; in order to surmount these obstacles and navigate the very rocky path, it would be best to get in touch with the Mexican Forestry Office (INIF) at the corner of Calle Mexico and Calzado Cortez in Ensenada. The forestry staff there were very helpful in arranging a trip to the small stand of pines, and it is suggested that the trip be attempted only with their help and only with a high-clearance, 4-wheel-drive vehicle.

NOTES AND COMMENTS—There is a striking resemblance between *P. attenuata* and *P. greggii*. Mature trees are similar in form and have smooth grayish brown bark on the upper stem and branches; both species bear tenacious, serotinous cones similar in color and form, and both species have stiff, erect leaves in fascicles of 3. Even the conelets are similar in size and shape, and the tiny scales of both species bear a minute, triangular, persistent prickle. Still another interesting similarity is the fascicle sheath that becomes quite short with age, decreasing in length from 12–15 mm in young leaves to 3–4 mm in old leaves.

While *P. attenuata* is certainly not a rare species in the U.S., it is quite rare in Mexico. The small populations near Ensenada should certainly be protected and could serve as a source of seed for test plantings along the Pacific coast of Baja California Norte. This might be particularly important since it is one of only three pine species native to Baja California Norte that are found growing at low elevations along the Pacific coast.

Pinus greggii Engelm.

Pino, Pino Prieto, Ocote

THE TREE—A small to medium-size tree 10–25 m high, the crown irregularly rounded, the lower branches horizontal to drooping. In open-grown trees branches are often close to the ground and the crown is thick and bushy.

BARK—On mature trees bark on the lower trunk is thick, grayish brown and divided by deep vertical fissures into long, scaly plates. On the upper trunk the bark is grayish brown and smooth. On young trees the bark is grayish brown and smooth; the crown is open and irregularly branched.

BRANCHLETS—Slender, erect, grayish brown, smooth; although bases of the leaf bracts are decurrent the scars soon merge into the bark, leaving the surface quite smooth.

LEAVES—In fascicles of 3, slender to medium-thick, erect, 10–15 cm long, light green color; the margins finely serrate, stomata present on the dorsal and ventral surfaces; resin canals 2–6, medial; exterior walls of the endoderm are not thickened, fibrovascular bundles 2, contiguous but distinct; sheaths 5–10 mm long, pale grayish brown, persistent, but when older occasionally deciduous.

CONELETS—On slender peduncles, borne singly and in groups of 3–6, occasionally more; the scales are wide and bear a small prickle.

CONES—Oblong-conical, polished yellow-brown, oblique, slightly curved, strongly reflexed, 10–14 cm long; sessile and very tenacious, they are serotinous, long-persistent and shed their seeds over a long period. The cones are borne in groups of 3–6 or as many as 8, often forming nodal clusters that become partially embedded in the trunk as it increases in diameter.

SCALES—Hard, strong, the apophysis often raised to subpyramidal particularly on the adaxial (dorsal) side of the cone. On the abaxial (ventral) side of the cone, apophyses are much smaller and flattened. The umbo is flat to depressed with a very small, weak prickle.

P. greggii Tree   Bark

Branchlet, cones, and leaves

Cluster of cones on upper stem of tree. Note also the very smooth bark.

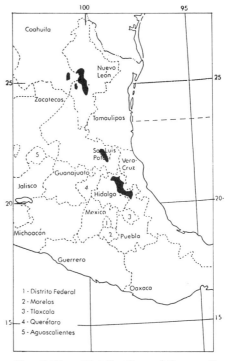

Fig. 3.58. Distribution of *P. greggii*.

SEEDS—Small, dark brown, 5–6 mm long, the seed wing about 15 mm long, articulate and thickened where it joins the seed.

WOOD—Not very resinous, pale yellowish color; used locally for firewood, mine timbers and hewn timbers for construction.

DISTRIBUTION—*P. greggii* has a rather limited distribution in the mountains of the Sierra Madre Oriental (Fig. 3.58). It has been reported in the states of Coahuila, Nuevo León, San Luis Potosí and Hidalgo. I also found a few small groups of trees in Veracruz and Puebla near the eastern border of Hidalgo.

HABITAT—Altitudinal range is 1,300–3,000 m though it seldom reaches the higher altitude. Annual rainfall over most of its range is 600–900 mm. However, in some areas along the eastern escarpment in Hidalgo, Veracruz and Puebla, rainfall is 1,000–1,500 mm annually. Frosts are common at the higher elevations during December and January. Associated pines are *P. leiophylla*, *P. teocote*, *P. montezumae*, *P. arizonica* var. *stormiae*, *P. pseudostrobus* var. *apulcensis* and *P. patula*. On one occasion I found it growing at 3,000 m with *P. ayacahuite* var. *brachyptera*, *P. rudis* and *Abies vejari*. At 1,500 m along the eastern escarpment, *Liquidambar styraciflua* was occasionally found as an associated species.

WHERE TO FIND *P. greggii*—At Saltillo take Highway 57 south for 25–30 km and look for a narrow paved road on the left with a sign to the town of Los Lirios. Drive to Los Lirios and continue through the town onto a dirt road that leads up into the mountains. This soon becomes a narrow, winding trail; however, *P. greggii* can be found as roadside trees where the trail drops downward and follows a narrow canyon eastward, deep into the mountains. This taxon can also be found as an occasional tree on the lower slopes of Cerro Potosí, north of Galeana. To reach the area from Saltillo, drive south on Highway 57 to San Roberto (about 120 km), turn left onto Highway 60 for about 18 km and left again to the town of Galeana (2–3 km). Ask for directions to Cerro Potosí or employ a guide who can take you to the trail leading up the mountain. Near the base of the mountain (the lower slopes) there are a few scattered, large trees near the trail. Either trip should be made only during the dry winter months and only in a high-clearance vehicle. The trip beyond Los Lirios should be made only with a guide who knows the region well.

NOTES AND COMMENTS—Cones of *P. greggii* are very similar to those of *Pinus patula*; however, the two species are easily distinguished in the field since *P. greggii* has leaves that are erect and never drooping while those of *P. patula* are invariably slender and pendent. Differences in the bark are even more pronounced; in *P. patula* bark on the upper trunk is thin, scaly and red, on *P. greggii* it is very smooth and grayish brown. *P. greggii* and *P. attenuata* share a number of very similar characters. In both species the leaves are ternate, stiff and erect; bark on the branchlets and upper trunk is smooth and grayish brown, cones are sessile, tenacious, long-persistent, and occur in nodal clusters (also in *P. patula*). Even the cone scales of *P. attenuata* and *P. greggii* are quite similar; in both taxa the apophyses on the adaxial (upper) side of the cone are raised to pyramidal. However, since the two species are widely separated geographically, identification in the field will present no problem.

Pinus patula Schl. et Cham.

Pino, Pino Triste, Ocote

THE TREE—A very fine pine that attains heights of 30–35 m and diameters of 50–90 cm. An occasional tree can be found with a height of 40 m and diameter of 1 m, but these are very rare. The trunk is usually straight and clear of branches for about 20 m. The branches are horizontal to somewhat drooping, forming an open, rounded crown.

BARK—In mature trees the bark is thick with deep vertical fissures on the lower trunk. However, at a height of 3–4 m the bark becomes thin, scaly and reddish to yellowish red. On young trees the bark is thin, scaly, yellowish red.

BRANCHLETS—Slender, often somewhat drooping, the bark scaly and yellowish red; bases of the leaf bracts are decurrent.

LEAVES—In fascicles of 3, occasionally 4, rarely 5; slender, 15–25 cm long, pendent, pale green to yellowish green in color, the margins finely serrate; stomata present on the dorsal and ventral surfaces; resin canals 1–4, mostly 3, usually medial, occasionally with 1 or 2 internal; exterior walls of the endoderm thin to slightly thickened, fibrovascular bundles 2, contiguous but distinct; fascicle sheaths pale, grayish brown, 10–15 mm long and persistent.

CONELETS—Short pedunculate, borne not only on the branchlets but also on the central stem in groups of 2, 3, 4 and up to 10 or more in thick clusters; the small cone scales are thick and pointed bearing a small, deciduous prickle.

CONES—Hard, strong, serotinous; conical–long-conical, generally slightly curved and reflexed; 7–10 cm long, they are sessile and extremely tenacious with a lustrous brown or yellowish brown color. Although the cones ripen during the winter months (November–February) they may remain closed for years. Since they are very persistent it is not unusual to find groups of 4, 5, 6 or 8 cones deeply embedded in the large branches or the trunk.

CONE SCALES—Stiff, hard, strong; the apophyses generally flat, occasionally depressed, often slightly raised on the basal scales; the umbo flat to depressed and armed with a small, early deciduous prickle.

SEED—Dark brown to almost black, very small, about 5 mm long with a pale brown wing about 17 mm long, slightly thickened at the base where it joins the seed. Cotyledons are 4–5, mostly 5 and number of seed/kg is about 115,000.

WOOD—Pale yellowish white with slightly darker heartwood, rather soft and light and not as resinous as *P. oocarpa*; it is used for general construction, hewn timbers, posts and of course for firewood.

DISTRIBUTION—*P. patula* grows in isolated stands and relatively narrow bands along the eastern escarpment of Mexico's Sierra Madre Oriental from about 24° N latitude (a few kilometers northwest of the city Ciudad Victoria, Tamaulipas state) to Oaxaca state (Sierra de Papalos, about 17° N latitude) (Fig. 3.59). The species has been reported in the states of Nuevo León, Tamaulipas, Queretaro, Hidalgo, Puebla,

Branchlet, cones, conelets, and leaves

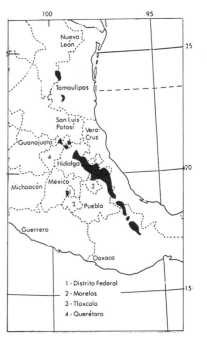

P. patula Tree   Bark

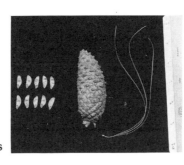

Cone, seeds, and leaves

1 - Distrito Federal
2 - Morelos
3 - Tlaxcala
4 - Querétaro

Fig. 3.59. Distribution of *P. patula*.

Veracruz, Oaxaca, the Distrito Federal and Tlaxcala. Some authors have described its range as extending into Chiapas state; however, I believe those collections should be referred to *P. patula* var. *longepedunculata*.

HABITAT—This species grows at altitudes of 1,500–3,100 m and makes its best growth on moist, well-drained sites with rainfall of 1,000–1,500 mm annually. Its principal range along the southeastern escarpment of the Sierra Madre Oriental receives moisture during the entire year in the form of heavy mists, clouds, fog and rain. On drier sites *P. teocote* and *P. leiophylla* take over. *P. patula* withstands heavy frosts and relatively dry periods but makes much better growth under warmer, more humid conditions. While most populations do not grow at 3,000 m, there is an interesting disjunct population of trees growing in the Federal Park, Desierto de Las Leones, on the outskirts of Mexico City at 3,000–3,100 m altitude. The trees are making excellent growth and regeneration is "fair." Over its more "normal" range, *P. patula* grows in pure stands and in association with *P. greggii, P. maximinoi, P. pseudostrobus, P. teocote, P. leiophylla* and in northeastern Oaxaca *P. patula* var. *longepedunculata*.

WHERE TO FIND *P. patula*—Very fine trees can be found in the Federal Park, Desierto de Las Leones, on the outskirts of

Mexico City. Here the trees will be found in association with *Abies religiosa, P. montezumae, P. ayacahuite* var. *veichtii* and *Quercus* spp.

An interesting day's trip would be to drive from Mexico City on Highway 130 toward Pachuca and the town of Tulancingo. Between Tulancingo and Huauchinango on Highway 130, look for stands of roadside trees. In this same area on Highway 129 between the towns of Teziutlán and Altotonga there are very fine stands of *P. patula* readily accessible from the highway.

NOTES AND COMMENTS—There should be no problem identifying this species in the field. The thin, scaly, reddish bark, the pendent leaves mostly in fascicles of 3 and the tenacious, sessile, lustrous brown cones are very positive identifying characters for *P. patula*.

This species was one of the first Mexican pines to be planted in Africa. In 1907 a small quantity of seed was planted at Tokai, South Africa, and since that date, additional small amounts of seed were obtained from Mexico. In 1924 these young trees began to produce sizable amounts of seed, and planting of young trees began on a large scale. Now the species is one of the most widely planted pines in Africa.

Pinus patula var. *longepedunculata* Loock

Ocote, Pino

THE TREE—A tall, straight pine with a clear trunk 20–35 m high and up to 1 m in diameter. Mature trees have an open, irregularly rounded crown. Young trees have an open, pyramidal crown with widely spaced branches.

BARK—On mature trees bark at the base of the trunk is grayish brown and deeply furrowed. At 3–4 m up the trunk the bark becomes thin, reddish and very scaly. Young trees also have reddish, scaly bark.

BRANCHLETS — Rather drooping, smooth when young but becoming reddish and scaly. Bases of the needle bracts are decurrent.

LEAVES—In fascicles of 3–4, occasionally 5, 15–25 cm long, very slender and flexible, pendent, pale green color; the margins finely serrate, stomata present on the dorsal and ventral surfaces; resin canals 2, occasionally 3, medial with occasionally 1 internal; exterior walls of the endodermal cells only slightly thickened, fibrovascular bundles 2, contiguous but distinct; fascicle sheaths persistent, 10–15 mm long.

CONELETS—Borne on long, scaly peduncles, in groups of 2–5, occasionally solitary, the small scales bearing a minute prickle.

CONES—Long-ovate to long-conical, 5–8 cm long, 2–3 cm wide, often slightly curved, oblique, lustrous brown, reflexed on peduncles 6–12 mm long. They open when mature and the open cones remain attached to the branch for some time after the seeds have fallen. The peduncle generally remains attached to the cone when it falls.

CONE SCALES—Not as hard and stiff as in *P. patula,* about 10 mm wide, the apophyses generally flat though occasionally raised particularly on the basal scales; umbo depressed or slightly raised with a small, deciduous prickle.

SEED—Small, very dark brown to almost black, 5 mm long and about 3 mm wide; the seed wing 15 mm long and 5 mm wide, thickened at the base where it joins the seed.

WOOD—Pale yellow sapwood and very light brown heartwood, rather soft, not very resinous. The trees are cut along with *P. patula* trees and sold for construction timbers. The trees are also cut for firewood.

DISTRIBUTION—Loock collected the type specimen at Rancho Benito Juarez in the mountains north of Oaxaca City. I have collected it in that area, in the Sierra Madre del Sur of southern Oaxaca and in Chiapas (Fig. 3.60). The range of var. *longepedunculata* is not yet clearly defined and may extend into Guatemala and Honduras.

HABITAT—Var. *longepedunculata* grows at 1,800–2,800 m altitude; annual rainfall over most of its range is 1,000–2,000 mm. Frosts occur at the higher elevations during the

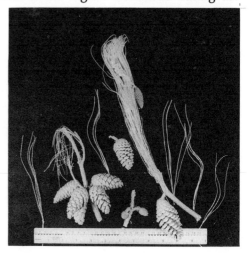

P. patula **var.** *longepedunculata* Trees   Bark   Leaves, conelets, branchlets with pedunculate cones

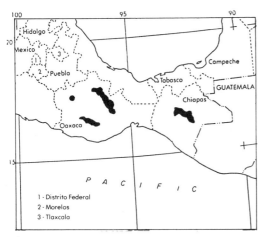

Fig. 3.60. Distribution of *P. patula* var. *longepedunculata.*

1 - Distrito Federal
2 - Morelos
3 - Tlaxcala

winter months and the warmest months are April, May and June. Although this taxon will grow on rather rocky dry sites, it makes its best growth on deep, well-drained soils. It is often found in association with *P. patula* (in Oaxaca), *P. pseudostrobus, P. rudis, P. douglasiana, P. ayacahuite, P. oocarpa* var. *ochoterenai,* and occasionally with *Liquid-ambar styraciflua.*

WHERE TO FIND var. *longepedunculata*— Drive to Oaxaca City and take Highway 175 north to Ixtlán. Before reaching Ixtlán, the pine-forested slopes begin to rise steeply and at 2,000 m altitude *P. patula* and var. *longepedunculata* can be found growing in mixed stands.

NOTES AND COMMENTS—When Loock described this taxon in 1950, he noted that it differs from the species in the following respects:

1. The cones are reflexed on relatively long peduncles and are never sessile.
2. The cones are much smaller than those of *P. patula,* measuring from 5.0–7.5 cm in length compared to about 10 cm for *P. patula.*
3. When mature the cones open quickly and do not remain closed for a long period.
4. The scales are relatively weak, not hard and stiff as in *P. patula.*
5. Seeds are black with brown marks, in *P. patula* seeds are pure black.

Barrett (1972) made a detailed study of needles, cones and seeds taken from *P. patula* trees over its range from Tamaulipas

southward into northeastern Oaxaca. From the 16 separate populations sampled, he concluded that the differences he found were minor and did not justify description of a separate variety viz. *P. patula* var. *longepdunculata* Loock.

I have reviewed Barrett's work and it appears to have been well done. Unfortunately, as he points out, he was not able to carefully measure peduncle length and cone serotiny in the four populations of northeastern Oaxaca (where variety *longepedunculata* occurs). He noted, however, that cones from trees in those four populations did have peduncles up to 12 mm long compared to peduncle length of 3–8 mm from the more northern collections. Trees from the four northeastern Oaxaca populations also had cones that opened in December while those from the other populations did not open in December. Other differences noted by Barrett were:

Northern Populations

Cone weight:	38 g
Cone size:	8.4 cm long, 3.4 cm dia.
No. scales:	145–193
Seed size:	5.6 mm long; 2.5 mm wide
Seed weight:	9 mg

Northeastern Oaxaca

Cone weight:	24 g
Cone size:	6.7 cm long; 2.9 cm dia.
No. scales:	118–138
Seed size:	5.2 mm long; 2.3 mm wide
Seed weight:	7 mg

Barrett's findings, particularly the peduncle length and early opening of the cones from the four northeastern Oaxaca populations confirm Loock's observation and description of var. *longepedunculata.* Nevertheless, Styles (1976) agreed with Barrett's conclusions and in addition, proposed that *P. oocarpa* var. *ochoterenai* Mart. is synonymous with var. *longepedunculata* and both taxa should be referred to *P. patula.*

I disagree with Styles' conclusions that var. *ochoterenai* and var. *longepedunculata* are synonymous with *P. patula.* Differences in cone, peduncle, cone scale and seed morphology are significant and I believe justify varietal status for both var. *ochoterenai* and var. *longepedunculata.* (See table of comparison under *P. oocarpa* var. *ochoterenai.*)

Subsection Oocarpa

This group is composed of four species and three varieties (Table 3.21). Although most of the trees have hard serotinous cones, none of them have sessile cones as in Subsection Patula.

Table 3.21. Characteristics of Species in Subsection Oocarpa.

Species	Leaves: number/fascicle; length, cm	Cone serotiny; length, cm	Peduncle: habit; persistence*
P. oocarpa	5; 20–25	Serotinous; 6–10	Not sessile; long-persistent
P. oocarpa var. ochoterenai	(3) 4–5; 17–25	Not serotinous; 5–8	Not sessile; semi-persistent
P. oocarpa var. trifoliata	3; 20–25	Serotinous; 3–5	Not sessile; long-persistent
P. oocarpa var. microphylla	5; 8–16	Serotinous; 3.5–4.5	Not sessile; semi-persistent
P. jaliscana	4–5; 12–16	Serotinous; 4–8	Not sessile; persistent
P. pringlei	3; 18–25	Serotinous; 5–8	Not sessile; long-persistent
P. tecunumanii	(3) 4–5; 14–21	Not serotinous; 4–7	Not sessile; semi-persistent

*As used here, "long-persistent" is 2–3 years or longer; "persistent" is about 2 years; "semi-persistent" is 1–2 years.

Pinus oocarpa Schiede

Pino, Pino Prieto, Pino Colorado, Ocote Chino

THE TREE—A medium to large pine 15–30 m high, occasionally 35 m, and 50–70 cm in diameter. An occasional tree can be found with a diameter of 1 m, but trees of this size are now very rare. Lower branches are mostly horizontal in older trees with the upper branches more ascending forming a thick, rounded crown.

BARK—Old, mature trees have bark that is 2–4 cm thick, dark grayish brown and formed by shallow vertical and horizontal fissures into rough, longitudinal, geometric-shaped plates. Young trees have thin, rough, reddish brown bark.

BRANCHLETS—Stiff, upright, rough and scaly, the bark reddish brown; bases of the leaf bracts are decurrent.

LEAVES—In fascicles of 5, occasionally 3 and 4, 20–25 cm long, occasionally somewhat shorter or longer; thick and stiff, only occasionally slender and flexible, the margins finely serrate; stomata present on the dorsal and ventral surfaces; resin canals 4–8, mostly septal; exterior walls of the endoderm not thickened; fibrovascular bundles 2, contiguous but distinct; fascicle sheaths brown, about 25 mm long and persistent.

P. oocarpa Tree

Bark

Branchlet, cone, and conelet

CONELETS—Subterminal, borne singly and in pairs on long (2–3 cm) scaly peduncles; the small cone scales are thick and rounded with a very small, deciduous prickle.

CONES—Cones of this species are very variable in form and size ranging from globose (almost round) to ovoid-conical, often tapering toward the apex, generally symmetrical, often oblique and usually reflexed on long (3–4 cm), strong peduncles. In some forms the peduncle may be very slender and weak, in others short (2 cm), thick and very tenacious. The cones vary in size from 6–10 cm long and are generally pale yellowish brown to polished ochre color; they ripen from November to January and remain closed for long periods of time, releasing the seed only during long dry periods. They are long-persistent, but when they do fall, the peduncle remains attached to the cone.

CONE SCALES—Hard, strong, stiff, the apophyses generally almost flat with a well-defined transverse keel. In some areas (Guatemala, Honduras, El Salvador) the apophyses may be raised to pyramidal with a small, recurved umbo; however, in most instances the umbo is small, almost flat to depressed, with a very small, early-deciduous prickle. It is interesting to note that in most instances when the scales are completely opened they form a characteristic symmetrical pattern or "rosette" type of cone that is in marked contrast to the

Cones and seeds

open cones of *Pinus patula* or *P. pringlei*.

SEED—Small, dark brown, 4–7 mm long; the seed wing 10–12 mm long, articulate and thickened at the base where it joins the seed. Cotyledons are 5–7, mostly 6, and seed/kg is about 120,000.

WOOD—The sapwood is yellowish white and the heartwood is pale brown, medium-hard and strong. Trees are cut for construction timbers and widely used in rural areas for firewood and hewn timbers. The wood is resinous, and throughout its range the trees are tapped for resin. In fact, *P. oocarpa* is the primary producer of pine resin in Mexico, Guatemala and Honduras.

DISTRIBUTION—*P. oocarpa* has the greatest north-south range of all the Mexican and Central American pines. From northwestern Mexico in Southern Sonora, it grows on the slopes of the Sierra Madre Occidental southward through Mexico into the mountains of Guatemala, Belize, El Salvador, Honduras and northwestern Nicaragua (Fig. 3.61). Only one pine, *P. caribaea* var. *hondurensis* grows at a more southerly latitude in North America.

HABITAT—Over a northwest-southeast range of 3,000 km, *P. oocarpa* is found growing under a variety of environmental conditions ranging from dry-temperate to humid subtropical. In Sonora, Chihuahua, Sinaloa, Nayarit, Durango and Zacatecas the species grows under dry, temperate conditions with annual rainfall ranging from 500–1,000 mm. In Jalisco, Michoacán, Mexico, Morelos, Guerrero and Oaxaca rainfall is still seasonal (June–September), but generally somewhat higher than in the more northerly states, averaging approximately 1,000–1,500 mm annually. In Chiapas, Mexico, Guatemala and El Salvador, annual rainfall is 1,500–2,000 mm. In Belize, Honduras and Nicaragua annual rainfall over its range is often 2,000–3,000 mm. The species has been collected at altitudes ranging from 200–2,500 m, but its best growth is made on well-drained slopes under warm-temperate to semi-tropical

conditions at about 1,500 m altitude and annual rainfall of 1,500–2,000 mm.

WHERE TO FIND *P. oocarpa*—The species is so widespread in Mexico there should be no difficulty in finding roadside trees along many of the main highways. A few collection localities are cited here; on the highway between Uruapan and Patzcuaro, Michoacán; near Guadalajara, Jalisco; near Cuernavaca, Morelos; near Juquila, Oaxaca; near the village of Nejapa, Oaxaca; between Tuxtla Gutierrez and San Cristobal de Las Casas, Chiapas.

In Guatemala there are fine stands of *P. oocarpa* east of Guatemala City in the departments of Santa Rosa, Jalapa and Chiquimula; also along a number of highways in the departments of Huehuetenango, El Quiché, Totonicapán, Baja Verapaz and El Progreso.

In Belize the species has been reported in the Maya Mountains, particularly in the Mountain Pine Ridge area.

In El Salvador excellent stands of trees were found in the department of Chalatenango near the town of La Palma and near Montecristo National Park where El Salvador joins Guatemala and Honduras. The species can also be collected in

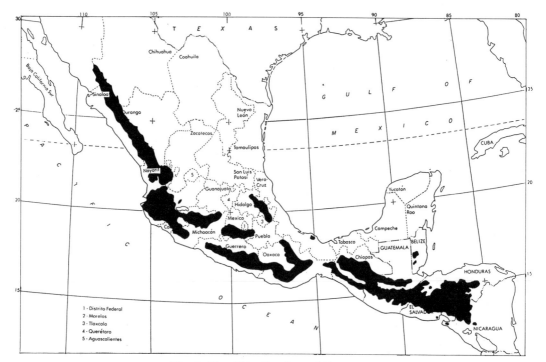

Fig. 3.61. Distribution of *P. oocarpa*.

Morazán department north of the city San Francisco. In Honduras *P. oocarpa* is widespread, occurring in almost all the departments. I collected it in the westernmost corner of the country in the department of Ocotepeque and along its range eastward across Honduras to Paraíso Department at the border of Nicaragua.

In Nicaragua the species forms extensive forests in the department of Nueva Segovia along the northwestern border with Honduras. Scattered populations extend southward in the department of Matagalpa, and roadside trees can be found along the highway from the city of Jinotega to Matagalpa. About 25 km east of Matagalpa there are sizable stands in the Cordillera Dariense. About 20–25 km south of the city Matagalpa, near the Rio Grande de Matagalpa, there is a small population of trees; possibly these are the southernmost occurrence of the species in North America (approximately 12° 30' N latitude). Only one other pine, *P. caribaea* var. *hondurensis* has a more southerly range in North America, growing on the Caribbean coast of Nicaragua near the city of Bluefields at approximately 12° 0' N.

NOTES AND COMMENTS—*P. oocarpa* is a very variable species, though this is not surprising in view of its very broad north-south distribution. Shaw described one variety, *P. oocarpa* var. *microphylla* from northwestern Mexico, and Prof. Martínez described three additional varieties. All of these are dealt with in the following pages.

From my field observations it appeared that in the northwestern part of its range (Sonora, Sinaloa, Durango, Nayarit) the species is, in general, a rather small, poorly-formed tree; in Central Mexico (Jalisco, Michoacán, Mexico) the form and size of the trees improved considerably; in southern Mexico and Central America *P. oocarpa* becomes a medium to large tree with fair to excellent form.

Over most of its southern range (Chiapas, Mexico, Guatemala, Honduras and Nicaragua) the species is subject to frequent ground fires. Although mature trees are fairly fire-resistant, young reproduction is often wiped out. Nevertheless, fire appears to be a very important factor in enabling the pines to compete successfully with the broadleaf vegetation in those semi-tropical areas. Heat from the fires coupled with the usually high temperatures of the dry season often causes the serotinous cones to open, and the burned-over terrain provides an excellent seedbed for the small seeds.

In addition to its serotinous cones, *P. oocarpa* possess another "fire-survival" character; very young trees 2–4 years old, have the ability to sprout from the root at ground line following fires that have killed the original young stem. This is a remarkable and very important survival mechanism for a pine that must compete with many broadleaf species possessing the same root sprouting ability. I believe that *P. leiophylla* may be the only other Mexican pine that has this ability. While *P. montezumae* and *P. michoacana* develop a "grass stage" that provides some fire-resistance during the first 2–4 years of growth, they do not have the ability to sprout from the root at ground line. I believe this "fire-survival" character is another example of *P. oocarpa's* wide range of adaptability that enables it to compete successfully in many different environments.

Pinus oocarpa var. *ochoterenai* Mart.

Pino, Ocote

THE TREE—A very fine pine that attains heights of 30–35 m and occasionally 45 m with diameter of 50–100 cm. The crown is rather narrow and in old trees somewhat rounded and dense.

BARK—On the lower trunk dark grayish brown, rough and divided into irregular plates by vertical and horizontal fissures;

higher up the trunk the bark often becomes brownish to reddish brown and scaly. Young trees have rather thin, scaly, reddish brown bark.

BRANCHLETS—Slender, stiff, the bark reddish brown and scaly; bases of the leaf bracts are decurrent.

LEAVES—In fascicles of 3, 4 and 5, mostly 4 and 5, generally more slender than in the species; erect to slightly drooping, not pendent, 17–25 cm long, the margins finely serrate; stomata present on the dorsal and ventral surfaces; resin canals 2–4, mostly 3 and 4, medial. Collections from some areas occasionally have leaves with 1 internal or 1 septal canal in addition to the medial canals. Exterior walls of the endoderm are thin to slightly thickened (occasionally thick); fibrovascular bundles are 2, contiguous but quite distinct; fascicle sheaths are pale brown, scaly, about 1.5 cm long and persistent.

CONELETS—Subterminal, borne in pairs and groups of 3 and 4 on long (1–2 cm), scaly peduncles, The small, thick scales have a short, stout prickle pointed toward the apex of the cone.

CONES—Smaller than those of the species, long-ovoid, 5–8 cm long, 5–6 cm wide, tapering toward the apex; oblique, reflexed on strong peduncles 1.0–2.5 cm long. Their color is a reddish yellow ochre somewhat darker than the species and they ripen during the dry, winter months. The small cones are not serotinous but often remain attached to the branchlet for a number of months. When the cone falls the peduncle remains attached to it.

CONE SCALES—Small, rather thin but hard and stiff, the apophysis flat to slightly raised; the umbo flat or depressed with a small, persistent prickle pointed toward the apex of the cone.

SEED—Small, dark brown, about 6 mm long and 3–5 mm wide, the seed wing 10–15 mm long, articulate and thickened at the base where it joins the seed.

WOOD—Hard, heavy, resinous; widely used for commercial timbers and cut locally for hewn timbers and firewood. The trees are routinely tapped for turpentine along with associated pines.

DISTRIBUTION—In his description of *P. oocarpa* var. *ochoterenai,* Martínez (1948) stated that he had seen specimens only from Chiapas, Mexico. It is now known that this variety occurs in Guerrero, Oaxaca and Chiapas, Mexico; Guatemala, El Salvador, Honduras, Nicaragua and Belize (Fig. 3.62).

HABITAT—Var. *ochoterenai* grows in pure stands and in association with *P. oocarpa, P. patula* var. *longepedunculata, P. maximinoi, P. oaxacana, P. tecunumanii, P. nubicola, P. ayacahuite, P. pringlei, P. teocote* and *P. caribaea* var. *hondurensis.* It grows under a variety of conditions ranging from semi-arid to humid-tropical and annual rainfall varies from 800 to 3,000 mm. It has been collected at altitudes ranging from 500 to 2,600 m but makes its best growth at 1,500–2,500 m with annual rainfall of about 1,600 mm.

WHERE TO FIND var. *ochoterenai*—A number of stands can be found near the city of San Cristobal de las Casas in Chiapas. In that area roadside trees were found along Highway 190 about 20 km south of the city and about 10 km north of the city on the same highway.

P. oocarpa var. *ochoterenae* Tree

Bark

Branchlet, cones, and leaves

Catkins and conelet

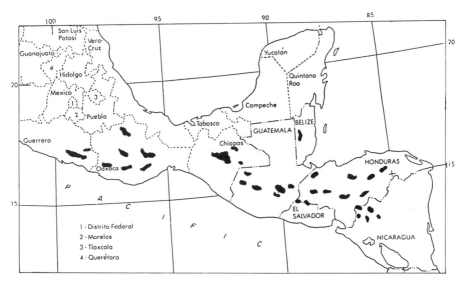

Fig. 3.62. Distribution of *P. oocarpa* var. *ochoterenae*.

In Guatemala fine trees were found along a partially paved road from San José Pinula to the village of Mataquescuintla (∿ kilometer 39 and 47, respectively).

In Honduras, at 800–900 m altitude, stands of excellent trees were encountered along an unpaved road near the village of Villa Santa, in the Department of El Paraíso near the Nicaraguan frontier. Trees were also observed in the hills north of Yoro at 600–700 m.

In El Salvador small stands of var. *ochoterenai* were found near the town of La Palma very near the Honduras border at about 2,100 m altitude. Trees were also found growing on Cerro Monte Cristo at 1,700 m altitude.

In Nicaragua the variety occurs with *P. oocarpa* in the department of Nueva Segovia along the northwestern border with Honduras.

NOTES AND COMMENTS—Foresters, botanists and taxonomists have disagreed for some time regarding the identification and classification of this taxon. Some believe that *P. oocarpa* var. *ochoterenai* and *P. patula* var. *longepedunculata* are the same and should be referred to *P. patula* (Styles, 1976).

There is no problem at all regarding identification of *P. oocarpa* and *P. patula*. The two taxa are so different in so many respects that they are easily separated in the field. If one keeps in mind the typical *P. patula* tree,

cone and needles and the typical *P. oocarpa* tree, cone and needles, it becomes easier to deal with the varieties, *P. patula* var. *longepedunculata* and *P. oocarpa* var. *ochoterenai*. The table on page 178 describes a number of similarities and dissimilarities between these taxa, all evidence supporting the belief that for millennia natural crossing has been occurring between these pines. (See also *P. tecunumanii* for table of comparison and notes on hybridization).

It is helpful to remember too that *P. oocarpa* is a very variable species with a number of described varieties. A recently described species, *Pinus jaliscana* (Pérez de la Rosa, 1983), is closely related to *P. oocarpa* and has small, tapering cones that closely resemble the cones of *P. patula* var. *longepedunculata*. This "new" species has only been reported from the state of Jalisco, Mexico.

One final word on these interesting taxa; *P. oocarpa* and *P. patula* have been successfully crossed at the Institute of Forest Genetics, Placerville, California. It would not be unusual to expect var. *ochoterenai* and var. *longepedunculata* to cross naturally in the field or to cross with the typical variety. Natural crosses of this kind could help to explain the introgression that appears to be taking place among these taxa.

The questions regarding identity and classification of *P. oocarpa* var. *ochoterenai* are much too complex to be completely answered here. However, it appears to me that var. *ochoterenai* is indeed quite separate and distinct from var. *longepedunculata* and certainly should not be referred to *P. patula*.

Table 3.22. Characteristics of *P. oocarpa* and var. *ochoterenai*; and *P. patula* and var. *longepedunculata*.

	P. oocarpa	P. oocarpa var. ochoterenai	P. patula	P. patula var. longepedunculata
Mature crown	Rounded, rather dense	Pyramidal, rather dense	Rounded, open	Rounded, open
Bark	Large, thick plates, reddish brown, scaly on upper stem	Not large plates, reddish to brownish, scaly	Very thin and scaly, reddish brown	Very thin and scaly, reddish brown
Branchlets	Thick, stiff, scaly, rough	Slender, stiff, scaly, rough	Slender, drooping, pruinose, later becoming scaly	Slender drooping, pruinose, later becoming scaly
Needles, number	Mostly 5, occasionally 3 & 4	3, 4, & 5, mostly 4 & 5	3, occasionally 4	3 & 4, rarely 5
Length	20–25 cm	17–25 cm	15–25 cm	15–25 cm
Habit	Stiff, erect, thick	Erect, often drooping, slender, not pendent	Slender, distinctly pendent	Slender, distinctly pendent
Resin canals	4–8, mostly septal, occasionally 1 or 2 medial or internal	3–4, occasionally 2, mostly medial, occasionally 1 internal or 1 septal	1–4, mostly 3, usually medial, occasionally 1 or 2 internal	2, occasionally 3, usually medial, occasionally 1 internal
Exterior wall of endodermal cells	Not thickened	Thin to slightly thickened to thick	Thin to slightly thickened	Thin to slightly thickened
Catkins	Large, loose clusters, rosy to light purple	Large, loose clusters, rosy to light purple	Small, tight clusters, pale yellow	Small tight clusters, pale yellow
Cones: number and habit	1–4, in groups on branchlets	1–4 or 5, in groups on branchlets	1–12 or more, often borne in clusters on stem of tree or branches	1–4 or 5, borne in groups on branchlets rarely on stem of tree or branches
Size and form	6–10 cm, long–ovoid to ovate, often broader than long, 6–12 cm, wide, symmetrical	5–8 cm, long–ovoid, tapering toward the apex, 5–6 cm wide, asymmetrical	7–10 cm, long-conical to conical; 5–7 cm wide, assymmetrical	5–8 cm,* long-conical to long-ovate, 2–5 cm wide slightly symmetrical
Serotiny and persistence	Serotinous and persistent for two or more years, cones opening in a year or two at most	Not serotinous, semi-persistent, i.e. not as long as *P. oocarpa*	Long serotinous and very persistent; cones not opening for years	Not serotinous and semi-persistent, i.e. not as long as *P. patula*

*See *P. patula* var. *longepedunculata* for detailed information on cone weight, number of scales, seed size, and seed weight.

	P. oocarpa	P. oocarpa var. ochoterenai	P. patula	P. patula var. longepedunculata
Cone scales	Thick, hard, stiff, opening widely to form a "rosette"	Smaller than those of P. oocarpa, hard but not so stiff, opening completely but not as widely as in P. oocarpa	Hard, stiff, not opening widely, scales at base of cone unopened for years	Small, hard but not as stiff as in P. patula, opening completely
Seed	7 mm long, dark brown, seed wing 10–15 mm long, articulate, dark brown	6 mm long, 3–5 mm wide, dark brown, seed wing 12–15 mm long, dark brown, articulate	About 5 mm long, 3 mm wide, dark brown almost black, seed wing 13 mm long, pale brown, articulate	5 mm long, 3 mm wide, black with brown marks; seed wing 15 mm long, 5 mm wide, light brown, articulate
Peduncle	3–4 cm long, stong, thick, generally recurved, tenacious	1.0–2.5 cm long, strong, generally thick, mostly recurved, not as tenacious as in P. oocarpa	Sessile very tenacious	0.5–1.5 cm long, generally recurved, slender, not as tenacious as in P. patula
Altitudinal range	200–2,500 m	500–2,600 m	1,500–3,100 m	1,800–2,800 m
Turpentine chemistry	Very high α-pinene, low limonene, carene and β-phellandrene, high longifolene	Moderately high α-pinene, high carene, usually low limonene and β-phellandrene, high longifolene	Low α-pinene, very high β-phellandrene, low carene, limonene and medium longifolene	Medium α-pinene, high carene, medium limonene and high β-phellandrene, high longifolene

Pinus oocarpa var. *trifoliata* Mart.

Pino, Pino Chino

THE TREE—A small, poorly-formed pine 10–15 m high and 40 cm in diameter. The branches are thick and mostly horizontal forming a thick, irregularly rounded crown.

BARK—Not thick and plated but rough, scaly and dark brown.

BRANCHLETS—Slender, reddish, scaly, the leaves borne in dense groups toward the ends of the branchlets; bases of the leaf bracts are decurrent.

LEAVES—In fascicles of 3, occasionally 4, 20–25 cm long, thick, stiff, the margins finely serrate, stomata present on the dorsal and ventral surfaces; resin canals 5–8, septal; exterior walls of the endoderm cells not thickened; fibrovascular bundles 2, contiguous but distinct. Fascicle sheaths brown, about 20 mm long and persistent.

CONELETS—Globose on long (15–20 mm), scaly peduncles, their small scales thick with a small, erect prickle.

CONES—Ovoid-globose, symmetrical, hard, 3–5 cm long; borne singly and in pairs on long (2.5 cm) peduncles, serotinous, per-

P. oocarpa **var.** *trifoliata* Tree   Bark

Cones, leaves, and conelets

sistent and a pale, lustrous ochre color.

CONE SCALES—Hard, thick, stiff, the apophyses flat to slightly raised, transversely keeled; the umbo depressed and bearing a small, early-deciduous prickle.

SEED—Brown to almost black, about 6 mm long, the seed wing about 16 mm long, articulate and thickened where it joins the seed.

WOOD—Pale yellow, not hard but resinous, used locally for hewn timbers and firewood.

DISTRIBUTION—Var. *trifoliata* has been reported from Durango and Jalisco (Fig. 3.63).

HABITAT—This small pine grows on the lower slopes of the Sierra Madre Occidental at about 1,500–2,000 m altitude. The climate is warm-temperate and rainfall amounts to about 1,000 mm annually.

WHERE TO FIND var. *trifoliata*—Specimens have been collected near the village of Pueblo Nuevo and at Las Azoteas about 60 km from the town of Chavarria. I found a few scattered trees south of Highway 40 near El Salto. A few kilometers before reaching El Salto, at the village of Coyotes, turn south on a winding road that leads to the villages of Ceballos, Cruz and Palo Gordo. Near Palo Gordo there are scattered pines on the nearby hillsides.

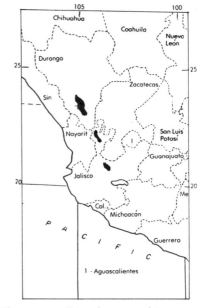

Fig. 3.63. Distribution of *P. oocarpa* var. *trifoliata*.

NOTES AND COMMENTS—With leaves in fascicles of 3 and its small, almost spherical cones, this variety is readily distinguished in the field from typical *P. oocarpa*. Although its distribution is quite limited, I believe that varietal classification is justified in this case.

Pinus oocarpa var. *microphylla* Shaw

Pino, Pino Prieto, Pino Chino

THE TREE—A small, generally poorly-formed pine about 15 m high, the branches irregularly spaced on the trunk and forming a somewhat rounded crown.

BARK—Not thick and plated but rough, scaly, grayish brown and about 1 cm thick.

BRANCHLETS—Slender, rough, yellowish brown; bases of the leaf bracts are decurrent.

LEAVES—In fascicles of 5, occasionally 4; 8–16 cm long, very slender, not thick and stiff as in the species, the margins finely serrate; stomata present on the dorsal and ventral surfaces; resin canals 1–4, internal; occasionally 1 septal; exterior walls of the endoderm cells thickened; fibrovascular bundles 2, contiguous but distinct; fascicle sheaths pale brown, about 7 mm long and persistent.

CONELETS—Ovoid on long, slender peduncles; the small scales pointed and bearing a long prickle.

CONES—Ovoid to ovoid-conical, generally symmetrical, 3.5–4.5 cm long and borne on slender, fragile peduncles 3.0–3.5 cm long. They are hard, strong, serotinous and a pale, polished ochre color.

CONE SCALES—Hard, stiff, the apophysis almost flat to very slightly raised, lightly transversely keeled; the umbo unusually depressed and the prickle very small and early-deciduous.

SEED—Dark brown with darker spots, 5–6 mm long, the seed wing 13–15 mm long, articulate and thickened where it joins the seed.

WOOD—Hard and strong, the sapwood pale brownish white and the heartwood light brown. The trees are of poor form and seldom cut for saw-logs but are used locally for firewood and hewn timbers.

DISTRIBUTION—Var. *microphylla* has been collected in the states of Sinaloa, Nayarit, Zacatecas and Jalisco on the western slopes of the Sierra Madre Occidental (Fig. 3.64).

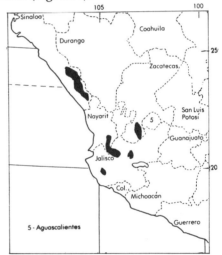

Fig. 3.64. Distribution of *P. oocarpa* var. *microphylla.*

P. oocarpa **var.** *microphylla* Tree   Bark   Cones and leaves

HABITAT—This variety grows under warm-temperate conditions on the lower slopes of the mountains at elevations of 1,000–1,300 m. Annual rainfall in those areas is about 1,000 mm and occurs mostly during the summer months of June–September.

WHERE TO FIND var. *microphylla*—Driving west from Durango to Mazatlan on Highway 40, I found roadside trees near the town of Concorcodia in the state of Sinaloa. Further south in Nayarit, on Highway 15, trees were found just before reaching the town of Ixtlán. On the same highway I collected specimens from roadside trees near the village of Tequila (1,300 m altitude) about 50 km west of Guadalajara.

NOTES AND COMMENTS—Var. *microphylla* is not difficult to distinguish from *P. oocarpa*. The short (8–16 cm), very slender leaves are in marked contrast to the leaves of typical *P. oocarpa* which are 20–25 cm long and very thick and stiff. The long, slender peduncle is quite different from that of *P. oocarpa* (most often thick, strong and tenacious). A number of writers have not recognized this variety. However, I believe that the consistent morphological differences summarized here justify its varietal status.

Pinus jaliscana Perez de la Rosa

Pino, Ocote, Jalisco Pine

THE TREE—A tall, well-formed pine, 20–30 m high and 50–80 cm in diameter. I saw a few trees that were 35 m high but they were unusual. In mature trees branches are clearly upraised, even the large, lower branches are characteristically ascending, the crown irregularly rounded and rather open. In young trees the crown is open and pyramidal.

BARK—In mature trees the bark is 1.5–3.5 cm thick and formed by shallow, vertical and horizontal fissures into longitudinal plates grayish brown in color. An unusual feature of the bark is its rapid exfoliation in large, very thin (0.5 mm) plates. These accummulate as small mounds around the base of old trees. Young trees have thin, rough, reddish brown bark in large, loose scales that form at a very early age (3–4 years).

BRANCHLETS—Long, slender, flexible; bases of the leaf bracts are early-decurrent leaving the branchlet relatively smooth.

LEAVES—In fascicles of 4 and 5, rarely 3; 12–16 cm long, very slender (0.5–0.8 mm wide) but not drooping, the margins finely serrate; stomata are present on the dorsal and ventral surfaces; resin canals 1–5, mostly 2–3, septal with occasionally 1 or 2 internal; exterior walls of the endoderm thickened; fibrovascular bundles 2, contiguous but distinct; fascicle sheaths pale brown, 8–15 mm long and persistent.

CONELETS—Subterminal, borne singly and in pairs on long (1.0–1.5 cm), scaly peduncles; the cone scales are very small, rounded and bear a minute, deciduous prickle pointed upward toward the apex of the cone.

CONES—Long conical to long-pointed, tapering toward the base and apex; almost symmetrical, lustrous ochre color turning grayish brown with age; 4–8 cm long (occasionally only 3 cm long) and 4–5 cm wide when open. They are borne singly and in pairs on slender, strong peduncles 1.0–1.5 cm long that are curved and twisted downward. The cones ripen during the winter months, are serotinous and persistent and when they fall, the peduncle generally remains attached to the cone.

CONE SCALES—Hard, strong, stiff; the apophyses mostly flat, slightly thickened and lightly transversely keeled; umbo very small, depressed and bearing a very small, weak, early-deciduous prickle. The scales open from the apex of the cone downward toward the base; the basal cone scales up to about one-third of the cone remain closed for years.

P. jaliscana Tree   Bark

Leaves, branchlets, and cones

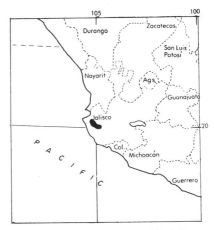

Fig. 3.65. Distribution of *P. jaliscana*.

SEED—Dark brown, small, 5–6 mm long and about 4 mm wide; the seed wing is pale brown, articulate, 12–16 mm long and 5–8 mm wide. The number of seed/kg has not been calculated; however, since they are about the same size as seed from *P. patula* and *P. oocarpa*, it is estimated that seed/kg is probably about 120,000.

WOOD—Hard, strong, resinous; the sapwood creamy white. Many trees had been logged along with *P. oocarpa*, *P. maximinoi* and *P. douglasiana*. The larger trees had been tapped for resin along with associated pines.

DISTRIBUTION—*P. jaliscana* has been reported as occurring only in the state of Jalisco, Mexico, in an area located about 25 km from the Puerto Vallarta-El Tuito highway (Fig. 3.65). Collections have been made from two locations within that area, near Minas de Zimapán and Rancho El Saucillo. The larger of the two populations is near Minas de Zimapán and covers an area of about 300 ha.

HABITAT—This species is found at elevations of 850–1,650 m. The climate is semi-tropical to tropical (banana, papaya and sugar cane growing nearby) with annual rainfall of 1,000–1,500 mm and mean annual temperature 22–26° C. The best trees were found growing on deep, well-drained soils of granite origin. Associated trees were *P. oocarpa*, *P. maximinoi* and *P. douglasiana*.

WHERE TO FIND *P. jaliscana*—From Puerto Vallarta take Highway MEX 200 south toward the town of El Tuito. A few kilometers before reaching El Tuito look for a narrow dirt road on the left with a large sign, Minas de Zimapán, near the entrance. Turn onto this road and drive for approximately 1 km to the offices and buildings of Minas de Zimapán. It will be necessary to stop there and obtain permission to proceed eastward on the dirt road. Once permission is granted, drive along the narrow winding road for about 25 km. Near a clear mountain stream spanned by a narrow concrete bridge, one can find scattered stands of *P. jaliscana*.

NOTES AND COMMENTS—*P. jaliscana*, described by Perez de la Rosa (1983), is a relatively "new" pine species. I agree with the author that this taxon is related to *P. oocarpa* (because of the serotinous, persistent cones and septal resin canals). The cones are very similar to the cones of *P. patula* var. *longepedunculata*; however, the plated bark and septal resin canals clearly indicate a closer relationship to *P. oocarpa* than to *P. patula*.

The leaves of this species are among the finest (most slender) of the Mexican and Central American pines and I find it strange that they are erect, never drooping. The strongly reflexed and twisted peduncle along with the rapid exfoliation of the bark

are also unusual characters.

Although the species apparently has a very limited range, it was dismaying to find that the small stands had recently been logged. Although *P. jaliscana* is not yet an endangered species, prompt action should be taken to protect the small populations.

Pinus pringlei Shaw

Pino Rojo, Pino, Ocote

THE TREE—A large tree 15–25 m high and up to 90 cm in diameter; in old trees the crown is generally rounded with large, irregularly spaced, horizontal to ascending branches.

BARK—On mature trees the bark is thick, grayish brown, scaly, and reddish color on the upper stem. On the lower trunk it is divided into large, scaly plates by deep fissures revealing an orange-red underbark.

BRANCHLETS—Stout, not slender or flexible, rough and scaly; bases of the leaf bracts are decurrent.

LEAVES—In fascicles of 3, occasionally 4, 18–25 cm long, 1.0–1.5 mm wide, stiff, erect and light green in color. Margins are finely serrate; stomata present on dorsal and ventral surfaces; resin canals 3–7, mostly internal, occasionally with 1 or 2 medial or 1 or 2

septal; outer walls of the endodermal cells are not thickened; fibrovascular bundles 2, close together but quite distinct; sheaths 10–20 mm long, brown, scaly, persistent and often resinous.

CONELETS—Borne on stout peduncles, singly and in groups of 2, 3 and 4; long-ovate, the scales bearing a minute prickle.

CONES—Long-ovate to long-conical, 5–8 cm long, asymmetrical, reflexed on short (5–10 mm), thick, tenacious peduncles; polished yellowish green color, persistent, opening very slowly over a long period of time.

CONE SCALES—Hard, stiff; apophysis generally flat but often slightly raised to pyramidal; umbo small, flat to depressed with a small, deciduous prickle.

SEEDS—About 5 mm long; dark brown

P. pringlei Tree   Bark   Branchlet, cones, conelets, and leaves

to almost black; the wing 15–17 mm long, articulate and thickened where it joins the seed.

WOOD—Hard and heavy; stronger and harder than wood of *P. patula*. The trees are logged along with associated pines for general construction timbers. It is also cut locally for firewood and hewn timbers and the trees are tapped commercially for pine resin.

DISTRIBUTION—*P. pringlei* has a rather limited range in Mexico, occurring in the warm, subtropical areas of Michoacán, Guerrero, Mexico, Morelos, Puebla and Oaxaca (Fig. 3.66).

HABITAT—Rainfall is 1,000–1,500 mm over most of its range, and temperature during the year varies from about 20°C during the cool, winter months to over 25°C during May and June. Its altitudinal range is from 1,500 to 2,500 m. Most rainfall occurs during the summer months of June–September. This species grows in pure stands and in small groups or individual trees often mixed with *P. pseudostrobus, P. michoacana, P. douglasiana, P. maximinoi, P. oocarpa, P. lawsoni, P. montezumae* and *P. patula* var. *longepedunculata*.

WHERE TO FIND *P. pringlei*—In Uruapan I made collections from very fine trees only 6 km from the city, on the slopes of Cerro de la Cruz at about 1,800 m altitude. Trees were

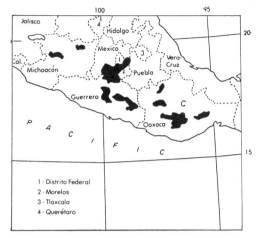

Fig. 3.66. Distribution of *P. pringlei*.

growing with *P. michoacana* var. *cornuta, P. douglasiana* and *P. lawsoni*.

NOTES AND COMMENTS—In the field this taxon is often difficult to distinguish from *P. lawsoni*. To identify *P. lawsoni* look for leaves in groups of 3, 4 and 5, small cones with apophysis irregularly raised and often slightly protuberant. *P. pringlei* has stiff, thick leaves most often in groups of three, the cones are generally a little larger than those of *P. lawsoni* and are very persistent. They are borne in clusters of 3–4, and occasionally in groups of 4–6. Another distinguishing character of *P. pringlei* are the internal resin canals, generally 4–8 in number, with often 1 or 2 septal.

Pinus oocarpa var. *manzanoi* Mart.

Martinez (1940) noted that this variety had been collected only near Huasca in the state of Hidalgo. He also pointed out that it could be distinguished from typical *P. oocarpa* by its more slender leaves in fascicles of 4 and 5 (occasionally 3), its long-ovoid cones, its resin canals often medial and at times septal, its cone scales with raised apophysis and its short, strong peduncle.

I collected cones and foliage of *P. oocarpa*

in Hidalgo and over most of its range in Mexico, Guatemala, Honduras and El Salvador. In all of these countries variation in cone size, form, thickness of the leaves, and peduncle length and thickness is unusually great in this taxon. This range of variation easily embraces Martinez' description of var. *manzanoi*. I believe then that the description of var. *manzanoi* does not merit classification as a distinct variety.

Pinus tecunumanii (Schw.) Eguiluz et Perry

Pino, Ocote

THE TREE—A beautiful pine that grows up to 50 m in height with a diameter of 50–120 cm. The trunk is straight and generally free of branches for 20–30 m. The crown in mature trees is narrowly pyramidal and rather dense. In young trees the branches are in distinct whorls and the crown is pyramidal.

BARK—On mature trees, generally 2–5 cm thick near the base; at 2–4 m becoming thinner, scaly and brown to brownish red. Young trees have thin, scaly, reddish bark.

BRANCHLETS—Slender, flexible, mostly horizontal, smooth when young but becoming scaly; bases of the leaf bracts are decurrent.

LEAVES—Light green to greenish yellow; 3–5 per fascicle, (mostly 4–5); 14–21 cm long, mostly 17–18 cm, slender, flexible, erect to drooping but not pendent as in *P. patula*, borne thickly along the branchlet, not in tufts or groups at the ends of the branchlet. The margins are finely serrate; stomata present on the dorsal and ventral surfaces; resin canals 2–5 (mostly 3–4) medial, occasionally with 1 internal and/or 1 septal; exterior walls of the endodermal cells slightly thickened to occasionally thick; fibrovascular bundles 2, quite distinct; fascicle sheaths are persistent, 15–20 mm long and grayish brown.

CONELETS—Borne singly and in 2s and 3s on slender peduncles. The small scales are pointed and bear a minute prickle.

CONES—Generally solitary or in pairs, (occasionally 3–4); symmetrical to slightly asymmetrical; 4–7 cm long, generally about 5 cm, 2.5–3.5 cm wide, long-ovoid to long conical, and a polished, grayish yellow color. Cones are borne on slender, slightly curved, strong but not tenacious peduncles 0.5–1.5 cm long that remain attached to the cone when it falls. The cones open when mature and are persistent for a year or more.

CONE SCALES—Small, medium-stiff, but not as stiff and hard as the scales in *P. patula* and *P. oocarpa;* the apophysis flat to slightly raised; umbo reddish brown while the cone is still green, very slightly raised, the margins often depressed, bearing a small prickle curved toward the apex of the cone.

SEED—Pale brown, quite small, 4–6 mm long and about 3 mm wide, the seed wing articulate, slightly thickened where it joins the seed, about 9 mm long and 5 mm wide. Cotyledons number 5–6, occasionally 4 or 7.

WOOD—Of excellent quality; specific gravity is high, 0.51–0.56, fairly hard and heavy but not as resinous as *P. oocarpa.* Trees are logged and sold along with associated pines and are also cut locally for firewood and hewn timbers.

P. tecunumanii Tree.
Thanks to W. Mittak.

Bark

Branchlets, cones, conelets, and leaves

DISTRIBUTION—The range of this variable species has not yet been clearly established. However, my own collections and some of those of CAMCORE (Central America an Mexico Coniferous Resources Cooperative) indicate that *P. tecunumanii* occurs in Guatemala, El Salvador and Honduras. It may also occur in Chiapas, Mexico (Fig. 3.67).

HABITAT—*P. tecunumanii* grows occasionally in small, pure stands but most often in association with *P. oocarpa* var. *ochoterenai*, *P. patula* var. *longepedunculata*, *P. maximinoi*, *P. oaxacana*, *P. nubicola*, *P. ayacahuite* and *P. oocarpa*. *Liquidambar styraciflua* is often present on the more humid sites. It has been collected at altitudes ranging from 1,500 to 2,600 m. Although rainfall measurements are not available for all the collection localities, it appears that annual rainfall over most of its range is approximately 1,200–2,000 mm. Best growth is made on well-drained slopes with deep, fertile soils. At higher elevations (2,200–2,600 m) frosts may occur during the coldest winter months (December and January) while at lower elevations the climate is subtropical to tropical.

WHERE TO FIND *P. tecunumanii*—In Guatemala, Schwerdtfeger (1953) found this species growing at 1,900 m altitude in the Department of Verapaz near Salamá and I collected it in this same area at the Federal Forest Preserve near the village of San Jeronimo. To reach this area drive east from Guatemala City on Highway CA-9 to the town of El Progreso. Approximately 7 km east of the town locate Highway 17 and turn sharply left onto it. Drive toward the city of Salamá to kilometer 135; near this point look for a sign "El Guatel" (telephone tower) near the village of San Jeronimo. This winding road leads to the Federal Forest Preserve. After entering the Preserve drive for about 4 km along a winding dirt trail. Very fine trees of *P. tecunumanii* will be found at 1,700–1,800 m altitude growing near the telephone tower.

In El Salvador drive north from San Salvador toward the town of La Palma near the Honduras border. At La Palma look for a narrow trail on the right that leads to the villages of Las Pilas, El Miramundo and El Aguacatal. Near these villages *P. tecunumanii* can be found at elevations

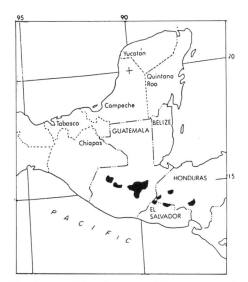

Fig. 3.67. Distribution of *P. tecunumanii.*

ranging from 1,700 to 2,200 m. I found it growing in association with *P. oocarpa* var. *ochoterenai*, *P. nubicola*, *P. oocarpa*, *P. ayacahuite*, *P. maximinoi*, *Abies guatemalensis* var. *tacanensis* (Lundell) Mart. and *Cupressus* sp. It would be wise to employ a guide at La Palma since the road to the villages is winding with many crossing trails. This is rather isolated country very near the Honduras border so the trip should be attempted only with a 4-wheel-drive vehicle equipped with good tires and a good supply of gasoline and water. The trip should only be made during the dry season and no night driving should be planned.

NOTES AND COMMENTS—I mentioned earlier the confusion surrounding the identification and classification of *P. oocarpa* var. *ochoterenai* and *P. patula* var. *longepedunculata*. A similar situation exists with regard to *P. tecunumanii*. Some botanists and taxonomists believe that *P. tecunumanii* should be considered a subspecies of *P. patula* (*P. patula* subsp. *tecunumanii* (Eguiluz & Perry; Styles, 1985) while others believe it is a valid species. As in the case of *P. oocarpa* var. *ochoterenai*, this is not the place for a complete review of the literature and pros and cons of its classification. However, a brief summary of its classification may be helpful in understanding its present taxonomic status.

There is very little difficulty in the field or herbarium in separating *P. tecunumanii* from

P. oocarpa and *P. patula.* However, the situation is quite different with regard to the identification of *P. oocarpa* var. *ochoterenai,* *P. patula* var. *longepedunculata* and *P. tecunumanii.* Styles (1976) has complicated the picture by referring both var. *ochoterenai* and var. *longepedunculata* to *P. patula* and, more recently (1985), proposing *P. tecunumanii* as a subspecies of *P. patula.*

Although the three taxa (*P. tecunumanii,* var. *ochoterenai* and var. *longepedunculata*) are difficult to separate in the field and particularly in the herbarium where one cannot see the entire tree and its surroundings, this does not justify the "disappearance taxonomically" of var. *ochoterenai* and var.

longepedunculata and the reclassification of *P. tecunumanii.* While I agree there are many similarities between the three taxa discussed here and those stressed by Styles (1976, 1985) in his morphological studies, there are also significant differences that I believe justify consideration of these taxa as separate varieties and species. In my description of var. *ochoterenai* I have tabulated a number of characters for *P. oocarpa,* var. *ochoterenai,* *P. patula* and var. *longepedunculata.* In Table 3.23 the characters of var. *ochoterenai* and var. *longepedunculata* are compared with those of *P. tecunumanii.*

Table 3.23.   Characterstics of *P. oocarpa* var. *ochoterenai, P. patula* var. *longepeduncula,* and *P. tecunumanii.*

	P. oocarpa var. *ochoterenai*	*P. tecunumanii*	*P. patula* var. *longepedunculata*
Mature crown	Pyramidal, rather dense	Narrow, pyramidal, dense	Rounded, open
Bark	Not in large plates; scaly, reddish–brownish	Near the base, dark brown, obscure, 2–5cm thick, at 3m becoming thinner, scaly reddish-brown	Thick at the base, at 3m becoming very thin, scaly, reddish-brown
Branchlets	Slender, stiff, scaly, rough	Slender, horizontal to raised, smooth but becoming scaly	Slender, drooping, smooth but becoming scaly
Needles, number	4 and 5, occasionally 3	4 and 5, occasionally 3	3 and 4, rarely 5
Length	17–25 cm	14–21 cm	15–25 cm
Habit	Slender, erect to drooping, not pendent; borne in clusters at ends of the branchlets	Slender, erect to drooping, not pendent; borne all along and at ends of branchlets	Slender, distinctly pendent; borne in clusters at ends of branchlets
Resin canals	3–4, occasionally 2, mostly medial, occasionally 1 internal or 1 septal	2–5, mostly 3, medial, occasionally 1 internal or 1 septal	2, occasionally 3, mostly medial, occasionally 1 internal
Exterior wall of endodermal cells	Thin to slightly thickened, to thick	Slightly thickened to occasionally thick	Thin to slightly thickened
Catkins	Large, loose clusters, rosy to light purple	Medium compact clusters, light yellow tinged with purple	Small, tight clusters, pale yellow
Cones; number and habit	1–4 or 5 in groups on branchlets	1–2 or 3 on branchlets	1–4 in groups on branchlets, occasionally on branches and stem
Size and form	5–8 cm, long-ovoid, tapering toward the apex, 5–6 cm wide, symmetrical	4–6 cm, conical to slightly ovoid, 2.5–3.5 cm wide, sub-symmetrical	5–8 cm, long-conical to long-ovate, 2–5 cm wide, slightly asymmetrical

	P. oocarpa var. ochoterenai	P. tecunumanii	P. patula var. longepedunculata
Serotiny and persistence	Not serotinous; semi-persistent, i.e. not as long as P. oocarpa	Not serotinous; semi-persistent, i.e. not as long as P. oocarpa or P. patula	Not serotinous; semi-persistent, i.e. not as long as P. patula
Cone scales	Small, hard, not as stiff as in P. oocarpa; opening completely but not in form of "rosette" as in P. oocarpa	Small, hard but not as stiff as in P. patula; opening completely	Small, hard but not as stiff as in P. patula; opening completely
Peduncle	1.0–2.5 cm long, strong, generally thick, mostly recurved, not as tenacious as P. oocarpa; remains attached to cone when it falls	0.7–1.6 cm long, slender, often recurved, not as tenacious as P. patula; remains attached to cone when it falls	0.5–1.5 cm long, generally recurved, slender, not as tenacious as P. patula; remains attached to cone when it falls
Seed	6 mm long, 3–5 mm wide, dark brown; seed wing 12–15 mm long, dark brown, thickened at the base	About 5 mm long and 3 mm wide, pale brown; seed wing pale brown, about 9 mm long and 5 mm wide, thickened at the base	5 mm long, 3 mm wide, black with brown marks; seed wing 15 mm long and 5 mm wide, light brown, thickened at the base
Cotyledons	Data not available, however P. oocarpa has 5–7, mostly 6	Mostly 5–6, occasionally 4 or 7	Data not available, however P. patula has 4–5, mostly 5
Wood	Fairly hard, heavy, resinous, specific gravity is high, about 0.60 (wood from mature trees, Mountain Pine Ridge, Belize)	Fairly hard and heavy, not as resinous as var. ochoterenai; specific gravity is high 0.51–0.56	Fairly soft, light not resinous, similar to P. patula, perhaps a little harder; specific gravity not available
Altitudinal range	500–2,600 m	1,500–2,600 m	1,800–2,800 m
Turpentine chemistry	High α-pinene, high carene, low limonene and β-phellandrene, high longifolene	Low to medium α-pinene and carene, high limonene and β-phellandrene, high longifolene	Medium α-pinene, high carene, medium limonene, high β-phellandrene, high longifolene

Without reviewing each item in the table, it is clear that *P. tecunumanii* has many characters that are similar to *P. oocarpa* var. *ochoterenai* and *P. patula* var. *longepedunculata*. There are, however, some important differences that I have found very helpful in distinguishing the species in the field. *P. tecunumanii* has the best formed trunk and crown of these three taxa. It is quite different from that of var. *longepedunculata* which has an open, rounded crown. The crown of *P. tecunumanii* is usually more pyramidal and dense than the crowns of both varieties. The brownish to reddish scaly bark has been cited by many taxonomists and botanists as positive proof of the close relationship of this taxon to *P. patula*, noted for its thin, scaly, reddish bark. *P. patula* var. *longepedunculata* does have the scaly reddish bark characteristic of *P. patula* and I expect that many trees formerly identified as var. *longepedunculata* are now incorrectly classified as *P. patula* subsp. *tecunumanii* based on this character alone. My own field observations are that the bark of typical *P. tecunumanii* is often reddish brown, thin and scaly and also often brownish red and not as thin and scaly as the bark of *P. patula* or var. *longepedunculata*. Var. *ochoterenai* also often has thin, scaly, brownish red bark somewhat similar to the bark of *P. patula* and var. *longepedunculata*. There are also many trees in this group with all gradations of bark characteristics that range from reddish, thin and scaly to brown, thin and scaly, brownish red and less thin and scaly, etc.

The thin, scaly, reddish bark beginning at 2–4 m on the trunk of *P. patula* and var. *longepedunculata* is indeed characteristic of the two taxa. In *P. tecunamanii* and var. *ochoterenai* it is much more variable and less definitive.

There should be no problem in separating var. *longepedunculata* from the other two taxa since the needles are similar to those of *P. patula* in number per fascicle (mostly 3) and in habit (pendent). Neither *P. oocarpa* var. *ochoterenai* nor *P. tecunumanii* have pendent needles. Needles of var. *ochoterenai* are usually longer, more erect, and usually not as slender as needles of *P. tecunumanii*. Needles of *P. tecunumanii* are usually borne all along the branchlet and in var. *ochoterenai* they are generally in groups at the ends of the branchlet.

The cones and peduncles too are different; careful observation of many cones and their peduncles, along with observations of the needles, tree form and bark usually (though not always) reveal the true identity of a particular tree. The cones of *P. oocarpa* var. *ochoterenai* are generally more ovate with a broader base (a *P. oocarpa* character) than the cones of *P. patula* var. *longepedunculata* and *P. tecunumanii*. Cones of *P. tecunumanii* are usually smaller than those of var. *ochoterenai* and var. *longepedunculata* and the base of the cone usually tapers slightly toward the peduncle. It also tapers slightly toward the apex of the cone. I have also observed that *P. tecunumanii* green cones often have a rusty red colored area on the umbo around the small prickle. I have not observed this small colored area on green cones of either var. *ochoterenai* or var. *longepedunculata*. The green cone scales of var. *longepedunculata* usually do not have a sharp prickle pointed toward the apex of the cone as in *P. tecunumanii* and var. *ochoterenai*. Var. *longepedunculata* scales do have a small, weak prickle that is soon deciduous.

Cones of var. *longepedunculata* are usually, though not always, longer and more tapering toward the base and apex of the cone than the cones of var. *ochoterenai* and *P. tecunumanii*.

In *P. oocarpa* var. *ochoterenai* the peduncle is generally long, quite stout, recurved and difficult to pull from the branchlet. In both *P. tecunumanii* and var. *longepedunculata* the peduncle is not as thick as in var. *ochoterenai* and though often curved, it is also often almost straight. The peduncles in both these taxa are neither as long as those of var. *ochoterenai* nor as difficult to pull from the branchlet.

Seed of the three taxa are also slightly different. *P. patula* var. *longepedunculata* seeds are black with brown markings (Loock stressed this difference from the seed of *P. patula*) while seeds from var. *ochoterenai* are dark brown and seeds from *P. tecunumanii* are pale brown. Seeds of all three taxa are quite small; however, the seed wings of var. *ochoterenai* and var. *longepedunculata* are longer than those of *P. tecunumanii*.

With regard to altitudinal range, both *P. tecunumanii* and *P. patula* var. *longepedunculata* are high-altitude pines (1,500–2,600 m and 1,800–2,800 m, respectively) compared to *P. oocarpa* var. *ochoterenai* which occurs at 500–2,600 m.

Turpentine chemistry of the three taxa is also different. See the table. (Terpene data is presented in more detail in a separate paper in preparation by Perry and Squillace). While certainly not a character identifiable in the field, gas chromatograph analysis of the turpentine is so objective that it makes a valuable contribution to identification of these taxa.

In summary it appears to me that these three taxa are indeed similar in many respects and different too. All three taxa occur sympatrically and with *P. oocarpa*. *P. oocarpa* and *P. patula* also occur sympatrically and among the natural ranges of all these taxa there are many trees with morphological characters that shade imperceptibly from one species to a variety and on to another variety and another species. At this point it is helpful to remember that no two trees are exactly alike. Almost certainly introgression adds to the complexity of these populations.

P. oocarpa and *P. patula* have been successfully crossed at the U.S. Forest Service, Institute of Forest Genetics, Placerville, California. I believe the two species also cross naturally in the field. Varieties *ochoterenai* and *longepedunculata* probably cross naturally and back-cross with *P. oocarpa* and *P. patula*. *P. tecunumanii* may well be of hybrid origin emerging from this com-

plex of closed cone pines as an unusually outstanding pine.

Test plantings of seed from provenances of most of these taxa have been planted in a number of countries in South America, Africa and in Australia. Some are now producing cones and some crossings are being made. These plantings will soon enable geneticists to more accurately trace the relationships of this complex group.

Section Teocote

Only three species make up this section. All have small cones and leaves 3–5 (mostly 3) per fascicle. Table 3.24 lists the species with some of their morphological characteristics.

Table 3.24. Characteristics of Species in Section Teocote.

Species	Leaves per fascicle; length, cm	Cone length, cm; form	Resin canals: number; location
P. teocote	3; 8–15 cm; thick, stiff	4–7; symmetrical	2–5; medial
P. lawsoni	4–5 (3); 15–20 cm; thick, stiff	5–8; asymmetrical	2–6; internal
P. herrerai	3; 10–20 cm; slender, flexible	2–4; almost symmetrical	1–4 internal

Pinus teocote Schl. & Cham.

Ocote, Ocotl, Pino Real, Pino Chino

THE TREE—Medium-sized, 8–25 m high; in mature trees the branches are horizontal to slightly drooping forming a dense, rather rounded crown. In young, open-grown trees the crown is dense and pyramidal in form.

BARK—On old trees thick, rough, dark grayish brown, divided by deep, wide fissures into irregular longitudinal plates. On young trees the bark is thin, scaly and reddish. This species, like *P. leiophylla*, often has epicormic shoots along the trunk.

BRANCHLETS—When very young are smooth, however, they soon become rough with thin, reddish scales; bases of the leaf bracts are decurrent.

LEAVES—In fascicles of 3, rarely 4, 8–15 cm, rarely longer; thick, stiff, often more than 1 mm wide, margins finely serrate; stomata present on dorsal and ventral surfaces; resin canals medial, 2–5, rarely more; exterior walls of endoderm cells thickened; fibrovascular bundles 2, close together but quite distinct; sheaths are persistent, dark brown, 5–10 mm long.

CONELETS—Borne singly or in groups of 2, 3 and 4, occasionally more, on short, thick, stiff peduncles; long-ovoid, shiny brown, the scales transversely keeled, bearing a small prickle.

CONES—Pale brown, ovoid-conical, 4–7 cm long, occasionally only 2.5–4.0 cm,

P. teocote Tree   Bark   Cones, conelets, shoot, buds, and leaves

almost symmetrical, reflexed on short (5–8 mm) peduncles. They mature during the winter months, are dehiscent and soon deciduous, the peduncle generally falling with the small cone.

CONE SCALES—Small, not thickened, rather flexible, the apophysis flat to slightly raised; the umbo clearly defined, generally flat, gray, with a small, weak prickle that is soon deciduous.

SEEDS—Very small, about 4 mm long; grayish brown, the wing 10–15 mm long; articulate.

WOOD—Strong, hard, resinous, the sapwood very pale yellow color and the heartwood slightly darker; used for general construction purposes and cut locally for posts and firewood. The trees are also tapped commercially for resin.

DISTRIBUTION—*P. teocote* has a very broad range in Mexico, extending from southern Chihuahua southward along the Sierra Madre Occidental into Chiapas (Fig. 3.68). In the Sierra Madre Oriental its range extends southward from Coahuila and Nuevo León into Hidalgo, Mexico and Puebla. It has been reported from Guatamala; however, I have not been able to find it there.

One very isolated population of *P. teocote* should be mentioned because it is only 60–65 km from the Gulf of Mexico in the state of Tamaulipas. The pines here grow at elevations of 1,000–1,300 m on rocky, limestone soils. The highest peaks in the Sierra

are 1,200–1,300 m and it is on these peaks that *P. teocote* is found in pure, open stands. No other pine species are found in the Sierra de Tamaulipas. In these isolated, almost inaccessible hills no records of rainfall and temperature are available; however, from other stations in the state it is estimated that annual rainfall is about 600–900 mm and average annual temperature is about 23–26° C. The climate is semi-tropical, frost-free with dry, winter months.

At about 700–1,000 m altitude a dense forest of oaks forms a broad zone around the pine stands, intermingling with the pines at 1,000–1,100 m altitude.

The pines that I saw on the highest peaks were good trees with straight, clear stems; at lower altitudes they were generally smaller and more limby. On large, mature trees the bark was smoother and more evenly plated than I have seen on *P. teocote* in other parts of its range. It is interesting to note, too, that in this isolated, semi-tropical location, *P. teocote* grows at its lowest altitude—1,000 m.

HABITAT—*P. teocote* grows over such a wide range of conditions that it is difficult to cite a typical environment for the species. Its altitudinal range is about 1,000–3,000 m. In the southern part of its range it is generally of poor form and grows on rather dry, gravelly or rocky slopes. In the northern portion of its range, in Durango and in Nuevo León, groups of trees with very fine form usually grow on moist, well-drained sites. At higher altitudes frosts and snow

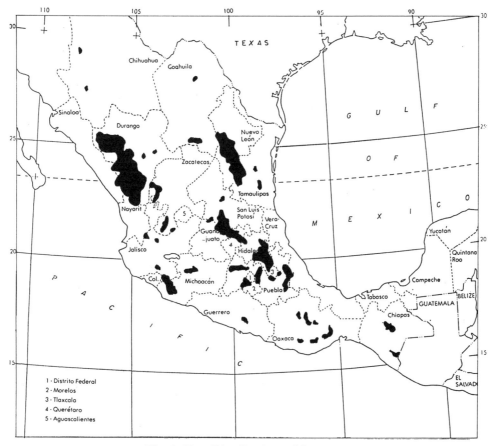

Fig. 3.68. Distribution of *P. teocote.*

occur during the winter months and at lower altitudes, on dry, rocky sites, this species survives very high temperatures. Over its very wide range *P. teocote* grows in rather open stands in association with many species of pines including *P. montezumae, P. leiophylla, P. rudis, P. chihuahuana, P. cembroides, P. engelmanii, P. oocarpa, P. patula* and *P. lawsoni.*

WHERE TO FIND *P. teocote*—With its very broad distribution this species can easily be found as a roadside tree along many of Mexico's principal highways. A fairly easy collecting trip could be made from Monterrey by driving to Chipinque Mesa (west on Highway 40 for about 30 km). This is a very interesting area at a much higher elevation than Monterrey and *P. teocote* attains very fine proportions here. Another short trip from Monterrey is south along Highway 85 to the town of Allende (about 45 km). Look carefully for signs on the right to "Cola de Caballo," a well-known tourist attraction—"Horse-tail Falls." Drive up past the falls on a very steep, winding, dirt road that will take you into the pine forest. Here *P. teocote* can be found growing along the road. This trip should be made only in a high-clearance vehicle and during the dry, winter months.

NOTES AND COMMENTS—In the southern part of its range *P. teocote* is found growing with *Pinus lawsoni,* another species that has very small cones and leaves in fascicles of 3, 4 and 5. The two species can be separated by checking the position of the resin canals; in *P. teocote* they are mostly medial, in *P. lawsoni* mostly internal. A simpler, field method is to make a slanting cut into the bark exposing the underbark, which in *P. lawsoni* is a deep reddish purple color. With such an extensive range and very variable environments, one would expect considerable variation in the species and this is indeed the case. Trees in Durango and Nuevo León are often of very fine form while trees from the southern part of its range are most often small, limby, and of poor form; leaves are mostly 3/fascicle and rather short, thick and stiff, yet in numerous locations trees can be found with longer, thinner leaves often 3,4 and 5 in a fascicle. Cones may vary too from 2.5 cm to as much as 8 cm long. It is clear then, that *P. teocote* is a variable species, yet with some experience in the field, it is not difficult to identify.

Pinus teocote forma *macrocarpa* Mart.

Pinus teocote forma *quinquefoliata* Mart.

I have decided to treat these two forms as synonymous with *Pinus teocote* because the few specimens cited are from widely scattered locations and appear to represent occasional individuals rather than population (or populations) of similar trees. Shaw (1909) in describing *P. teocote* var. *macrocarpa*, cited the cones as considerably larger than the typical form and the leaves in fascicles of 3, 4 and 5. He also pointed out that the "variety may easily be confused with some forms of the variable *P. lawsoni*, between which and *P. teocote* it seems to be intermediate." He mentioned too that he found the variety growing in mixed stands of *P. teocote* and *P. leiophylla* and noted that "it resembles the latter in cone and leaf but lacks the peculiar character that distinguishes *P. leiophylla* from other Mexican pines—the 'triennial cone'." Martínez (1948) reduced Shaw's variety *macrocarpa* to the status of "forma" and also referred to another form, i.e. *P. teocote* forma *quinquefoliata* that he described as having leaves in fascicles of 4 and 5, mostly 5. Loock (1950) followed Martínez' classification and noted that he had collected specimens of both forms near Huasca, Hidalgo growing in association with *P. teocote, P. oocarpa* var. *manzanoi, P. leiophylla, P. montezumae* and other species.

most interestingly, in his description of forma *quinquefoliata*, Loock states

> ... at first mistook the tree for *P. leiophylla*, but the cones resemble those of *P. teocote* more closely and the sheaths of the leaves are more or less persistent. The leaves are rather slender and mostly in fascicles of 4 and 5, predominantly 5, up to about 5 inches along. Their internal structure corresponds with that of *P. teocote*. The cones are about 2½ inches long with flat to slightly raised apophyses, resembling both those of *P. teocote* and *P. lawsoni*, with which it can easily be confused, if the leaves are not closely examined. To me it appears to be a hybrid between *P. leiophylla* and *P. teocote* or *P. lawsoni*.

Fortunately in 1981 I was able to locate a similar, or what may have been the same, population of trees visited by Loock in 1947. The small group of trees were growing on a hillside at 2,500 m altitude and, at a distance, appeared to be *P. leiophylla*. Most of the trees were rather low, limby and of poor form. Some had thick, bushy crowns with epicormic shoots on the trunk and others had more open, low crowns with no epicormic shoots on the trunk. On closer examination four trees were found with leaves in fascicles of 3, 4 and 5 (mostly 5), longer and thicker than the leaves of typical *P. leiophylla*, their sheaths only partially deciduous, i.e. some sheaths on two of the trees had been shed. On another, all of the sheaths had been shed and on one tree none of the sheaths were shed. On four trees all the fascicle sheaths were deciduous; however, the leaves were thick and stiff. The cones too were quite variable in length and width; on five of the trees the cones were much larger and the cone scales much harder and stiffer than typical *P. leiophylla* cones. In all instances the cones were long-persistent, very tenacious, and the scales appeared to open very slowly. Among the group of trees there appeared to be typical *P. teocote* and *P. leiophylla*. Loock (1950) mentioned that the cones resembled those of *P. teocote* more closely than those of *P. leiophylla*. However, I found the cones much larger than cones of typical *P. teocote* and also different from cones of typical *P. leiophylla*. The hard, stiff cone scales and tenacious peduncle reminded me more of *Pinus greggii* which also occurs in the area (however, no trees were found in this small group of pines). In summary, it appeared to me that a number of the trees were hybrids, possibly between *P. leiophylla* and *P. teocote* and/or *P. leiophylla* and *P. greggii*.

One final note: in his description of *P. greggi*, Martínez (1948) mentions that on mature trees the fascicle sheath is often deciduous; also that in specimens collected at Apulco, Hidalgo (not far from this population near Huasca) the cones are somewhat smaller than typical *P. greggii* cones.

Pinus lawsoni Roezl.

Pino, Ocote, Pino Chino

THE TREE—A medium-size tree 20–30 m high, the branches mostly horizontal, the crown rather limby and irregularly rounded. On young trees the crown is pyramidal and dense.

BARK—On mature trees rough, dark brown, divided by deep furrows into longitudinal, scaly plates. A slanting cut into the bark reveals a dark red to purple-red inner bark that is characteristic of this species. On young trees the bark is thin, reddish and very scaly.

BRANCHLETS—When very young are rather smooth but soon become rougher with thin reddish scales; bases of the leaf bracts are decurrent.

LEAVES—In fascicles of 3, 4 and 5, rarely 2, mostly 4 and 5, grayish green, 15–20 cm long, thick (1.0–1.5 mm) and stiff; generally grouped toward the ends of the branchlets. The margins are finely serrate, stomata on dorsal and ventral surfaces; resin canals 2–6 mostly internal, occasionally 1 or 2 medial; outer walls of the endoderm not thickened; fibrovascular bundles 2, clearly separated; sheaths 10–15 mm long, brown and persistent.

CONELETS—Solitary or in pairs; ovoid, on long, rather stout peduncles; brown, the small scales bearing a minute prickle.

CONES—Ovate-conical, asymmetrical, 5–8 cm long, reflexed on slender peduncles 6–8 mm long; yellowish brown to dull brown. The cones open at maturity and are

P. lawsoni Tree   Bark   Cones, conelets, and leaves

mostly deciduous; some appear to be semi-persistent; the small peduncle falls with the cone.

CONE SCALES—Small, rather thin, not hard or stiff, the apophysis irregularly developed, often protuberant on the basal scales, on some cones flat to slightly pyramidal, clearly transversely keeled; the umbo large, flat to slightly raised and armed with a small deciduous prickle.

SEEDS—Small, dark brown, 4–5 mm long with an articulate, brown wing 10–15 mm long.

WOOD—Hard, resinous, yellowish; the trees are cut commercially along with other associated pines and the lumber sold for construction purposes. Locally it is cut for firewood and hewn timbers; the trees are also tapped commercially for resin.

DISTRIBUTION—As scattered trees and small stands on lower slopes of the mountains forming the east-west Volcanic Axis and southward on lower slopes of the Sierra Madre del Sur (Fig. 3.69). This species has been reported from the states of Jalisco, Michoacán, Mexico, Morelos, Puebla, Guerrero and Oaxaca.

HABITAT—*P. lawsoni* grows in temperate and warmer zones and occasionally in subtropical areas; its altitudinal range is from 1,300 to 2,500 m and rainfall is 600–1,500 mm over most of its range. Temperature ranges from 25° C in May to 18° C in December and January; the winter months are generally dry and most rain falls during the summer months of May–September. Associated pine species are often *P. montezumae, P. pseudostrobus, P. pringlei, P. herrerai, P. teocote, P. oocarpa* and *P. leiophylla.*

WHERE TO FIND *P. lawsoni*—From Mexico City drive west on Highway 15 toward the city of Toluca; bypass the city and continue on Highway 15 for 10–12 km. Look for a paved road turning off to the left to the towns of Amanalco and Valle de Bravo (about 50 km). Valle de Bravo is well known and there should be no problem finding it. There are many trails and roads in the area, and *P. lawsoni* should not be difficult to find. If one is driving west to Morelia and Patzcuaro, it would be an easy drive to continue to Uruapan; along the highway are

Fig. 3.69.   Distribution of *P. lawsoni.*

P. lawsoni trees growing with a number of other pine species.

If there is not enough time for the journey west a quick trip could be made from Mexico City east toward Puebla but turning off soon onto Highway 115 which will take you near Amecameca. Look for the twin, snow-capped volcanoes on the left— Ixtaccihuatl and Popocatepetl. A good road from Amecameca leads up into the park where *P. lawsoni* can be found (though not common) growing with *P. montezumae, P. pseudostrobus* and *P. leiophylla.*

NOTES AND COMMENTS—Although most *P. lawsoni* trees are of poor form, I found very fine trees growing in Michoacán about 6 km from the city of Uruapan at the Forest Experiment Station, Barranca Cupatítzio. Here the trees were growing at an altitude of 1,750 m; tree height was about 20–25 m and diameter ranged from 30 to 60 cm. This was an excellent site, perhaps because no grazing or woodcutting was permitted and no fires had occurred during the past 10 years. Interesting, too, I found leaves only in groups of 3 and 4, no 5s at all.

The thick, stiff needles and small, asymmetrical cones on rather weak peduncles, plus the irregularly protuberant apophyses, all help to distinguish the trees from *P. pringlei* (tenacious, persistent cones) and *P. herrerai,* (slender, delicate leaves).

Pinus herrerai Mart.

Ocote, Pino Chino

THE TREE—A large tree 25–35 m high, branches on old trees horizontal to drooping, the crown rather rounded and open.

BARK—On mature trees thick, divided by longitudinal fissures into reddish brown, scaly plates. On young trees the bark is thin, scaly and reddish brown.

BRANCHLETS—Smooth to slightly scaly, also reddish brown; bases of the leaf bracts are decurrent.

LEAVES—In fascicles of 3, 10–20 cm long, slender, flexible, occasionally somewhat drooping but most often erect; margins finely serrate, stomata on dorsal and ventral surfaces; resin canals 1–4 internal, occasionally with one septal or medial; outer walls of the endodermal cells are thickened; fibrovascular bundles 2, contiguous but distinct; fascicle sheaths persistent, 8–14 mm long, pale brown.

CONELETS—Subglobose, borne on short, stout peduncles, solitary or in groups of 2 and 3, the scales bearing a sharp, minute prickle.

CONES—Long-ovoid, almost symmetrical, 2–4 cm long, reflexed on stout peduncles about 5 mm long; light brown, opening when mature and soon deciduous.

CONE SCALES—Small, about 5–6 mm wide, not hard and stiff, the apophysis flat to only slightly raised, lightly keeled; the umbo slightly raised with a small, early-deciduous prickle.

SEEDS—Very small, 3–4 mm long, dark brown, the seed wing 5–7 mm long and articulate.

WOOD—Pale yellowish color, of good quality; the trees are logged along with *Pinus pseudostrobus, Pinus michoacana, Pinus douglasiana* and other pines. Locally the trees are cut for firewood and construction timbers.

DISTRIBUTION—*P. herrerai* is not a very well known species and, while it has been collected in Sinaloa, Durango, Jalisco, Michoacán and Guerrero, the limits of its range are still not clearly established (Fig. 3.70).

HABITAT—This species grows at altitudes that range from 1,200 to 2,400 m. It is generally found on moist, well-drained slopes where rainfall is 900–1,200 mm/yr. Associated pines are often *P. montezumae, P. pseudostrobus, P. douglasiana, P. maximinoi, P. lawsoni, P. teocote* and *P. michoacana*. While the species is often found in mixed stands with other pines, I observed it growing in small, pure stands in southwestern Michoacán.

WHERE TO FIND *P. herrerai*—I collected this taxon west of Durango and El Salto on Highway 40 near the village of Ciudad as a roadside tree. I recommend, however, that

P. herrerai Tree, center foreground

Bark

Cones and leaves

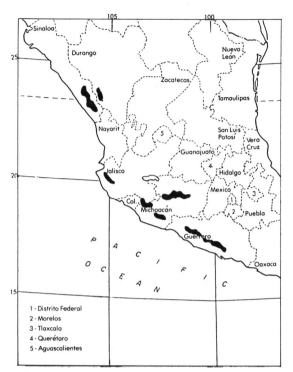

Fig. 3.70. Distribution of *P. herrerai*.

collection be made in Michoacán where I observed the finest trees of this species. From Mexico City drive west to the city of Uruapan; there take Highway 37 south to the village of Neuva Italia and turn right onto Highway 120. Drive westward for about 25 km to the town of Apatzingán and find a guide who is familiar with the region south and west of Apatzingán. Drive on a dirt road to the village of Aguililla and con-

tinue about 20 km westward to the village of Dos Aguas, a small "sawmill village" in the heart of extensive pine forests. Around Dos Aguas are numerous logging trails into the forest and it will not be difficult to find specimens of *P. herrerai* on some of the trails. The trip only should be attempted during the dry season and in a high-clearance vehicle with a reserve supply of gasoline and water. If the guide you have is not familiar with the forest around Dos Aguas, it would be best to hire an additional guide at Dos Aguas and to make arrangements for lodging for at least one night.

Still further west, I collected this taxon in Jalisco not far from the village of Tuito, south of Puerta Vallarta. The trees were growing with *P. ayacahuite* var. *veichtii* at 2,200 m altitude and may represent the westernmost occurrence of the species.

NOTES AND COMMENTS—Near Dos Aguas this species was found growing in small, pure stands, and in the same area very good reproduction had taken place where logging activity had disturbed the soil. Some of the mature trees were of excellent form and obviously were competing successfully with other associated pine species. Although the Mexican Forest Service is actively engaged in field studies of pine regeneration in the Dos Aguas area, this species merits particular attention. Seed should be collected from exceptional parent trees and distributed for experimental plantings in Mexico, Central America and other tropical and semi-tropical countries.

Section Caribaea

In Mexico and Central America a single variety, *P. caribaea* var. *hondurensis*, is included in this section. It is the only completely tropical pine in Mexico and Central America and is found primarily in Belize, Honduras and Nicaragua. A few small populations occur in eastern tropical Guatemala and a small group of trees has been reported in Quintana Roo, Mexico.

Pinus caribaea var. *hondurensis* (Sénécl) Barr. et Golf.

Honduras Caribbean Pine, Pino, Ocote

THE TREE—A fine tree 20–30 m high, often 35 m, with a diameter of 50–80 cm and occasionally up to 1 m; the trunk generally straight and well-formed; lower branches large, horizontal to drooping, the upper branches often ascending forming an open, rounded to pyramidal crown. Young trees have a dense, pyramidal crown.

BARK—On old trees reddish brown, thick, formed in rough plates by deep vertical and horizontal fissures; on young trees it is reddish, rough and scaly.

BRANCHLETS—Rather smooth when young but becoming rough and scaly; bases of the leaf bracts are decurrent.

LEAVES—Mostly in fascicles of 3–4, rarely 2 and 5; thick (1.0–1.6 mm), stiff, erect, usually 15–25 cm long; yellowish green and borne in groups at the ends of the branchlets. The margins are finely serrate, stomata present on the ventral and dorsal surfaces; resin canals 2–3, occasionally 4, generally internal though occasionally there are 1 or 2 medial; outer walls of the endodermal cells are not thickened; fibrovascular bundles 2, clearly separated; fascicle sheaths are persistent, about 12 mm long, pale grayish brown.

CONELETS—Brown, reflexed on long, thick peduncles, in clusters of 2–4, the small scales bearing a sharp prickle curved upward toward the apex of the cone.

CONES—Generally symmetrical, cylindrical to ovoid-conical, occasionally oblique, 5–12 cm long, 3–8 cm wide, borne singly and in groups of 2–5 on stiff, stout peduncles 1–2 cm long. They are brown, not hard, ripening mostly during the late summer months, and are early-deciduous, the peduncle generally remaining attached to the branch.

CONE SCALES—Thin, weak, not hard and stiff, the apophyses raised, often pyramidal and recurved, transversely keeled; the umbo dorsal, erect, prominent and bearing a sharp, persistent prickle.

SEED—Small, brown, 5–6 mm long and about 4 mm wide, the seed wing about 20 mm long and 5–7 mm wide. Viable seed/kg is about 45,000. Although the wing is articulate, it partially covers one side of the seed.

WOOD—Rather hard and heavy, sapwood pale brown, the heartwood darker brown, resinous. The trees are tapped commercially for resin and when logged, are sawn into commercial timbers and boards for export. The wood is also used locally for construction of homes, posts and firewood.

DISTRIBUTION—*P. caribaea* var. *hondurensis* is a tropical pine found in Nicaragua, Honduras, Belize and as small isolated populations in Guatemala and Quintana Roo, Mexico (Fig. 3.71).

HABITAT—This taxon grows in frost-free

P. caribaea **var.** *hondurensis* Trees.   Young tree   Leaves, branchlet, and cones
Thanks to W. M. Mittak.

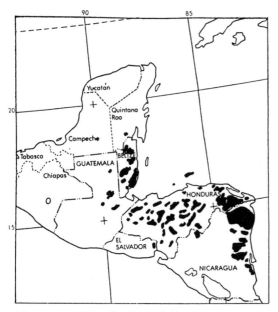

Fig. 3.71. Distribution of *P. caribaea* var. *hondurensis.*

areas from sea level (occasionally) up to about 700 m altitude. Trees are occasionally found at 1,000 m though a more "normal" altitudinal range is 100–700 m. Soils are often sandy to sandy-clay and in many areas are poorly-drained. Best growth is made on more fertile sites with good subsoil drainage and annual rainfall of 2,000–3,000 mm. Many writers believe that the extensive stands of var. *hondurensis* found in the coastal areas of Belize, Honduras and Nicaragua are the result of recurring fires that kill the broadleaf tropical species and allow the pines to reseed the burned-over sites. I believe there is no question that fires do play an important role in the establishment and maintenance of *P. caribaea* var. *hondurensis* stands.

This taxon is often associated with *P. oocarpa* and *P. oocarpa* var. *ochoterenai,* generally at elevations of 600–800 m. While var. *hondurensis* grows best with annual rainfall of 2,000 mm or more, there are scattered stands growing under very dry conditions east and south of Tegucigalpa near the village of Los Limones and in the department of Choluteca.

WHERE TO FIND *P. caribaea* var. *hondurensis*—In Belize City arrange for a car and guide and drive west on any road or trail for a few kilometers; the first pines that

you see will be var. *hondurensis.* Also in Belize, a two-hour drive from Belmopan will take you to the village of San Augustin at Mountain Pine Ridge. Fine trees are growing around the Federal Forestry offices at 400–500 m altitude. In Honduras drive south from the city of San Pedro Sula on Highway 1 for about 20 km to the town of Pimienta; there turn left toward the towns of El Negrito, Morazán and Yoro (about 100 km). At Yoro look for a guide who can take you on the dirt trails north of Yoro. In the hills at 300–500 m there are fine stands of var. *hondurensis.*

At Tegucigalpa drive east on Highway 4 to Zamarano; a few kilometers east of Zamarano look for a dirt road on the left that leads to the village of Los Limones. This is a winding road that passes through widely scattered stands of var. *hondurensis.* At all locations in Belize and Honduras, collecting trips should be undertaken only during the dry season with a reliable guide and a high-clearance, 4-wheel-drive vehicle.

NOTES AND COMMENTS—*P. caribaea* var. *hondurensis* is one of the most interesting Mexican and Central American pines. A number of unusual qualities set it apart from the other pines; over its natural range it is completely tropical, growing only under frost-free conditions; it grows at the lowest elevation of all the Mexican and Central American pines—sea level to 600–700 m; of all the North American pines, var. *hondurensis* grows furthest south, reaching the southernmost limit of its range near Bluefields, Nicaragua at 12° N latitude.

Partly because of these qualities this taxon has been successfully planted in many countries with climates similar to those of coastal Honduras, Belize and Nicaragua. This worldwide interest has focused attention on rapid-growing selections and races of the variety, and it has been found that var. *hondurensis* crosses naturally with *P. oocarpa* and *P. oocarpa* var. *ochoterenai.* Progeny from these crosses, in general, have better form and are faster growing than the parents. Foresters and botanists have long suspected this to be the case and have often commented on the presence, in the field, of outstanding trees in areas where var. *hondurensis* overlaps the range of *P. oocarpa* and var. *ochoterenai.* This has been observed in Belize at Mountain Pine Ridge (600–800 m altitude) and in Honduras at Los Limones (650 m altitude), in the foothills of the Sierra de Omoa (600–700 m altitude), at Ocotillos, near Yoro (650 m altitude) and near Lake Yohoa (1,000 m altitude). Here I found trees shedding pollen on 15 February.

The disjunct population of var. *hondurensis* at Poptún in eastern Guatemala (about 75 km, straight-line distance from Mountain Pine Ridge, Belize) has long been considered a source of seed noted for the production of fast-growing and unusually well-formed trees. Some writers believe that many of these outstanding, low-elevation populations should be identified as *P. patula* ssp. *tecunumanii* rather than *P. oocarpa* var. *ochoterenai*. I am one of a group that believes such a classification is incor-

rect since, among other reasons, *P. tecunumanii* occurs at 1,500–2,600 m and the low-elevation populations referred to here, occur mostly at 600–800 m altitude. Very briefly, I believe we are dealing with two very distinct populations, one that occurs at 600–800 m (possibly 500–1,000 m) altitude involving *P. oocarpa*, *P. oocarpa* var. *ochoterenai* and *P. caribaea* var. *hondurensis* and another population that occurs at 1,500–2,500 m (possibly 1,300–2,700 m) altitude that may involve *P. maximinoi*, *P. oocarpa*, var. *ochoterenai*, *P. patula* var. *longepedunculata* and *P. tecunumnaii*. There seems to be no question that natural hybridization occurs between some of these taxa. Further morphological studies and analyses of turpentine from parents and progeny are needed to clarify these complex relationships.

Section Macrocarpae

A single species, *P. coulteri*, is included in this section. It occurs only in California and Baja California Norte. The trees bear very unusual cones as noted in the description below.

Pinus coulteri D. Don

Coulter Pine, Pitch Pine, Pino

THE TREE—A small to medium-size tree 10–25 m tall, the crown open and irregular, lower branches quite long particularly in open-grown trees, often pendulous with the ends upturned; the upper branches more slender and ascending.

BARK—In mature trees the bark is 3–5 cm thick, dark brown and divided into rough, irregular, longitudinal scaly plates.

BRANCHLETS—Thick, rough, reddish brown, the leaf bracts large, rough and decurrent.

LEAVES—Borne in fascicles of 3 in dense groups at the ends of the branchlets; stiff, erect, 15–28 cm long, very thick, about 2 mm wide, the margins finely serrate;

stomata present on the dorsal and ventral surfaces; resin canals 3–4, medial, occasionally one internal; walls of the endodermal cells not thickened; vascular bundles 2, clearly separated and distinct; fascicle sheaths pale brown and not deciduous.

CONELETS—Unusually large, 4–5 cm long and 5–6 cm wide, the scales long, narrow, sharply pointed and curved upward; very stiff and bearing very small droplets of resin. They are very pale to tawny brown color and borne on a stout, stiff, erect peduncle 3–4 cm long.

CONES—Oblong-conical, oblique, 20–35 cm long, 13–15 cm wide when open, reflexed on a short (1–2 cm), stout

P. coulteri Tree   Bark   Cone and seed

peduncle. They are borne singly, very persistent, pendent, resinous, and a remarkable lustrous, pale yellow color. When
green the cones may weigh up to 2 kg.

CONE SCALES—Hard and stiff, the
apophyses often as much as 3 cm wide, very
protuberant, curved upward toward the
apex of the cone, horizontally keeled and
terminating in a remarkable umbo 2–3 cm
long, hard, stiff, sharply pointed and
resembling more than anything else the
talons of an eagle.

SEED—Rather flattened, 10–16 mm long
and 8–10 mm wide, dark brown with an
articulate wing that is quite thick (as much
as 2 mm) where it joins the seed. The wing
is brown, 20–25 mm long and 12–15 mm
wide. The average number of seeds/kg is
3,000 and cotyledons number 12–15,
mostly 13. The seeds are gathered for food
by the natives although the seed coat is very
hard and thick.

WOOD—Since most populations of this
pine in Baja California Norte are quite small
and isolated, the rather light, soft wood is
used only occasionally for firewood.

DISTRIBUTION—*P. coulteri* occurs principally in small scattered forests along the
coastal mountains of central and southern
California. However, a few, small isolated
populations occur in Baja California Norte,
Mexico, in the Sierra de Juárez and San
Pedro Mártir Mountains (Fig. 3.72).

HABITAT—This species grows on the
dry–arid rocky slopes and basins of the

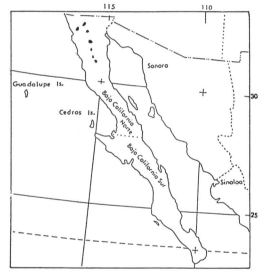

Fig. 3.72.   Distribution of *P. coulteri*.

mountains in Baja California Norte at altitudes of 1,200–2,100 m. Rainfall in the
Sierra de Juárez is 300–500 mm annually,
about 15% occurring during the winter
months from November to March. The
coldest months are December, January and
February and temperatures often fall below
freezing with occasional snowfall. Associated pines are *Pinus jeffreyi*, *Pinus
quadrifolia* and *Pinus juarezensis*.

WHERE TO FIND *P. coulteri*—Collections
of *P. coulteri* can be easily made in the
Cleveland National Forest, San Diego
County, California. U.S. Highway 8 passes
directly through the forest in an east-west

direction, and the species can be found as a roadside tree by driving north from U.S. 8 on California Highway 79. If collections are sought in Baja California Norte, take California Highway 94 south along the California-Mexico border to the town of Tecate located directly on the Baja California border. Cross the border there and turn east on Highway MEX 2. Follow the highway east for about 20 km and look carefully on the right for a sign, Colonia El Hongo. Turn off the highway there and drive south on a narrow, winding, paved road for about 4 km. The paved road ends here and soon forks; take the southeast fork and look for signs to the villages of Neji, La Hechicera, San Faustino and San Juan de Dios. The pines along this winding trail are mostly *P. jeffreyi*; however, just southwest of San Faustino there is a small grove of *P. coulteri* trees. Just northwest of Laguna Hanson scattered groves have also been reported. It would be wise to obtain a reliable guide at one of the villages and plan on a full day for the trip from Tecate and return. Plans should not be made to drive along the trail at night, and the trip should only be made during the dry season in a high-clearance, 4-wheel-drive vehicle with an adequate supply of water and gasoline.

NOTES AND COMMENTS—The cones and seeds of this species are quite unique; the massive development of the cone scales and prolongation of the apophyses and umbo make it immediately recognizable. The large, dark, thick-shelled seed with unusually thickened seed wing is another very distinctive feature. *P. coulteri* is rare in northern Baja California. Apparently it becomes established following ground fires, but mature trees are now found primarily on rocky sites that are generally protected from fire. Although the species is usually described as a low, scrubby tree of poor form, Bruce Zobel (1951a) found fine trees growing on a number of favorable sites. Since it hybridizes naturally with Jeffrey Pine, it would appear that selections from those trees might have an important potential for planting in many mountainous areas particularly in northern Baja California. A final note on this interesting pine; when the wind is blowing, it could be very dangerous to sit under one of these trees bearing a heavy cone crop.

CHAPTER 4

PRESENT STATUS OF THE PINE FORESTS

This assessment, like the descriptions of the species, is based on my observations of the forests, conversations with local botanists and foresters, and articles by authors knowledgeable in this field. I have given considerable weight to the opinions of Mexican and Central American writers simply because they know and care deeply about the forest resources of their own countries.

MEXICO

Mexico's total land area amounts to 1,972,547 km² (761,605 square miles) and the population is about 80 million. Mexico City, the world's largest city, staggers under a population of approximately 20 million people. With a growth rate of 2.6%, the country's population will be over 100 million by the year 2,000. For hundreds of years the people have literally "scratched out" an existence on mountain slopes and dry plateaus. Now with exploding population growth, about 25 million people are unemployed. Even with its very large oil reserves, Mexico simply cannot provide opportunities for its people to make a living so about 4,000 of them, every day of the year, illegally enter the United States looking for jobs. Now, with a tremendous international debt and the value of its currency declining daily, the country is facing an economic crisis.

What relevance do the pine forests have against this background? Even an untrained observer can see that the forests are rapidly disappearing. And the cause? No single factor has led to the phenomenal reduction in Mexico's pine forests; however, the many causes may be grouped into three major categories; diseases, insects and human activities.

Disease

Although the Mexican pines are attacked by various pathogens (needle cast, needle rusts, stem rusts, stem canker and heart rot), disease does not appear to be a major factor in reduction of the pine forests. However, a parasitic plant, dwarf mistletoe (*Arceuthobium*), is found throughout the pine forests and in some areas causes extensive damage, particularly in stands of young trees.

Also in a number of forests I found pines with many cones infected by *Caeoma conigenum*. Although the trees were not killed by the disease, the cones were killed and thus reproduction of the species was reduced. In Cerro Potosí I found a number of *P. rudis* populations with 60–70% of the cones destroyed by this disease.

Insects

In all Mexico's pine forests it is possible to find, at some time, a number of insect pests attacking the trees. Often these are species of *Rhyacionia* spp. pine tip moth, *Pissodes* spp. shoot weevil, defoliators (*Tortricidae*) and cone weevils (*Curculionidae*). While these pests do have an impact on the pine forests, they are minor when compared to the damage caused by the Mexican pine bark beetle, *Dendroctonus mexicanus* Hopk.

Early records show that in 1900–1903 pine forests in the states of Mexico, Morelos and Michoacán were severely damaged by widespread bark beetle outbreaks. In 1949–50 I observed three major bark beetle outbreaks in the pine-forested mountains near Mexico City and Puebla. In that area alone I estimated that not less than 4,000 ha (10,000 acres) of pines were completely destroyed by the beetles (Fig. 4.1). During subsequent visits to most of Mexico's pine-forested areas, I found repeated evidence of epidemic outbreaks of bark beetles. No records are available as to total damage to the pine forests by these outbreaks; however, there is no doubt whatever that the losses are enormous. Of course every insect kill is not a permanent reduction of the pine forest; many areas are soon reseeded and in a few years are covered again with a dense forest. However, many areas are never reforested due primarily to human activity.

Fig. 4.1.   Pines killed by the Mexican pine bark beetle, *Dendroctonus mexicanus* Hopk. Approximately 4,000 hectares near Amecameca, Mexico, were destroyed during a single epidemic outbreak in 1949–50.

Human Impacts

It would be impossible to summarize here the literature on this subject. I can, however, state briefly how I see it. I believe that Mexico's population explosion fuels most of the nation's problems including that of the disappearing forests. It is not a very complicated picture and looks like this; for about 200 years Mexico's rural population survived as subsistence farmers living under primitive conditions. Isolation, malnutrition, disease, revolution and civil war took their toll and population increase was minimal. During the past 100 years the situation has changed dramatically. With greater political stability roads began to penetrate the rural areas, often bringing for the first time medicines that controlled many of the great killers—smallpox, malaria and pneumonia. World wars brought a demand for construction timbers so sawmills by the hundreds moved into Mexico's forests. In a few years logging trails became roads opening new lands far into the mountains. With medicines, jobs (road building, sawmills, logging, small stores, shops, etc.) and mobility (roads and cheap bus transportation) rural populations began to increase.

The population explosion had been ignited but food production remained at earlier levels and rural poor, mostly farmers, pushed into the formerly forested areas. Wherever forests were cut and abandoned the small subsistence farmer looking for "new land" followed. With him came his animals; a few cattle, burros and always goats. Of course he brought his wooden plow and, most importantly, fire. Fire to help him clear the brush and weeds for his first corn crop and to encourage a "crop" of green grass for his animals. And if the ground fire became a wild fire raging across the mountain slopes, it was only a step toward more grass for his goats, sheep and cattle.

I believe the picture is clear now; every year there are a million *more* hungry people searching for food. While thousands flock to the cities, thousands more push into the mountains and valleys looking for a plot of land where they can plant a few rows of corn and beans (Fig. 4.2). I realize this is a very "simplified picture" but it is also a "real picture" that "describes" the destruction of Mexico's forests. What then is the future of Mexico's forests? They will continue to disappear, first becoming fragmented then reduced to small patches and parcels and finally to small groups of trees on inaccessible mountain slopes and valleys.

Fig. 4.2. Cow and horse manure drying on the walls of an abandoned hacienda. Forests in the area have been completely destroyed, so the dry manure will be used for fuel.

GUATEMALA

Guatemala's total area is 108,889 km² (42,042 square miles). Population is about 8.5 million; Guatemala City, the capital, has about 1.5 million people. With an annual growth rate of 2.8%, Guatemala's population will pass the 10 million mark by the year 2,000. Like Mexico, Guatemala is experiencing a population explosion and rural farmers, barely existing in a land of mountains, are flocking to the cities in search of jobs. Those remaining in the countryside constantly push up the mountain slopes and into the steep valleys in search of land for their small plots of corn, (Fig. 4.3) beans and vegetables. Conflict between large land owners and small, poor farmers, often landless, occasionally erupts into violence and thousands of peasant families have fled across the border into Mexico. Under these conditions, what is happening to the pine forests of Guatemala? As in Mexico, disease and insect pests are important natural factors affecting the forests. Human activity is another factor but certainly not a natural one.

Fig. 4.3.   Here in Guatemala the forest has been cut and cleared for corn planting. The few trees of *P. michoacana* shown were left for fuel wood. The branch stubs are left so the trees can be climbed and the higher branches cut for firewood. They will soon die from the intensive pruning.

Disease

The pine forests of Guatemala are similar to those of Mexico and are subject to the same diseases. The trees are attacked by rusts, cankers and mistletoe and while many die, many more survive and the forests are not endangered by these losses.

Insects

The cone weevils, shoot moths and defoliators are all minor pests of the pines. The pine bark beetle (*Dendroctonus mexicanus*) falls into another category; it can, and often does, destroy great sections of a forest. Infestations that reach epidemic proportions can spread rapidly through a pine forest and in less than a year kill most of the pines in a 10,000–20,000 ha (25,000–50,000 acre) forest. What happens to the dead pines? Portable sawmills move in to salvage the larger trees before wood borers (*Cerambycidae* and *Buprestidae*) and decay ruin the timber. Rural farmers reap a bonanza from the sale of firewood. Horses, carts, burros and trucks, large and small, all move into the dead forest and in a short time most of the trees are salvaged for firewood and hewn timbers.

Some of the denuded areas will be reseeded by nearby pines. But many areas will become open pastureland grazed by herds of goats, sheep and cattle from nearby villages. If grazing is not too intensive and if ground fires are not too frequent, pines may gradually reforest most of the area. Generally, though, there is a net loss of pine forests.

Human Activity

It seems clear to me that Guatemala's rapidly increasing population is the principal force generating pressure on the pine forests. Children of poor, rural farmers, when (if) they reach adulthood, have very few work options. Since they are largely uneducated and illiterate, they either move to a large city to take work as unskilled laborers or they remain in their own small villages and try to survive as subsistence farmers. Since they own no land, many turn to the forest for "free land". Large beetle-killed areas are a "made-to-order" opportunity since the trees are already dead and some income can be obtained from the sale of firewood. I saw this sequence of events many times in Guatemala where an epidemic of the pine bark beetle was moving steadily through forests of *P. rudis* in the departments of Totonicapán and El Quiché. Wild fires create similar opportunities for land-hungry, subsistence farmers.

In the area of "human activity" there are other factors exerting pressure on the forests. The demand for construction timbers and lumber, charcoal and firewood is always present—and increasing.

Admittedly this is a rather "uncomplicated" picture of Guatemala's forest problems but the events as pictured here take place every day. I believe then, that Guatemala's pine forests are rapidly disappearing under the human pressures outlined here.

HONDURAS

Honduras has a land area of 112,088 km² (43,277 square miles), a little larger than Guatemala. Its population is approximately 4.5 million (one-half that of Guatemala); its capital, Tegucigalpa, has a population of about 550,000. Politically, Honduras has unresolved border problems with El Salvador and Nicaragua. Since both of those countries are caught in the upheaval and violence of civil wars, tens of thousands of refugees have moved across these borders into Honduras. Although Honduras has a high population growth rate, 2.5–3.0%, it is still sparsely populated relative to Mexico, Guatemala and El Salvador.

How, then, are the pine forests faring in this country? Not too badly (with one exception) in comparison to those of Mexico, Guatemala and El Salvador. The exception noted has to do with an epidemic infestation of pine bark beetles that swept through the pine forests of Honduras during 1963–66. Coyne and Critchfield (1974) called this "perhaps the most severe epidemic of bark beetles ever observed in North America." At the peak of the epidemic in 1964, about 77,000 trees/day were killed by the beetles. Pine mortality averaged 25% for the entire infested area but reached 70% in some compartments (Coyne and Critchfield, 1974).

At the time of the epidemic, about 60% of the nation was forested with pines and Honduras exported more timber than any country in Central America. Fortunately many pines survived the epidemic and most of the beetle-killed areas were reseeded by those survivors. Nevertheless, the nations timber economy was dealt a severe blow and is only now recovering as the young trees reach merchantable size. I should add that the bark beetles have not disappeared, they are still present in the pine forests and no one knows if or when another epidemic outbreak may occur.

Human Activity

Although a great part of the beetle-kill described above was reseeded by pines, there was a net loss of pine-forested area. As I pointed out earlier, most poor rural farmers in Mexico and Central America are always alert for an opportunity to enlarge their parcels of cultivated land. The enormous beetle-kill opened many areas for grazing livestock and establishing new milpas for corn and beans, so these areas will not return to forest.

The tens of thousands of refugees from Nicaragua and El Salvador are mostly poor, subsistence farmers all too familiar with what they must do to survive on the land. When the crisis in their home countries subside, many will return to their native villages. Others, however, having found a niche where they "fit," will remain and gradually be absorbed as a part of Honduras' population of rural farmers.

Despite the enormous beetle-kill and the constant pressure of poor farmers searching for "new" land, the pine forests of Honduras are probably in a better position to survive than the forests of Mexico, Guatemala, El Salvador and Nicaragua.

NICARAGUA

Nicaragua, with an area of 130,000 km² (50,193 square miles) is the largest Central American country; with 3 million people, it is sparsely populated when compared to Guatemala, El Salvador and Honduras. Its capital, Managua, contains about 1 million people and is growing rapidly as rural families move to the city seeking employment. These area and population figures are somewhat misleading though, since most of the population is concentrated in the central and northeastern highlands north of Lake Nicaragua. The eastern half of the country bordering the Caribbean Sea is very sparsely populated. Politically unstable since civil war erupted in 1978, Nicaragua has lost tens of thousands of families as refugees to Honduras and Costa Rica.

How are Nicaragua's pine forests faring under these conditions? From all reports, poorly. The tremendous bark beetle epidemic in Honduras reached part of the pine forests in Nicaragua's central highlands. Although damage was not as severe as in Honduras, still large areas of forest were killed. Since this is a densely populated area, the pine forests are always under pressure by the rural farmers and, as pointed out earlier, beetle-kills open the door to grazing, and new corn and bean milpas.

Although pine forests in the central highland are disappearing due to population pressure, Nicaragua has a very large forested area along its Caribbean coast. From about 12 degrees N latitude a single species, *Pinus carribaea* var. *hondurensis,* extends northward to the Honduras border forming Central America's largest remaining tropical pine forest. Without becoming involved in a long description of the ecology and silvicultural requirements of these pines, controlled fire seems to be the key to regeneration and maintenance of this unique forest. If wild fires continue to burn through the forests, Nicaragua will lose one of its most important natural resources.

EL SALVADOR

With a total area of 21,041 km² (8,124 square miles), El Salvador is the smallest Central American country. It is also the most crowded. Its population of about 5.5 million places it ahead of Honduras and Nicaragua, both countries five times larger in land area than El Salvador. About 1.5 million people live in and around the capital, San Salvador. Politically, the nation seems constantly on the verge of collapse. With civil war and violence throughout the country, tens of thousands of families have crossed the borders into Guatemala and particularly into Honduras.

How have the pine forests fared under these conditions? From my own observations I would say they have practically disappeared. With approximately 5.5 million people trying to survive in an area of only 21,000 km² of mountains, semi-arrid terrain, pine forests simply do not have a chance. The last tree will eventually be cut for firewood, and then the people will scour the hillsides for shrubs, the roots of corn stalks and the manure of horses and cows for fuel to cook their tortillas (Fig. 4.4).

Fig. 4.4. The three classic stages in destruction of the environment are shown here. Pine forests on the ridge in the background are being destroyed by cutting for firewood and clearing for milpas; the ridge in the center is overgrazed following cutting of all pines; the steep slope in the foreground is destroyed by erosion. El Salvador, near the border with Honduras, Dept. of Chalatenango, altitude ca. 2,000 m, 1973.

BELIZE

Belize, with an area of 22,965 km² (8,867 square miles), is almost as small as El Salvador. The similarity stops there since its population is only 200,000; one twenty-fifth that of El Salvador. Belmopan, the capital, has a population of 4,000 and is not over-whelmed with rural poor looking for jobs. An independent nation since 1981, Belize appears to have a stable government even though Guatemala claims sovereignty.

Although this is a tropical country, there are extensive pine forests along the Caribbean coast and on a low range of hills near its western border with Guatemala. Like the Caribbean pine forests of Nicaragua and Honduras, these forests require ground fires at intervals in order to compete successfully with the broadleaf, tropical vegetation. Unlike most Central American countries, Belieze has a forest management program aimed at encouraging pine reproduction. Forest management practices of controlled harvesting of the pines, controlled burning, hand-weeding and thinning have been instituted by the Department of Forestry. I saw much of their Mountain Pine Ridge pine forest and was very impressed with the many stands of young pines bearing testimony to the value of their management practices.

With absolutely no population pressures and with a working forestry management program, Belize's pine forests appear to have an excellent future; barring, of course, the possibility of a disastrous bark beetle outbreak like that in Honduras!

CHAPTER 5

RARE AND ENDANGERED PINES
OF
MEXICO AND CENTRAL AMERICA

In descriptions of the pines I have called attention to a number of species that are quite rare. Another group, in addition to being rare, is definitely endangered. Unless protective action is taken immediately, some of the species could be wiped out by a single wild-fire. Others are growing in such isolated desert conditions that fire is not a problem. Constant grazing by goats, sheep, cattle and burros and, most serious of all, cutting for firewood, are the hazards that will finally, silently and unnoticed, push them over the brink into extinction.

The small boys and girls, the old men and women who herd the goats and burros across the arid, desolate hills will never know that they were slowly and inexorably pushing the populations of *Pinus pinceana* toward extinction. And then, one by one the scattered trees disappeared as the flashing machete took the branches and then the stem, until one day there were no more—ever. When that moment occurs, something terrible has happened to our planet. A shock-wave should pass around the earth, a deep quiver should be felt in the earth and sea, all sentient life should sense a moment of deep alarm. For man has struck another blow against life on our planet. Another thread has been withdrawn from the intricate web of life and we are all weakened by the loss.

So, too, may man disappear; first destruction of the environment and finally the "machete" flashing in the brilliant sun, taking first the cities and then the nations, one by one.

Many writers say this is an absurd view of civilization and our planet, and marshall volumes of evidence to prove that through advances in science "we shall overcome". If they would but take seriously the increase in world population that has occurred during the past 100 years and then project what will happen to the world's population in the next 100 years (the figures are all there!) they might glimpse an unimaginable picture of life in Mexico, Central America, South America, Africa and South Asia in the year 2100.

I don't have a civilized solution to our planet's problem of overpopulation. Nature may have one waiting in the wings. We do need green, growings things though, and trees were here millions of years before we were. If we were smart we would start to really use them—not exterminate them. We could start by helping Mexico and Central America save a few of their pines that now hang on the brink of extinction.

The pines I have listed in Table 5.1 are rare and endangered, globally. They are not found anywhere else on our planet.

Table 5.1.   Rare and endangered pines.

Species	Present status	Description and map page number	Endangering human activity
P. culminicola	Very rare and very endangered	77, 78	Fire
P. maximartinezii	Very rare and very endangered	83, 84	Grazing and fire
P. rzedowskii	Very rare and very endangered	86, 87	Fire
P. pinceana	Very rare and very endangered	81, 82	Grazing and cutting for firewood
P. johannis	Rare and endangered	71, 72	Grazing and cutting for firewood
P. radiata var. *binata*	Rare and endangered	159, 160	Grazing
P. lagunae	Rare	72, 73	Fire and cutting for firewood
P. jaliscana	Rare	182, 183	Fire, cutting for lumber, and firewood
P. nelsoni	Rare	84, 85	Grazing, fire and cutting for firewood

CHAPTER 6

CONCLUDING REMARKS

As I review the descriptions of the pine species in Mexico and Central America in this book and recall the thousands of intermediate forms and varieties I observed in the field, I can only conclude, like Mirov, "that in the tropical highlands of Mexico and Central America, there has developed a secondary center of evolution and speciation of the genus *Pinus*" (Mirov, 1967). He refers repeatedly to the widespread interspecific hybridization of the Mexican and Central American pines. Martínez (1948) also noted the close relationship between a number of pine species. Shaw, as early as 1914, pointed out,

> In mountainous countries, where there are warm, sheltered valleys with rich soil below cold, barren ledges, the most variable Pines are found. The western species of North America, for instance, are much more variable than the eastern species, while in Mexico, a tropical country with snow-capped mountains, the variation is greatest.

It seems then, that a number of writers are in general agreement that among the Mexican and Central American pines there are indeed many very variable species and that there is widespread interspecific hybridization.

This is an ancient process and at the same time a very real and current one. Evolution in these pines is not something that only happened a million years ago, it happens every year. Seed from natural crosses are disseminated along with millions of other pine seeds and a few survive to produce pine trees that "fit" a particular environmental niche and perform a little better than other seedlings. Ten, twenty, forty years later those trees may backcross with their parents, or cross with one another (or both!) and their progeny will be tested in the same manner.

My point is: The pine forests of Mexico and Central America are a natural forest genetics laboratory for foresters, botanists, taxonomists and geneticists. All the recent evidence points to this. I believe there is a tremendous opportunity here to realize a "giant step forward" by the entire field of forestry. But this step will never be taken if strenuous and immediate steps are not taken to prevent further destruction. I cannot emphasize strongly enough that one of the world's giant plant laboratories borders on the verge of extinction. Foresters and botanists the world over must join with their colleagues in Mexico and Central America to preserve this quite remarkable and infinitely precious natural experiment.

SELECTED BIBLIOGRAPHY

Aguilar, G. José Ignacio. 1961. *Pinos de Guatemala* 3d. ed. Ministerio de Agricultura: Guatemala. 32 pp.

Andresen, J. W. and J. H. Beaman. 1961. A new species of *Pinus* from Mexico. *Journal of the Arnold Arboretum*, 2, XLII, 437–41.

Ascencio C., Victor. 1979. Investigaciones sobre palagas forestales realizadas in Tixtlancingo, Gro. *Ciencia Forestal*, 1(18), 33–57.

Axelrod, D. I. 1960. The evolution of flowering plants. In: *The Evolution of Life. Its Origin, History and Future (Evolution after Darwin* Vol. 1). University of Chicago Press: Chicago. pp. 227–305.

Bailey, D. K. 1983. A new allopatric segregate from, and a new combination in, *Pinus cembroides* Zucc. at its southern limits. *Phytologia*, 54(2), 89–100.

Bailey, D. K. and F. G. Hawksworth. 1979. Piñons of the Chihuahuan desert region. *Phytologia*. 44, 129–33.

Bailey, D. K. and F. G. Hawksworth. 1983. Pinaceae of the Chihuahuan desert region. *Phytologia*, 53, 226–34.

Bailey, D. K. and F. G. Hawksworth. 1987. *Phytogeography and Taxonomy of the Piñon Pines*, Pinus *subsection Cembroides*. II Simposio Nacional Sobre Pinos Piñoneros. México, D. F.

Bailey, D. K. and T. Wendt. 1979. New Piñon records for northern Mexico, *Southwestern Naturalist*, 24, 389–90.

Barnes, R. D. and B. T. Styles. 1983. The closed-cone pines of Mexico and Central America. *Commonwealth Forestry Review*, 62, 81–4.

Barrett, W. H. G. 1972. Variacion de Characteres Morfologicos en poblaciones naturales de *Pinus patula* en Mexico. IDIA. Suplemento Forestal No. 7, 9–35.

Beaman, J. H. 1962. The timberlines of Ixtaccihuatl and Popocatepetl, México. *Ecology*, 43,(3), 377–85.

Birks, J. S. and R. D. Barnes. 1985. Multivariate analysis of data from international provenance trials of *Pinus oocarpa/Pinus patula* subspecies *tecunumanii*. *Commonwealth Forestry Review*. 64, 367–373.

Blanco, C. E. 1949. *Pinus cooperi* sp. nova. *Anales del Instituto de Biología*, 2D, Mexico, 185–87.

Burley, J. and C. L. Green. 1977. Variation of gum turpentine between provenances of *Pinus caribaea* Morelet and *Pinus oocarpa* Schiede in Central America. In: *EEC symposium on Forest Tree Biochemistry*: Brussels. pp. 73–108.

Burley, J. and C. L. Green. 1979. Relationships of terpenes between exotic and natural populations of *Pinus caribaea* Morelet and *P. oocarpa* Schiede. In: *Proceedings of the Conference on Biochemical Genetics of Forest Trees*, ed. D. Rubin. Umea, Sweden. pp. 118–135.

Chavelas, P., Javier. 1981. El *Pinus caribaea* Morelet, en el estado de Quintana Roo, México. *Nota técnia* No. 10: 1–8. INIF, México, D. F.

Coyne, J. F. & W. B. Critchfield. 1974. Identity and terpene composition of Honduran pines attacked by the bark beetle *Dendroctonus frontalis* (Scolytidae). *Turrialba* Vol. 24: No. 3, 327–31.

Critchfield, W. B. 1957. *Geographic Variation in Pinus contorta.* Maria Moors Cabot Foundation. Pub. No. 3, Harvard Univ., Cambridge, Mass. pp. 1–118.

_____ . 1966. *Crossability and Relationships of the California Big-cone Pines.* U.S. Forest Service Research paper NC–6N. Central Forest Experiment Station, St. Paul, Minn.

_____ . 1967. Crossability and relationships of the closed-cone pines. *Silvae Genetica.* 16: 89–97.

Critchfield, W. B., and E. L. Little. 1966. *Geographic Distribution of Pines of the World.* USDA Miscellaneous Publication, 991:91.

Dallimore, W. and A. B. Jackson. 1948. *A Handbook of Coniferae & Ginkgoaceae,* 3rd edition. Edward Arnold, Ltd., London.

Deloya, M. C. 1967. *Estudio comparativo de dos especies de pinos mexicanos (P. pseudostrobus* Lindl. y *P. montexumae* Lamb) *con base en caracteristicas de plantula y semilla.* Bol. Tecnico No. 20, 1–45.

Denevan, W. M. 1961. The upland forests of Nicaragua: a study in cultural geography. *Geography,* 12, 251–320.

Donahue, J. K. and M. Arizmendi. 1986. *Natural Range of P. chiapensis* and *P. ayacahuite Found to Overlap in Ixtlán, Oaxaca, México.* CAMCORE technical note No. 1. North Carolina State University.

Dressler, R. L. 1954. Some floristic relationships between Mexico and the United States. *Rhodora,* 56(665), 81–96.

Duffield, J. W. 1951. *Interrelationships of the California Closed-cone Pines with Special Reference to Pinus muricata* D. Don. Unpublished Ph.d Thesis. University of California, Berkeley.

_____ . 1952. Relationships and species hybridization in the genus Pinus. *Zeiteschriftes fur Forstgenetik und Forstpflanzenzuchtung,* I, 93–7.

Dvorak, W. S. 1983. Strategy for the development of conservation banks and breeding programs for coniferous species from Central America and Mexico. In: *Proceedings of the 17th Southern Forest TRee Improvement Conference,* Athens, Georgia. June 7–9. pp. 22–9.

_____ . 1985. One year provenance/progeny test results of *Pinus tecunumanii* established in Brazil and Colombia. *Commonwealth Forestry Review,* 64(1), 57–65.

_____ . 1986. Provenance/progeny testing of *Pinus tecunumanii.* IUFRO Conference, Williamsburg, Virginia. pp. 1–11.

Dvorak, W. S. and J. Brovard. 1987. An evaluation of *Pinus chiapensis* as a commercial plantation species for the tropics and subtropics. *Commonwealth Forestry Review,* 66(2), 165–76.

Dvorak, W. S. and J. K. Donahue. 1988. *Pinus maximinoi Seed Collections in Mexico and Central America.* CAMCORE Bulletin on Tropical Forestry, No. 4. North Carolina State University.

Dvorak, W. S. and J. G. Laarman. 1986. Conserving the genes of tropical conifers. *Journal of Forestry,* 84(1) 43–5.

Equiluz Piedra, T. 1982a. *Natural Variation and Taxonomy of Pinus tecunumanii from Guatemala.* Unpublished Ph.d Thesis, North Carolina State University, School of Forest Resources, Raleigh, North Carolina.

_____ . 1982b. Clima y distribución del género *Pinus* en México. *Ciencia Forestal,* 38(7) Julio-Agosto, México.

_____ . 1984. Geographic variation in needles, cones and seeds of *Pinus tecunumanii* in Guatemala. *Silvae Genetica,* 33(2–3), 72–9.

Equiluz, T. P. and J. P. Perry. 1983. *Pinus tecunumanii:* una especie nueva de Guatemala. *Ciencia Forestal,* 8, 3–22.

Garcia, E. 1969. Distribución de la précipitación en la Republica Mexicana. *Boletin Instituto*

Geografia, Universidad Nacional Outónoma de Mexico, 1, 3–30.

Gomex-Pompa, A. 1965. La vegetación de México. *Boletin Sociedad Botanico de México,* 29, 76–120.

Greaves, A. 1982. *Pinus oocarpa. Forestry Abstract* 43(9), 503–32.

Griffin, J. R. and W. B. Critchfield. 1976. *The Distribution of Forest Trees in California.* U.S. D. A. Forest Service Research Paper PSW-82: Washington, D.C.

Haller, J. R. 1962. Variation and hybridization in ponderosa and Jeffrey pines. University of California, *Publications Botanical,* 34, 123–66.

Hawksworth, F. G. and D. Wiens. 1972. *Biology and classification of Dwarf Mistletoes (Arceuthobium).* U.S. D. A. Agricultural Handbook 401: Washington, D.C.

Hazlett, D. L. 1979. A first report on the vegetation of Celaque. *Ceiba,* 23(2), 114–28.

Hernandez, X. E., H. Crun, W. B. Fox and A. J. Sharp. 1951. A unique vegetational area in Tamaulipas. *Bulletin of the Torrey Botanical Club,* 78, 458–63.

Howell, T. R. 1972. Birds of the lowland pine savanna of northeastern Nicaragua. *The Condor,* 74(3), 316–40.

Hunt, D. R. 1962. Some notes on the pines of British Honduras, *Empire Forestry Review,* 41, 134–45.

Jarquín, Tirso G., Manuel A. Rodriguez Peña, and Ignacio V. Cázares. 1979. La produción de resina en pinares de ciertas áreas del estado de Michoacán baja condiciones experimentales. *Ciencia Forestal,* 4(21), 17–64.

Johnston, I. M. 1943. Plants of Coahuila, eastern Chihuahua and adjoining Zacatecas and Durango. I. *Journal of the Arnold Arboretum,* 24, 306–39.

Lanner, R. M. 1974a. A new pine from California and the hybrid origin of *Pinus quadrifolia. The Southwestern naturalist,* 19(1), 75–95.

_____ . 1974b. Natural hybridization between *Pinus edulis* and *P. monophylla* in the American Southwest. *Silvae Genetica,* 23(4), 108–16.

Larsen, E. 1964. A new species of pine from Mexico. *Madroño* 17(5), 217–18.

Libby, W. J. 1978. The 1978 Expedition to collect Radiata seed from Cedros and Guadalupe Islands. *IUFRO Working Party 52-03-09, Newsletter,* No. 2, pp. 9–12.

Libby, W. J., M. H. Bannister & Y. B. Linhart. 1968. The pines of Cedros and Guadalupe Islands. *Journal of Forestry,* 66, 846–53.

Lindley, J. 1839. *Pinus apulcensis. Edwards Botannical Register.* Vol. XXV, 63–4.

Little, E. L. 1953. *Check List of Native and Naturalized Trees of the United States (including Alaska),* U.S. Department of Agriculture Handbook No. 41. Government Printing Office: Washington, D.C.

_____ . 1962. *Identificación de especies de Pinos mexicanos in Seminario y Viaje de estudio de coniferas latinoamericanas.* Esp. Publicación especial, Instituto Nacional de Investigaciones Forestales, México, D. F. 1, 73–5.

_____ . 1966. A new piñon variety from Texas. *Wrightia,* 3(8), 181–5.

_____ . 1968. Two new piñon varieties from Arizona. *Phytologia,* 17, 329–42.

Little, E. L. and W. B. Critchfield. 1969. *Subdivisions of the Genus Pinus (Pines).* U.S. Department of Agriculture, Miscellaneous Publication, 1144. Forest Service: Washington, D.C.

Lockhart, Linda A. 1985. Investigation of tropical pine resin terpenes, M.S. thesis, Oxford University, 206 pp. *Forestry Abstracts,* 48, 254 (1987).

Loock, E. E. M. 1950. *The Pines of Mexico and British Honduras.* South Africa Department of Forestry Bulletin 35.

Martínez, M. 1948. *Los pinos Mexicanos.* Segunda edición, Ediciones Botas. México, D. F. 361 pp.

_____ . 1963. *Las pináceas Mexicanas.* Tercera edición. Instituto de Biología. México. Universidad Nacional Autonoma de Mexico, México, D. F. 400 pp.

Masters, N.J. 1891. *Pinus Donnell-Smithii, Botannical Gazette* Vol. XVI, No. 6: 199–200.

McCarter, P. S. and J. S. Birks. 1985. *Pinus patula* subspecies *tecunumanii:* the application of numerical techniques to some problems of its taxonomy. *Commonwealth Forestry Review,* 64(2), 117–32.

Millar, C. I. 1983. A steep cline in *Pinus muricata. Evolution,* 37, 311–19.

Millar, C. I. 1985. *Genetic Studies of Dissimilar Parapatric Populations in Northern Bishop Pine (Pinus muricata).* Unpublished Ph.d dissertation, University of California, Berkeley.

———. 1986. The California closed cone pines (subsection *Oocarpae* Little & Critchfield): a taxonomic history and review. *Taxon,* 35, 657–70.

Millar, C. I. & W. B. Critchfield. 1988. Crossability and relationships of *Pinus muricata (Pinaceae). Madroño,* 35(1) 39–53.

Minnich, R. A. 1987. The distribution of forest trees in northern Baja California, Mexico. *Madroño,* 34(2), 98–127.

Miranda, F. 1952. *La vegetación de Chiapas.* Ed. del Gobierno del Estado, 2 vol. Tuxtla Guttierez, Chiapas, México.

Miranda, F. & X. E. Hernandez. 1963. Los tipos de vegetación de México y su clasificación. *Boletin Sociedad Botanico de México,* Mexico, D. F. 28, 1–179.

Mirov, N. T. 1938. Phylogenetic relations of *Pinus jeffreyi* and *Pinus ponderosa, Madroño,* 4, 169–71.

———. 1948. The terpenes (in relation to the biology of genus *Pinus). Annual Review of Biochemistry,* 17, 521–40.

———. 1958. *Pinus oaxacana,* a new species from Mexico, *Madroño* 14, 145–50.

———. 1961. *Composition of Gum Terpentines of Pines.* U.S. Department of Agriculture, Forest Service Technical Bulletin 1239. Washington, D.C. pp. 1–158,

———. 1967. *The Genus Pinus.* Ronald Press Co. New York.

Mittak, W. L. 1977. *Estudios para la reforestación nacional.* FAO Number 25. FO:DP/GUA/72/006: Guatemala, C. A.

Mittak, W. L. & J. P. Perry. 1979. *Pinus maximinoi:* its taxonomic status and distribution. *Journal of the Arnold Arboretum,* 60, 386–95.

Molina, A. 1964. Coniferas de Honduras. *Ceiba,* 10(1), 5–21.

Muller, C. H. 1947. Vegetation and climate of Coahuila, Mexico. *Madroño,* 9, 33–57.

Murillo, O. 1988. *Natural variation in wood specific gravity of Pinus greggii, Pinus leiophylla* and *Pinus pringlei.* CAMCORE Bulletin on Tropical Forestry No. 5·, North Carolina State University, Raleigh, N.C.

Passini, M.-F. 1982. *Le forets de Pinus cembroides au Mexique.* Etudes Mísoaméricaines II–5. Editions recherche sur les civilisations: Paris.

Pérez de la Rosa, J. A. 1983. Una neuva especie de pino de Jalisco, México. *Phytologia,* 54, 289–98.

———. 1987. *Notas del herbario del Instituto de Botánica de la Univ. de Guadalajara.* (IBUG). Julio-Sept. pp. 37–40.

Perry, J. P. 1951. Pine bark beetles of Central Mexico. *Unasylva,* 5–4, 158–65, F. A. O., Rome.

———. 1982. The taxonomy and chemistry of *Pinus estevezii. Journal of the Arnold Arboretum,* 63, 187–98.

———. 1987. A new species of Pinus from Mexico and Central America. *Journal of the Arnold Arboretum,* 68, 447–59.

Puig, H. 1970. Etude Phytogéographique de la Sierra de Tamaulipas (Mexico). *Buletín Sociedad de Historia Natural,* Toulouse, 106,(1–2), 57–79.

Righter, F. I. & J. W. Duffield. 1951. Hybrids between Ponderosa and Apache Pine. *Journal of Forestry,* 49, 345–9.

Riskind, D. H. & T. F. Patterson. 1975. Distributional and ecological notes on *Pinus culminicola. Madroño,* 23(3), 159–61.

Robbins, A. M. J. & C. E. Hughes. 1983. *Provenance regions for Pinus caribaea Mor. and P. oocarpa Schiede within the Republic of Honduras, C. A.* Tropical Foresty paper No. 18.

Escuela Nacional De Ciencias Forestales, Siguatepeque, Honduras.

Robert, M.-F. 1978. Un nouveau pin pignon mexicain: *Pinus johannis*. M.-F. Robert, sp. nov. *Adansonia*, sér. 2(18), 365–73.

Roezl, B. & Cie. 1857. *Catalogue de Graines de Conferes Mexicains*.

Rzedowski, Graciela C. 1957. *Vegetación del Valle de San Luis Potosí*. Tesis professional al titulo de Biologo, Institute Politecnico Nacional, México D. F.

Rzedowski, J. 1964. Una especie neuva de pino piñonero del Estado de Zacatecas (México). *Ciencia*, México, D. F., XXIII, 17–20.

———. 1965a. *Relaciones geographicas y posibles origenes de la flora de Mexico*. Colegio de Post-gradudos, Escuela Nacional de Agriculture, Chapingo, Mexico. 29, 121–77.

———. 1965b. Vegetación del estado de San Luis Potosí. *Acta Cientifico* Potosí, México, D. F., 5, 1–291.

———. 1966. *Pinus strobus* var. *chiapensis* en la sierra madre del sur de Mexico, *Ciencia*, México, D. F. XXIV(5–6), 211–6.

———. 1978. *Vegetación de México*. Editorial Limusa: México, D. F. 432 pp.

Rzedowski, J., L. Vela & X. M. Sánchez. 1977. Algunas consideraciones acerca de la dinamica de los bosques de coniferas en Mexico. *Ciencia Forestal*, 5.

Sánchez, X. M. 1967a. *Contribución al conocimiento de la ecológico de los bosques de oyamel, Abies religiosa* (H. B. K.) Schl. et Cham. en el valle de México. Boletín Tecnico, 18, Instituto Nacional Investigaciones Forestales, México.

———. 1967b. Algunos aspectos ecológicas de las bosques de coniferas mexicanas. Revista México y sus bosques. *Epoca*, III, 16, 11–19.

———. 1970a. Observaciones botanicos generales de la Isla de Cedros, Baja California (México). *Boletín divulgación*, 18, 1–17.

———. 1970b. Caracterización fito—ecologica preliminar de las volcanes de Fuego y Nevada de Colima (México). *Boletín divulgación*, 33, 1–36.

———. 1977. Caracteristicas generales de la vegetación del estado de Durango, México. *Ciencia Forestal*, 7(2), 30–58.

———. 1982. *Claves para la identificacion de las coniferas silvestres del estado de Michoacán*. Boletín Divulgativo No. 58, Secretaria de Agricultura: México.

Sánchez, X. M. & M. C. Deloya. 1969. *Una nueva especie mexicans de Pinus*. Boletín Tecnico, 26, INIF: Mexico.

Schmutzenhofer, H. 1975. *Mapa de los pinares de El Salvador*. Proyecta PNUD-FAO, ELS/74/004 (unpublished).

Schwerdtfeger, F. 1953. Informe al Gobierno de Guatemala sobre la entomología forestal de Guatemala I. *Los pinos de Guatemala*. Informe FAO/ETAP, FAO No. 202: Rome.

Sharp, A. J. 1953. Notes on the flora of Mexico: world distribution of the woody dicotyledonous families and the origin of the modern vegetation. *Journal of Ecology*, 41, 374–80.

Shaw, G. R. 1909. The pines of Mexico, *Journal of The Arnold Arboretum*, 1, 1–30.

———. 1914. The genus *Pinus, Journal of The Arnold Arboretum*, 5, 1–96.

Shreve, F. 1939. Observations on the vegetation of Chihuahua, *Madroño*, 5(1), 1–13.

Smith, J. Donnell. 1891. Undescribed plants from Guatemala. IX. *Botanical Gazette*, 16(6), 199–200.

Squillace, A. E. 1976. Analyses of monoterpenes of conifers by gas-liquid chromatography: In *Modern Methods in Forest Genetics*, ed. J. P. Miksche. Springer-Verlag: Berlin and Heidelberg. pp. 120–57.

Squillace, A. E., O. O. Wells & D. L. Rockwood. 1980. Inheritance of monoterpene composition in cortical oleoresin of loblolly pine. *Silvae Genetica*, 29, 141–152.

Standley, P. C. 1929. Trees and shrubs of Mexico. *Contributions U.S. National Herbarium*, 23, 1–848; 1, 1–169.

Standley, P. C. & J. A. Steyermark. 1958. Flora of Guatemala. *Fieldiana, Botany*, 24(1), 20–63.

Stead, J. W. 1983a. Studies of variation in Central American pines V: a numerical study of variation in the Pseudostrobus group. *Silvae Genetica,* 32, 101–15.

———. 1983b. A study of variation and taxonomy of the *Pinus pseudostrobus* complex. *Commonwealth Forestry Review,* 62, 25–35.

Stead, J. W. & B. T. Styles. 1984. Studies of Central American pines: a revision of the 'pseudostrobus' group (Pinaceae). *Journal of the Linnaen Society Botany,* 89, 249–75.

Stebbins, G. L. 1950. *Variation and Evolution in Plants.* Colombia University Press: New York.

———. 1959. The role of hybridizaion in evolution. *American Philosophical Society Proceedings,* 103, 231–51.

Styles, B. T. 1976. Studies of variation in Central American pines I. The identity of *Pinus oocarpa* var. *ochoterenai* Martínez, *Silvae Genetica,* 25, 109–18.

———. 1985. The identity of Schwerdtfeger's Central American Pine. *Forest Genetic Resources Information,* 13, 47–51.

Styles, B. T., J. W. Stead & K. J. Rolph. 1982. Studies of variation in Central American Pines 2. Putative hybridization between *Pinus caribaea* var. *hondurensis* and *P. oocarpa*. *Turrialba* 32(3), 229–42.

Taylor, B. W. 1963. Outline of the vegetation of Nicaragua. *Journal of Ecology,* 51, 27–54.

USDA. 1974. *Seeds of Woody Plants in the United States,* Agriculture Handbook No. 450. Forest Service, USDA: Washington, D.C.

Williams, L. 1955. *Pinus caribaea. Ceiba,* 4, 299–300.

Wolffsohn, A. 1982. *The Pine Forests of Honduras.* Technical Report No. 1, Overseas Development Administration: London, UK. 34 p. (Unpublished).

Wormald, T. J. 1975. *Pinus patula. Tropical Forestry Papers* No. 7: 1–172, plus appendices and plates.

Zamora, S., Crisóforo. 1981. Algunos aspectos sobre *Pinus oocarpa* Schiede, en el estado de Chiapas. *Ciencia Forestal,* 6(32), 25–53.

Zamora, S.C. & V. F. Valentín. 1977. *Pinus strobus* var. *chiapensis,* una especie en peligro de extinción en el estado de Chiapas. *Ciencia Forestal,* 2(8), 3–23.

Zamora, S.C. & V. F. Valentín. 1978. *Contribución al estudio ecológico de los pinos del estado de Chiapas.* Boletín técnico, Instituto Nacional Investigacion Forestal, No. 56; 1–32, México, D. F.

Zobel, Bruce. 1951a. The natural hybrid between Coulter and Jeffrey pines. *Evolution,* 5, 405–13.

———. 1951b. Oleoresin composition as a determinant of pine hybridity. *Botanical Gazette,* 113, 221–7.

Zobel, B. J. & F. Cech. 1957. Pines from Nuevo León, Mexico, *Madroño,* 14(4), 133–44.

INDEX

225